Rethinking Knowledge

SUNY Series in the Philosophy of the Social Sciences

Lenore Langsdorf, Editor

Rethinking Knowledge

Reflections Across the Disciplines

Edited by
Robert F. Goodman and
Walter R. Fisher

With a Foreword by Stephen Toulmin

State University of New York Press

Published by
State University of New York Press, Albany

© 1995 State University of New York

Printed in the United States of America

For information, address State University of New York Press,
State University Plaza, Albany, N.Y. 12246

Production by M. R. Mulholland
Marketing by Fran Keneston

Library of Congress Cataloging-in-Publication Data

Rethinking knowledge : reflections across the disciplines / edited by
  Robert F. Goodman and Walter R. Fisher : foreword by Stephen
  Toulmin.
      p.   cm. — (SUNY series in the philosophy of the social
  sciences)
    Includes bibliographical references and index.
    ISBN 0-7914-2337-9 (alk. paper). — ISBN 0-7914-2338-7 (pbk. :
  alk. paper)
    1. Knowledge, Theory of. 2. Social sciences—Philosophy.
  3. Postmodernism. I. Goodman, Robert F. II. Fisher, Walter R.
  III. Series.
  BD161.R484 1995
  121—dc20   94-14442
                                                                   CIP

10 9 8 7 6 5 4 3 2 1

Contents

Part III
Values, Reason, and Responsibility

Part IV
Knowledge and Schema Theory

Acknowledgments

We wish to express our sincere thanks to C. S. Whitaker, who, in his capacity as Dean of the Social Sciences and Communication, provided intellectual and financial support for the two-year project "Epistemology in the Social Sciences." The project led to the conferences featuring the presentations on which the essays collected here are based. We would also like to express our deep appreciation to the informal group of scholars who were our partners in the discussions leading up to the conferences and in their planning: Michael Dear, Anne Dunlea, Dallas Willard, John Crossley, Florence Clark, Scott Davis, Philip Youderian, Edna Bonacich, Michael Arbib, and James Holston. We have been very fortunate in having the clerical assistance of Clare Walker and Jennifer Claussen.

Foreword

Stephen Toulmin

I

The twentieth century has been a time of extraordinary change in every branch of philosophy and the social sciences, above all episte-mology. In all the fields of inquiry concerned with the analysis of knowledge—how it is created and improved, the mental and neuro-physiological processes involved in its acquisition, and the relations between individual and collective human knowledge—the questions that occupy the center of our attention in the 1990s are unlike those that preoccupied philosophers, psychologists, and social scientists a hun-dred years earlier. The leading epistemological questions of the 1890s would be directly intelligible, even familiar, to Immanuel Kant in the 1790s or to John Locke in the 1690s; but our current preoccupations would strike them as having drastically changed the subject—even, from their point of view, as having missed the central point of episte-mology. (As we shall see, philosophically minded writers in the 1590s saw these issues very differently.)

Historically, the last time our ideas about knowledge went through such a deep change was the mid-seventeenth century. Between 1630 and 1690, a set of fundamental issues was framed which, for most of the next 300 years, defined the Received Program of epistemology and human sciences. Contemporary critics of this program refer to it as the "Cartesian" program, and attribute it to the writings of René Descartes, notably to his *Discourse on Method* and *Meditations*, both of which first appeared in the 1630s. Advocates of the program, for that matter, do the same: In their eyes, the fact that the whole agenda of modern philosophy took complete and convincing shape in the mind of one man is a mark of Descartes's supreme genius: His work seems to supersede all that had gone before, so removing any need for us to inquire into his relations with his forerunners. In the great chess game of modern philosophy, Descartes played white, and his classic texts represent the opening "P to K4."

By now, however, this attribution is open to doubt. The place of Descartes's work in the "canon" of modern philosophy is beyond question; but it is less clear if he meant us to interpret it just as his followers did. After his death, the Cartesian program for philosophy took on a life of its own; and, looking back, we find ourselves forced to ask just how wholeheartedly René Descartes himself was ever committed to being a "Cartesian."

All the essays in this volume, then, focus on issues that arise in the late twentieth century, in the death throes of the "research program" for philosophy that took hold in Western Europe in the latter part of the seventeenth century: having been shaped as much by Descartes's successors as by Descartes himself. This program relied on three underlying assumptions which, at the time, appeared so obvious and beyond question that they did not need to be made explicit:

1. The true locus of "knowledge" is *personal and individual*, not public or collective: The possibility of knowledge is intelligible to Descartes (say) only insofar as he can recognize what is "known" as part of *his own* knowledge.
2. Any account that philosophers give of the nature of "knowledge" must accommodate itself to accepted ideas about the *physiological mechanisms* in the knower's sensory nerves and brain. So, most plainly in John Locke's writing, the picture took hold of the Mind as the *sensorium—a camera obscura*, or "inner theater," in the depths of the Brain.
3. Finally, if "knowledge" is to have any claim on our intellectual loyalty or attention, its building blocks (at least) must be *demonstrably certain*, so that, for Descartes as for Plato, "knowledge" ideally takes the form of a deductive system, such as the classical Greeks created for geometry.

As the essays in this collection make clear, the debate about knowledge in the last years of the twentieth century can no longer be committed to—or constrained within—any of these axiomatic assumptions.

Yet these axioms had remarkably long lives. The first radical challenge to their validity carrying general conviction with philosophers and social scientists came only in the mid-twentieth century. Precursors of the critique (it is true) existed at the turn of the century (e.g. in Wilhelm Wundt's *Volkspsychologie*, or "cultural psychology"; yet the

axioms of the Received Program were still insisted on, in the late nineteenth and early twentieth centuries, by authors as notable as Thomas
Henry Huxley, William James, and Bertrand Russell. In *Science and
Culture*, for example, Huxley takes care to explain at length that our
bodily sense organs are not (as we suppose) instruments or servants
that help us to acquire reliable knowledge: On the contrary, we should
see them as *obstacles* to knowledge. The Inner Mind is located at the
wrong end of the sensory nerves, and it can gain access to the External
World only by relying on inference to circumvent the physiological
machinery between it and the World.

In the *Principles of Psychology*, again, William James emphasizes his
belief that *every thought is part of a personal consciousness* (all the high-
lights are his):

> No thought even comes into direct *sight* of a thought in another
> personal consciousness than its own. Absolute insulation, irre-
> ducible pluralism, is the law. It seems as if the elementary psychic
> fact were not *thought* or *this thought* or *that thought*, but *my thought*,
> every thought being *owned*.

Since "thoughts" were the building blocks of James's epistemology,
even the founder of Pragmatism could not free himself from the
assumptions of his Cartesian forerunners, and he even veered toward
solipsism. As for the role of "certainty" in knowledge, Russell's philosophical oeuvre testifies to the charm of this third axiom; and this makes
it the more remarkable that, in his 1929 Gifford Lectures, published as
The Quest for Certainty, John Dewey was able to free himself so completely from all three assumptions.

The mid-twentieth century saw an avalanche of changes in the epistemological debate, particularly after 1960. Much of the material for this
transformation had been available before the Second World War, not just
in Dewey's writings but also in the work of L. S. Vygotsky and Mikhail
Bakhtin in Russia, George Herbert Mead in the United States, and R. G.
Collingwood in England. But it was only in the late 1950s and early '60s
that these different pieces began to fall into place relative to one another.
One catalytic event was the posthumous publication of Wittgenstein's
Philosophical Investigations. This book was little more accessible to general
readers than the author's earlier, mystifying *Tractatus Logico-Philosophicus*;
but, since its publication in 1953, its central message has rippled outward
into all disciplines concerned with knowledge and its ramifications.

In the *Investigations*, Wittgenstein tackled head-on the central paradoxes in John Locke's model of the Mind as an inner theater. If that

model is inescapable, we have no way of crediting language/concepts/ideas with *meaning*. Like Mead and Vygotsky before him, Wittgenstein treats all knowledge as socially and culturally situated: If it is to be meaningful, its primary locus must be collective, not individual. So everything to do with knowledge (and/or cognition) has to be understood as acquiring its "meaning" *in the public domain*. When we learn to speak, each of us masters the language games and other collective procedures current in his or her particular community. Some of these procedures may prove to be cultural universals, and the bodily mechanisms that they call into play may prove to be genetically transmitted; but this does not undermine the basic epistemological point.

Meanwhile, two other changes were under way. On the one hand, philosophers of science moved away from their earlier commitment to the Vienna Circle's program for inductive logic, and began to pay more attention to the historical and social contexts of knowledge. To the extent that knowledge belongs to scientific *collectives* (they saw), the evolution of disciplines and professions—within their intellectual and social contexts—must play a significant part within the Theory of Knowledge itself. Correspondingly, in the analysis of communication and argumentation, the barriers that the seventeenth-century philosophers had erected to separate logic from rhetoric were at last dismantled. So, patterns of communication and reception took their place alongside the structure of formal scientific inferences, as topics of epistemological inquiry.

II

The situation created by the abandonment of the Cartesian program is stressful and confused. For some, it has been the occasion for desperate intellectual gestures. Those who were earlier committed to that program react to its disappearance with an unappeased sense of loss, which is expressed in their complaints about the absurdity of human claims to knowledge, let alone rationality. In France, where Cartesianism has its deepest roots, philosophers and critical theorists are tempted (if anything) to revel in generating paradoxes, by hanging on to Cartesian categories and methods of argument, in a world in which they are no longer appropriate. So understood, the philosophical agenda of "deconstruction" can be seen as pulling down the Cartesian Temple *from within*. (For Samson, it was courage—not absurdity—to die with the Philistines in the ruins of their temple.)

Others recognize the end of Cartesian epistemology as bringing with it the need to rethink its critical categories: Like the fly that retraces its way out of Wittgenstein's fly bottle, the philosopher who escapes from the Cartesian cul de sac is liberated from the received interpretation of these categories, and can set about rethinking their meaning and application in a new context. But this point calls for historical comment. In itself, a bare claim that the critical categories of epistemology may be "rethought" is so vague as to be only programmatic. The question, How can that be done?, leaves us in a fog of uncertainty. Just that fog shrouds the current debate about *post*modernity: having renounced the excess certainty of Cartesianism, people do not know where else to turn.

However, the step onward from the Cartesian program of "modern philosophy" is also in some ways—I would argue—a step backward in time, to the tolerance of ambiguity we find in the *pre*modern humanists. The agenda of epistemology from 1650 to 1950—I said—was not yet accepted in the 1590s; and we can learn something by looking to see how far the twentieth-century rejection of Cartesian foundationalism frees us to reappropriate some central issues from the High Renaissance. For instance, Michel de Montaigne's skeptical humanism is closer to the later ideas of Wittgenstein than either position is to the intervening epistemologies of Descartes and Locke, Mach, and Russell.

The standard accounts of "objectivity" within the Received Program, again, make it dependent on a wider theory of the relation of Mind to the World: The question is, Does the External World comprise *facts* which the Mind can establish with certainty? Yet, long before Descartes was born, questions about "objectivity" were intelligible— quite aside from epistemological theory—as turning on the presence or absence of *bias*. A judge's rulings, for instance, demonstrate his judicial objectivity—or lack of it—by the extent to which they are exempt from prejudice against, or partiality to, one of the parties.

In different ways, all of the authors in this collection address issues that moved to the front of the philosophical stage only in the last thirty years, with the abandonment of the Cartesian Program. Aaron Ben-Ze'ev, for example, sets out to show how we can reformulate the problems of philosophical psychology, such as the role of the senses, in terms that free us from John Locke's inner theater or *sensorium*: by following his suggestions, we are led back to the road originally opened up in Aristotle's *de Anima*. For her part, Helen Couclelis deliberately moves away from an individualist conception of "cognition," or mental activity, and invites us to reflect on the role of "evolutionary imagination"—a field of inquiry she shares with Mihaly Csikszentmihalyi. (The issues raised in these two essays are dealt with in technical detail by Michael Arbib, whose post-Kantian analysis of mental schemata extends into the social sciences.)

Some readers may wonder whether, in their subject matters, the essays in this collection have anything in common; so one thing is worth repeating: The authors may go off in different directions, but *they all start from the same place.* All of these essays are products of the changes by which philosophy and social science have been emancipated, after three hundred years in which epistemology was shaped by a fallacious agenda. In different ways, for instance, Donald Schon and Charles Taylor recognize our need to be freed from the conception of knowledge as the property of human *individuals.* At the least, knowledge is "dialogical"; and, often enough, it is a property of organized collectives. Nor can the human sciences remain dominated any longer by considerations of *theory*: In economics, which is particularly blighted by its addiction to theory, much is learned—as Donald McCloskey has shown—by bringing in the categories of rhetoric and practice to counterbalance those of formal logic and theory.

III

At the end of the day, then, we are left with the question, Why did the Cartesian Program carry conviction initially, and for so long? The compelling attractions of this view—I would argue—sprang originally from ideological problems associated with the Thirty Years War and from the spiritual and intellectual crises that went on around it. In the last thirty years, historians of early modern Europe have written at length about a "general crisis" in the early seventeenth century: Far from being economic, social, and political alone, this crisis embraced the ideological conflicts arising at the climax of the religious wars that followed the breach between the Protestants and the Roman Catholic Church. This trauma is, perhaps, best seen as the final collapse of confidence in the collective intellectual tradition of Medieval and Renaissance Europe. As a result, thinking people were thrown back on their individual thoughts; and, for the time being, philosophers saw no escape in epistemology from the narcissistic self-absorption that is represented by seventeenth-century models of the Internal Mind.

Why, then, was the Cartesian Program not abandoned once the stresses of the Religious Wars had been overcome, and Western Europe was reconstructed on a new basis? That is another, more complex issue. The intellectual foundations of the new political system of nation-states, and the social system of "classes" embodied in those states, rested on moral and intellectual compromises which would take three hundred years to overcome. Jean-Jacques Rousseau rightly asked about the origins of human inequalities; but the forms in which he encountered those inequalities had, by his time, lasted some two or three generations at most. Radical changes were needed—across the whole intellectual spectrum from physical theory ("natural philosophy") to social and political institutions ("practical philosophy")—before the last of the conceptual presuppositions taken over from that late seventeenth-century compromise could be dismantled.

At the end of the twentieth century, we have the same tasks that faced European thinkers in the 1650s: to rebuild not merely our intellectual account of "knowledge," but also a social and political order within which epistemology will be free of the excess individualism of the Cartesian tradition. All of the essays in the present volume can be seen as tentative forays into this new territory, whose comprehensive mapping will keep philosophers and social scientists busy well into the third millennium.

Introduction

Robert F. Goodman

I

At the center of the contemporary clash between modernist and postmodernist thinking is a struggle over questions regarding the nature, procedures, justification, and outcomes of scholarly inquiry. Regardless of the stance taken on these questions—defense of modernist aims, resistance to them, the reconstruction of inquiry, or the radical advocacy of postmodernist forms of skepticism—rethinking is the order of the day. It is the motif of the essays in this volume.

Most of the essays are written by and for social scientists, but the issues they address and the arguments they make are pertinent to the interests of scholars across the academy. That it is not only the social sciences that are engaged in the intellectual ferment of our time is amply demonstrated by the inclusion in this volume of essays written by representatives of the humanities and natural sciences. In all, the disciplines represented include economics, English, philosophy, administrative and organizational theory, anthropology, psychology, political science, rhetoric, geography, and computer sciences.

Clearly there is a conversation going on within and across disciplines, however discordant the voices may appear on the surface. While essay themes vary—from method to operations of the mind to the concept of the self, from social responsibility to reason and wisdom—common themes and questions appear throughout the volume: how knowledge should be understood, what the relationship is between values and knowledge, and how knowledge should be pursued, justified, and put into use in practical affairs. The essays are at one in trying to move the conversation in productive ways, and this—as Richard Rorty would have it—is about as much as we could expect or want in these turbulent times.

II

Part I presents general theoretical perspectives. We lead off with McCloskey's broad-gauged assault on the ramparts of methodism. The notion of method takes on different coloration within the various disciplines. In philosophy, it has entailed the dominance of epistemology (the study of the methods and grounds of knowledge) over moral and political philosophy; whereas in the social sciences, as Sheldon Wolin has explained, it has involved the presupposition that "the fundamental purposes and arrangements served by [social science] techniques have been settled"[1] and a consistent effort to separate out or bracket questions of morality and practical action.[2] According to the "methodist" perspective, the social scientist is a "neutral" observer whose values are kept in abeyance insofar as his or her research is concerned.

McCloskey pokes holes in this still widely accepted view of social science methodology. He argues that the love for demarcating Science (with a capital S) from the rest of culture ought to be abandoned in favor of a looser, less methodologically oriented understanding of what science (with a small s) entails. He argues that the preoccupation with method distorts our understanding of the true nature of science and has created a false barrier between Science and the humanities.

McCloskey's landmark work on the rhetoric of economics has established him as a leading figure in the scholarly efforts to break down this barrier and to bring to light essential commonalities that are shared by all the formal disciplines. It is difficult to assess the impact of this message on the ongoing work of the individual social science disciplines. One obvious outcome of the attack on, and loss of faith in, methodism has been the creation of small pockets of resistance within the individual disciplines. Scholars of resistance, like McCloskey and George Marcus, want nothing less than a complete realignment of guiding paradigms. At present, their efforts have encountered a considerable degree of counterresistance and indifference; and the question of whether or not the social sciences in time will take new and quite different forms remains an open one.

McCloskey also gives us a brief introduction to his candidate for a new guiding paradigm, the notion of rhetoric, which he considers the theory and practice of argumentation. Regardless of discipline, he believes, all scholars argue. This paradigm is closely aligned to Walter R. Fisher's concept of *homo narrans*, which entails viewing all communication, from the informal conversations of everyday life to the highly formal presentation of scientific theories, as instances of narration. As

McCloskey and Fisher indicate, the concepts of rhetoric and narration have attracted wide interest, and a considerable body of new literature which explores their uses and implications has grown up in recent years.

Barbara Herrnstein Smith advances the claim that thought and action are infused with what she calls "the conditionality of value," "all the way down" and without exception. Her position is rightly understood as representing a direct denial of philosophical and scientific claims of absolute neutrality and objectivity. Some believe that a position such as the one that she takes leads us into the abyss of relativism, a charge that she takes some pains to refute.

Insofar as Herrnstein Smith's essay is taken to be a comment about science, it expresses a view that has gathered great force in recent years. A series of studies of how scientists actually conduct their work—beginning with Thomas Kuhn's landmark work, *The Structure of Scientific Revolutions*, and including David Hull's *Science as a Social Process* and Martin Rudwick's *The Great Devonian Controversy*—have emphasized the extent to which scientific research is a social process in which competing values and interests have a crucial role to play.[3] None of these authors is led to adopt a skeptical view of scientific knowledge as a result of their findings, but each does maintain that the rigid view of scientific objectivity must be abandoned.

Herrnstein Smith employs an economic model to explain how values operate, and incorporates the activities of science within a general value framework. Fisher's concept of narration likewise encompasses science within a general framework that includes questions of value. However, while she allows, at best, for the rationality of the individual actor trying to find a sensible way in the vast supermarket of late modernity, Fisher presents narrative thought as a kind of overarching reason. My own sympathies are with Fisher and other thinkers who are struggling to develop a concept of reason that is suitable to the complex times in which we live.

The collection's most direct analysis of fundamental epistemological questions is to be found in Aaron Ben-Ze'ev's chapter on cognitive organization. He presents two paradigms of how knowledge is structured in the mind: the container model, which he associates with John Locke, and the schema model, which he and Helen Couclelis and Michael Arbib claim is the best available general account of what the cognitive sciences are learning about the basic nature of cognitive organization. This approach to epistemology is to be distinguished from the alternative and more prominent one which focuses, instead, upon the question of how "reality" is represented in the mind or, as Rorty has put it, how the mind can "mirror reality." Ben-Ze'ev's analysis of the operations of schema provides the basis for the defense of an episte-mological position that he calls "constitutive realism."

However, his position in the debates between realists and idealists is of less interest to me than two other implications that follow from the line that he is following. First, the cognitive approach establishes a bond of common interest between philosophy and the cognitive sciences. We no longer are limited, as were Locke and Kant, to armchair speculation about the nature of mental processes. Methods for testing and exploring the implications of various models of the mind facilitate the mutual influence of philosophy and cognitive science. These connections are explored further in the chapters by Couclelis and Arbib in Part IV. Second, the notion of schema is consistent with a generally holistic understanding of reality and with theories and methods that are in accord with holistic assumptions.

There is, thus, a strong, familial resemblance between the chapters on schema theory and Charles Taylor's discussion of the "dialogical self." Taylor maintains that the modern conception of the "self" as an isolated entity and the reification of "the disengaged first-person-sin-gular self [are] already evident in the founding figures of the modern epistemological tradition, for instance, in Descartes and Locke." The essay brings to light the extent to which the individualist view of the subject is taken for granted within the social sciences, and advocates a revision of basic social science thought that would take into account the sense in which human action might be comprehended as being of a "dialogical" nature.

> From the standpoint of the old epistemology, all acts were mono-logical, although often the agent coordinates his/her actions with those of others. But this notion of coordination fails to capture the way in which some actions require and sustain an integrated agent. Think of two people sawing a log with a two-handed saw; or a couple dancing. A very important feature of human action is rhythming, cadence. Every apt, coordinated gesture has a certain flow.

Taylor, however, is a moral and political philosopher, not a social sci-entist. From a moral perspective, the replacement of the notion of the discrete and separate moral agent with a dialogical one creates a con-ception of an "ethical space" that is integrated in such a way as to call into question the individualistic biases that are to be found in many forms of moral philosophizing.

Part II is devoted to three essays by social scientists. Superficially, these essays share very little in common. Their concerns, problems, and basic orientations are those of specific disciplines. Each author, though, makes a very significant break with dominant social science paradigms; and each would agree, I think, that it is much more important for the social scientist to attempt to understand and explain significant social questions in all their complexity than it is for him or her to adhere to methodological orthodoxy.

Donald Schon, a leading organizational theorist with extensive experience as an advisor to large public and private institutions, finds that the "technical rationality" of the social scientist researcher

leads to a dilemma of rigor and relevance. If researchers tilt toward rigor, according to the standards of normal science, they risk becoming irrelevant to practitioners' demands for knowledge that is usable under the pressured and often confusing conditions of everyday practice; if they tilt toward relevance, on the other hand, they tend by the same standards to become unrigorous.

The essay focuses on alternative understandings of the concept of causality. Its application within the paradigm of technical-rationality, he maintains, fails "to provide knowledge usable by practitioners in the everyday world of organizations." This troubling observation leads him to redefine his own role as a social scientist. The task that he sets for himself is that of clarifying the ways in which practitioners employ causal thinking to try to understand and control critical events that occur from time to time in organizational life. This critical shift of perspective has far-reaching consequences. The social scientist ceases to be a strictly disengaged observer, and he or she abandons the assumption that the formal, technical knowledge of the detached, disinterested analyst is superior to that of the practitioner who is immersed in the daily problems of organizational life. This is not to deny the extent to which the posture of the observer, enjoying as she does a certain distance from events, enables her to identify commonalities across individual cases and to construct theoretical generalizatons about the significance of these commonalities. However, in the kind of work that Schon is doing here, generalities emerge from the concreteness of experience rather than being imposed upon it.

Concern about the dubious role of the disengaged observer is a central theme in the extended critique of ethnography in anthropology presented by Marcus. He writes, for instance, that the belief that the ethnographer can be a competent translator of the distinctive forms of life that are the objects of field study ignores "the various blindnesses, evasions, and indeed fictions that had to be created to reap the very important insights that ethnography has produced." Anthropology, he tells us, is moving toward a conception of reflexive interaction between the observer and the world he is trying to describe and understand.

Marcus' hope is that

> ethnography within anthropology now has the possibility of redefining its position within Western intellectual discourse by freeing itself of its historic identification with the exotic and the primitive, objects of highly dubious empirical and ethical value in the late twentieth century anyway, and by exemplifying a discipline that not only heeds the continuing critique of its practices and discourses but embraces such critique as the very source of its projects of knowledge.

His essay makes an important contribution to our understanding of the difficulties confronting social scientists who adopt a critical posture with respect to their own disciplines. The discussion of some of the strategies available to them should be of interest to social scientists in other fields, and what he has to say might well inform the work of outside critics who often distance themselves from the problems of the researcher to such an extent that their proposals can find no practical application.

The last chapter in this section is written by the research psychologist Mihaly Csikszentmihalyi. Csikszentmihalyi is best known for his creative work in the area of "flow experience." In this essay, he tackles the notion of wisdom, a very different sort of topic. Now wisdom, quite obviously, is not the sort of phenomenon that can be treated as a clearly defined dependent variable that is the unambiguous result of the operations of other, clearly defined independent variables. In taking up this topic, Csikszentmihalyi is abandoning the classic experimental model in psychology.

He takes leave of that model in other very important respects. Psychologists assume that the aspects of behavior which they observe and explain are both timeless and universal. The particular qualities of their subjects—say the fact that they are young adults studying at an American university—are of no consequence. The method that Csikszentmihalyi employs, what he calls "evolutionary hermeneutics," takes the historical development of behavior into account. Furthermore, wisdom is by no means a universal human characteristic. Wise people are few and far between. Nor is wisdom a quality that tends to be encouraged by late modern society, which places so much emphasis on immediate gratification, short-term concerns, and cleverness rather than thoughtfulness. The essay, among other things, constitutes a plea for greater appreciation of the value of wisdom and for an enhancement of its role in our lives.

The primary emphasis in Part III is on values. When viewed from the perspective of knowledge acquisition, values tend to be understood as particular beliefs, needs, and interests that either threaten to or, in fact, do subvert our best efforts to achieve the universal posture of "objectivity." This perception of the matter is consistent with the logical-positivist school of philosophical thought. In fact, the breakdown of the logical-positivist conception of knowledge forces us to reconsider the basic problem of moral philosophy, that being on what grounds, if any, we can justify moral judgments. For instance, rational moral philosophy, particularly the Kantian version, attempts to supply logical justification for universal moral principles. Utilitarianism grounds morality on a single, hedonistic principle, and situational ethics explores modes by which moral judgments can be made when principles or norms are in conflict. The general opposition to Enlightenment rationality presented in this collection applies to values and morality no less, but also no more so, than it does to knowledge. Just as social scientists such as McCloskey, Schon, Marcus, and Csikszentmihalyi are searching for reconstructed conceptions of knowledge and methods of knowledge acquisition, so also are some theorists exploring the question of whether or not it is possible to sustain reasoned discourse about questions of value. The chapters by Jane Flax and Fisher take up this question.

Flax, who devotes the major portion of her analysis to the breakdown of the Enlightenment project, analyzes three principal developments in twentieth-century thought that have contributed to this development. The first of these is Freudian psychology. Freud, she suggests, undermined the rationalist faith in the "mind's capacity to be at least partially undetermined by the effects of the body, passions, and social authority and convention." Second, she maintains that postmodernist deconstruction has shattered Enlightenment conceptions of "mind, truth, language, and the Real." Third, she argues that feminism has begun to delineate the gender qualities of reason.

As a consequence of this analysis, her position with respect to the possibility of basing moral judgments on reasoned argument is entirely pessimistic; in fact, she describes such efforts as indicative of "a refusal to grow up." All attempts to build and sustain reasoned discourse are constraining rather than facilitative. But how, then, can she justify her own deeply felt moral concerns and sense of moral responsibility? Her answer to this question is that we have no choice but

> to firmly situate ourselves within contingent and imperfect con-
> texts, to acknowledge differential privileges of race, gender, geo-
> graphic location and sexual identities, and to resist the delusory
> and dangerous recurrent hope of redemption to a world not of
> our own making.

"Responsibility beyond innocence," she writes, "looms as a promise and as a frightening necessity."

In contrast to Flax, Fisher's aim is to reconstruct our understanding of the nature of reason rather than to escape from its clutches. The need for reconstruction derives from the fact that "the dominant notion of knowledge, which is the legacy of positivism, ill serves questions of justice, happiness, and humanity." These questions fall under the category of Aristotle's conception of practical wisdom. They are questions involving "knowledge of whether" rather than "knowledge of what." However, the fact that these are very different kinds of questions should not be taken as a justification for the traditional division between fact and value. To the contrary, they can be encapsulated within a single unified framework, the framework of narration. The narrative view of human discourse (including the individual's internal ones) encompasses the scientific, the historical, the philosophical, the political, and the religious "insofar *as they lay claim to our reason*" (Fisher's emphasis).

Various forms of reasoned discourse should be viewed as "stories" for which their narrators are making "truth claims." While the Enlightenment version of "truth" is based upon an absolute and timeless standard or criterion is not relevant to their evaluation, the reasonable person can judge them on the basis of the criteria of coherence and fidelity. In this sense, the sorts of communication among scientists that he discusses in the chapter are an extension and formalization of our everyday, commonsense efforts to persuade others of the truth of our beliefs and of our claims about the nature of reality. Thus, whereas Flax argues that the belief in reason establishes false barriers and differential power and privilege among people, Fisher insists that it has the potential for uniting them.

In the final section, we return to the discussion of schema theory that was introduced earlier by Ben-Ze'ev. Couclelis and Arbib argue that the notion of "schema," while emerging from the cognitive sciences, provides us with a view of reality that enables us to explain psychological and social processes in a new light and to redefine traditional epistemological issues.

The proposed shift from "container" to "schema," Couclelis suggests, may be something which runs a good deal deeper than simply a disagreement among scientists concerning the appropriateness and utility of alternative paradigms. She presents evidence that the image of the "container" may be one that is shared by all members of the human race. This suggests to me that the emergence of the dynamic, developmental, holistic notion of "schema" may be at the cutting edge of a reconceptualization of psychological and social life, not only in academia but also in the human community as a whole.

Couclelis maintains that schema theory enables us to bridge the gap between cognition and knowledge. Rather then depending on a representational view of knowledge, we are able to conceive of schemas

which 'make sense' because they cohere with our accumulated experience of the world, which are meaningful because they elicit dispositions and actions leading to pragmatically successful outcomes, and which are intellectually fruitful because they help connect together disparate pieces of the broader network of meanings, thus leading to ever more appropriate, though ever-shifting, truths.

Arbib, a leading computer theorist and cognitive scientist, adds several other dimensions to the understanding of the notion of schema. He begins by providing the lay reader with a brief explanation of its applications in scientific research. He then considers how it might be usefully applied by social scientists and by policy analysts.

III

If there is any single philosophy with which these essays might be associated, it is probably pragmatism. The breakdown of the distinction between practical and formal knowledge, the integration of knowledge and value, the distrust of "methodism," even something similar to the notion of schema—all these themes can be found in the philosophical work of the leading American pragmatists, C. S. Peirce, William James, and John Dewey.

In particular, one might imagine the giant figure of Dewey presiding over these proceedings. Like the authors of these essays, Dewey opposed the notion of a "purified" realm of "true" knowledge, entirely separate from the needs and activities of human beings. He nevertheless placed very great stock in the utility of knowledge gained by means of scientific research, and had high hopes for the future of the social sciences.

In *The Quest for Certainty*, which presents, perhaps, the clearest expression of his mature philosophy, Dewey argued that the problem of the relationship between knowledge and value ought to be the central focus of modern philosophy.[4] The most important questions facing modern society, he wrote, are about "conflicts between things which are or have been satisfying, not between good and evil."[5] Instead of a morality based on timeless moral principles, he attempted to construct an empirically oriented moral theory that deals with the changing circumstances of human existence and that employs scientific methodology as a means of addressing value questions.

Now, several generations after Dewey's passing, we find ourselves renewing this project. The task is more daunting now than it was then. It encounters a deeply entrenched methodism and the reality of a social science that has not achieved the kinds of results that Dewey anticipated. There is, moreover, a general spirit of skepticism in the air. Yet we might draw sustenance from Dewey's abiding optimism. He maintained his efforts to promote a philosophy enmeshed in the practical problems of human existence, even as other philosophers distanced themselves from them; and he retained his reformist zeal despite the limited success or outright failure of some of his own practical projects. His is not the inflated and unrealistic optimism of the Enlightenment rationalist who believes that all knowledge can be encapsulated within a static framework and that the problems of human existence can be "solved" once and for all. The Deweyan faith is based upon a recognition of the limitations of rational philosophy and an open-eyed encounter with the complexities and constantly changing character of human existence. The fact that the struggles of life are never-ending and that the solutions to the problems of existence are imperfect and transitory do not deter him. Such, I think, is the spirit of this collection.

Notes

1. Sheldon Wolin, "Political Theory as a Vocation," in *Machiavelli and the Nature of Political Thought*, ed. Martin Fleisher (London: Croom Helm, 1972), p. 27.

2. Ibid., p. 37.

3. Thomas S. Kuhn, *The Structure of Scientific Revolutions*, 2d ed. (Chicago: University of Chicago Press, 1970); David L. Hull, *Science as a Process: An*

Evolutionary Account of the Social and Conceptual Development of Science (Chicago: University of Chicago Press, 1988); Martin J. S. Rudwick, *The Great Devonian Controversy: The Shaping of Scientific Knowledge among Gentlemen Specialists* (Chicago: University of Chicago Press, 1985).

4. John Dewey, *The Quest for Certainty*, in *The Later Works*, vol. 4, ed. Jo Ann Boydston (Carbondale: Southern Illinois University Press, 1988).

5. Ibid., p. 212.

I

Fundamental Issues:
Method, Values, Mind, and Self

1

Economics and the Limits of Scientific Knowledge[1]

Donald N. McCloskey

For all their quarrels, economists know a lot. Some of it is obvious, the common sense of adults, such as that many things are scarce and that therefore we cannot have everything. The postulate of scarcity is what makes economics hard to teach to young adults, who believe they live among the blessed.

But a lot of economics is not so obvious, even to the middle-aged. The sociologist Randall Collins wrote an illuminating book subtitled *An Introduction to Non-Obvious Sociology.*[2] His job would have been easier in economics, not because economists are superior to lesser breeds without the law, but because economists have loved since the beginning the nonobvious, the counterintuitive, the paradoxical.[3] Even more than other social scientists, economists love to dumbfound the bourgeoisie. Did the Oregon Plan, selling gasoline by license plate number, cut lines at service stations? No. It had no effect on the lines, because the lines needed to be long enough to ration out the existing supplies (which were low at the controlled price). Is it a good idea to restrict American imports of Japanese cars, thereby saving jobs in Detroit? No. The last time we did so, the price of all cars rose by $1,000 each, costing American car buyers $160,000 a year in higher costs for each job saved (at $30,000 a year). Were unions the main reason that wages rose in the United States? No. Only 10 percentage points out of the 900 percentage points that wages have risen since 1865 can be explained by unions. Is America rich because of abundant natural resources? No. Less than 2 or 3 percent of the income of a modern economy is attributable to the original and indestructible properties of the soil.

As sociologists and political scientists and geographers can also claim, doubtless, we economists know a lot. We know for a fact that slavery was profitable. We know for a theory that first-place sealed-bid common-value auctions have a winner's curse. Economics is, to use the magic word, a Science.

That word capitalized, as it will be here when used in its magical sense—*Science*—is dangerously potent. English speakers over the past century and a half have used the word in a peculiar way, as in British academic usage—arts and sciences, the "arts" of literature and philosophy as against the "Sciences" of chemistry and geology. A historical geologist, in modern English, is a Scientist; a political historian is not. The usage in English is recent, a point which is difficult for a current English speaker to grasp or to believe. The evidence is overwhelming that *Science* in English has come to be specialized to "lab-coated, quantitative, dealing with physical nature"; whereas in all other languages the word is meant to mark off serious thinking from journalism. The English usage would puzzle an Italian mother boasting of her studious son, *mio scienziato* (my learned one). She does not mean that he is a physicist. Italians use the word to mean simply "systematic inquiry"— as do French, German, Dutch, Spanish, Swedish, Polish, Hungarian, Finnish, Turkish, Korean, Hindi, Tamil, and every other language where testimony has been collected. Only English, and only the English of the past century, has made physical and biological Science (definition 5b in the old *Oxford English Dictionary*) into, as the *Supplement* and the new *OED* describe it, "the dominant sense in ordinary use."

Economics has acquired, since the Second World War, the trappings of the dominant sense in ordinary use: numbers, models, and, above all, a tough mathematization that evokes envious squeals from other social scientists. Modernists in English long ago appropriated the word *Science* for their purposes. The word has ever since been a club with which to batter the arguments that the modernists do not wish to hear. Economists get into the National Academy of Science because they are armed to the teeth, in the English-speaking manner, with the weapons of Science.[4] Political scientists, if mathematicians can prevent it, do not get in, because the mere name of Science is not enough.

The weapons of Science are in daily use around the culture. The standard sneer is to attack the appropriation of "Science" in social Science, judging economics or anthropology as failing to make the cut. Science must enumerate: That lets out political philosophy as true Science (that it also lets out most of biology does not worry the attacker). Science must be mathematical: That lets out anthropology (and again much of biology). Science must predict: That lets out history (and paleontology and historical geology and cosmology). Science must experiment: That lets out every social science except parts of psychology and tiny bits of economics, archeology, and sociology (along with astronomy). Science must be about the physical world: That lets out the rest, with no remainder except certain branches of physics as understood by nonphysicists in 1900.

The Science-weapon, backed by the English use of the Science-word, has consequences. A good deal of money has been spent by the National Science Foundation since the 1950s to examine periodic stars and subatomic particles. A good deal of money has been spent by the National Institute of Health to examine genes and cell walls. The big expenditures on Big Science has been justified on the grounds that these are core Scientific activities and that such activities account for modern economic growth and modern improvements in health.

Such grounds for supporting Big Science are false, scientifically speaking. A sociologist of science could attest that the triumph of the physicists in chemistry and biology is a postwar accident. An economic historian could attest that Science had effectively nothing to do with economic growth until well into the twentieth century, and even at century's end its contribution is modest beside the big factors of peace, literacy, shop-floor ingenuity, and sound economic policies. A historian of public health could attest that most of the decline in the death rate since the eighteenth century occurred before medical Science could save more people than it killed (a date that Lewis Thomas once put in the 1920s, or perhaps as late as penicillin). And she might note that despite the enormous expenditure by the National Institute of Health on cancer research, cancer rates have gently but steadily increased in the past twenty years.

Not much is spent to test such hypotheses in history or in economics. The National Science Foundation does not support history, which is not a Science, and the Foundation's budget for economics (about $11 million) would not pay the light bill for high-energy physics.

So our English usage puts physical and biological Scientists in charge. The grounds are verbal, as must be the case in a human world or in a science run by humans. We cannot avoid using words, though we can use them poorly or well. The people who sneer about social "science" being un-Scientific are using childish verbal categories. The world, they think, comes in paired and correlated flavors of hard/soft, thing/word, fact/opinion, is/ought, male/female, Science/art. But people who scrutinize the hard facts about things in science usually come to the conclusion that the facts are constructed by words of art.[5] I can attest that in economic science the statistics central to its being are grounded in values, though no less scientific on that account.

Nonscientists and nonhumanists are in love with the project of demarcating Science from the rest of the culture, declaring the demarcation problem to be the central problem of epistemology.[6] In their view, the set of correlated dichotomies popular among English speakers over the past century occur naturally, like the ocean. The view is provincial. Except for government funding and a few other matters of persuading the electorate to go on paying for it, the demarcation of Science from non-Science, when you think of it, is lacking in point.

The pointless provinciality, an English-speaking one, is to think of Science and literature as two cultures. The two cultures are not natural territories, though department chairs and college deans in defense of the territories sometimes behave like border guards in the Eastern Europe of old, erecting barbed wire and shooting escapees. A dean of research at a large state university gave a speech a couple of years ago in which she described the humanities as what is left over after the (physical and biological) Sciences, and then after them the social sciences, have expended their eloquence. The humanities, in her mind, are a residuum for the mystical and the ineffable. (I have a friend, a remarkable economic scientist, who, when he learned that I was reading books about literature, asked me amiably whether I had become, as he put it, a "mystic.") The dean and my friend were being good-natured. The bad-natured remarks muttered from each side are worse: that if we mention "metaphors" we are committed to an arty irrationalism; that if we mention "logic" we are committed to a Scientific autism.

One wants to shake both sides and say, "Get serious." The better definition of *science* is the broader and more serious and less English one, as for instance in de Felice and Duro, *Dizionario della Lingua Italiana*: "the speculative, agreed-upon inquiry which recognizes and distinguishes, defines and interprets reality and its various aspects and parts, on the basis of theoretical principles, models, and methods rigorously cohering." The contrast is not with the humanities but with, say, bad journalism or the untutored opinion of the street. Nothing is said about using calculus or test tubes. The "rigor" can come from any argument that coheres. And so the speakers of German have their *Altertums wissenschaft*, the "science" of olden times, Greek and Roman classics; *klassische Wissenschaft*, similarly, is what English speakers call the humanities.

In non-English worlds of language, it is perhaps more evident that the sciences, such as chemistry, history, or economics, require "humanistic" methods, right in the middle of their sciences. They are sciences, not Sciences. The Sciences with a capital *S* are figments of the philosophical imagination. The real argumentative work gets done by lower case sciences. Newton used logic and metaphors. Darwin used facts and stories. And likewise, the arts and humanities require fact and logic, right in the middle. Leonardo, the scientist-artist, used stories and logic.[7] Shakespeare and John Donne made pointed use of alchemy and astrology (prestigious sciences in their day, to which that same Newton devoted most of his life). Goethe wrote a scientific (*wissenschaftlich*) treatise on colors. Science is literary, requiring metaphors and stories in its daily work, and literature is scientific.

Like other arts and sciences, to put it another way, economics as one of the social sciences uses the whole "rhetorical tetrad"—the facts, logics, metaphors, and stories necessary for completed human reasoning. Pieces of the four are not enough. The allegedly Scientific half of the tetrad, the fact and logic, falls short of an adequate economic science, or even a science of rocks and stars. The allegedly humanistic half falls short of an adequate art of economics or even a criticism of form and color. Scientists and scholars and artists had better be factual and logical. They had also better be literary—able to frame good models and tell true histories about the first three minutes of the universe or the last three months of the economy.[8] A scientist with only half of the culture is going to mess up her science.

The idea that fact and logic are enough for Science puts one in mind of the rural Midwestern expression "a few bricks short of a load." The program over the past fifty years of narrowing down our arguments in the name of rationality was a few bricks short of a load. The experiment in getting along with fewer than all the resources of human reasoning was worth trying and had plenty of good results; but it has done its work. To admit now that metaphor and story matter also in human reasoning does not entail becoming less rational and less reasonable, dressing in saffron robes or tuning in to "New Directions." On the contrary, it entails becoming more rational and more reasonable, because it puts more of what persuades serious people under the scrutiny of reason. Modernism, the ugly if fruitful experiment of the past fifty years, was rigorous about a tiny part of reasoning and angrily unreasonable about the rest. It's time to move on, without losing the permanent gains.

Bertrand Russell, the master of modernism in philosophy, is a case in point.[9] Santayana describes Russell during the First World War exploiting his retentive memory without the check of comprehensive reason:

This information, though accurate, was necessarily partial, and brought forward in a partisan argument; he couldn't know, he refused to consider everything; so that his judgments, nominally based on that partial information, were really inspired by passionate prejudice and were always unfair and sometimes mad. He would say, for instance, that the bishops supported the war because they had money invested in munition works.[10]

Modernists in philosophy or architecture or economics cannot reason with most of their opponents; on most matters they can only shout and sneer. They would say you are an unscientific fool if you do not believe that in building downtown Dallas in the 1970s the form should follow the function; you are an ignorant knave if you do not believe that political science in the 1990s should be reduced to secondhand econometrics.

Resistance to reason is faith. It is entirely unoriginal and uncontroversial to point out that Science is the modern faith; it arose after the sea of religious faith retreated down the vast edges drear and naked shingles of the world. Scientists, especially in the English sense, are ordained priests; winners of the Nobel Prize are granted a cardinal's hat, and in exceptional cases are canonized, to intervene for us in God's game of dice. The Science-faith is practiced on many college campuses. When forced into contact with Scientists, the economists, historians, and, most embarrassingly of all, the political scientists live in dread of Scientific sneers. The California Institute of Technology is a case in point. There and everywhere in our Science-faithful culture, the Scientific ayatollahs, mainly from physics and mathematics, have gotten into the ugly habit of mounting holy wars against other disciplines or at least initiating a diverting heresy trial now and then.

You know the rankings in Science itself: physics, math, chemistry, biology, geology, engineering. The chemist who made the trigger for the atom bomb was sneered at by the physicists and mathematicians; one of them—John von Neumann, I think—congratulated him with this rib-rocking jest: "You're a wonderful chemist—that is, a good third-rate physicist." The notion that Science is whatever most closely approximates the higher-status parts of physics showed in the fury of the physicists in New Haven and Los Angeles against the chemists in Utah ("Utah!" one could hear the Coasties sneer) who had the temerity to claim to have made fusion in a test tube. I wonder if physicists realize that we bystanders pray nightly in another faith that the chemists turn out to be right.

I do not mean all this to be funny. Soberly, really, religion and Science serve similar functions. An eminent anthropologist was asked by the anticreationist side in the Arkansas case if he would testify for the good guys. The lawyer argued something like this: "As a cultural anthropologist, you are an expert in both religion and Science, since you study one and practice the other. Therefore, you would be an excellent witness testifying that creation 'science' is not Science and that our blessed martyred Science is not a religion." The anthropologist thought about it for a while and then declined. He knew that on the witness stand he would have to admit that he could see no great difference between religion and Science, and especially not between Bible Belt Christianity and the Science myth we have created in the newspapers and public assemblies over the past century.

It is revealing how the scientist-customer is treated by workers in the service industries of Science—deans, journalists, book editors, foundation executives, and grant administrators. You would expect them to have the most cynically realistic view of Science. After all, they know what goes into the sausage. They know the unguarded remarks of scientists, the petty jealousies and the rejected proposals, and they know from the outside, unindoctrinated in the special topics of a particular science. Yet, despite this knowledge, they adhere to the Science religion of our culture.[11] They seem to get their prestige from pretending that Scientists are holy. They will claim that they support Science out of a devotion to truth (or, as they would put it, Truth); but, in fact, they define truth to be Science, squeezing out what does not fit the 3×5 card. Again, these service people of science are quick to adopt the Scientistic apologies for fallibility, such as that, after all, we are only approximating the truth. They forget that the only certitude is that yesterday's certitude in science will become tomorrow's laughingstock: a Newtonian universe, for example, or a Lamarckian theory of inheritance. Always in the theology of Science is today's credo that is timelessly True.

The service sector is forced into this position in part by its other customers, the attending and reading and, in any case, paying public, who have a magical view of Science. Either it's a heap good medicine, this Science, or its just a charlatan's trick. The attitude accounts for the genre of Fads and Fallacies in the Name of Science and the careers of some professional magicians devoted to unmasking nonconventional science (oddly, the magicians do not examine the magic in conventional laboratories; you would think they would want some controls on their experiments). The average person, educated or not, views Science as on/off, true/false, real/phony. He understands it with certain crude theories—the theory which has come to be called "Baconian," for example (I have never found it in Bacon), that speaks of "generalizing from data," and which Darwin, from the first sentence of *The Origin of Species*, had to pretend he followed.

When on board H.M.S. *Beagle* [1831-1836], as naturalist, I was much struck with certain facts. . . . On my return home, it occurred to me, in 1837, that something might perhaps be made out . . . by patiently accumulating and reflecting on all sorts of facts. . . . After five years' work I allowed myself to speculate on the subject.[12]

In private, Darwin himself scorned this 3 × 5-card version of scientific method. As he remarked in a letter to a colleague in 1861, "How odd it is that anyone should not see that all observation must be for or against some view if it is to be of any service!"[13] Nowadays, a 3 × 5-card version of Karl Popper's thinking has taken the place of Baconianism as the credo of the Scientistic, with a line or two from Thomas Kuhn in the Eastern rite. The ceremonies are closer to what happens in science, but not very close withal.

Modernist Scientism, in brief, is simple-minded and does not work. It does not deliver the miracles it promises, and erects pointless hierarchies to conceal the fact. The dilemma of practice in the postmodern world is that the experts have failed us, repeatedly, in Vietnam and in outer space and in the classroom. The experts' arrogant, muddled, intolerant, undemocratic, and unreasonable way of making social decisions comes from the elevation of Science and its correlate expertise into a religion. We need again an eighteenth-century scepticism about crude religions. Voltaire, where are you when we need you?

Fortunately, I am in possession of an answer to this problem and numerous others, a word to the wise that I am willing to share with you, at no extra charge. In an early scene of *The Graduate*, an uncle buttonholes Dustin Hoffman and gives him a bit of career advice: "Plastic," he says, "plastic." Plastic was a good bet, to tell the truth, in 1967. The uncle was right. For 1990, the avuncular advice is, in a word, "Rhetoric."

By the ancient definition, rhetoric is the whole art of argument— not ornament and bombast alone. If science is to cohere, it must use the art of argument; and if it is to be agreed upon by free people, it must be argued persuasively. Rhetoric is not a new foundation. It is merely a way of talking about the business we scholars are already in. The most fundamental epistemological implication of the rhetorical turn is simply that fundamental implications are useless for work in science. We do our work with words; and, to be responsible about words, the scientist must recognize her rhetoric, not ruminate on epistemology.

Even the Nobel science of the economy cannot bypass rhetoric. This is no bad thing. Speaking of a science such as economics in literary terms, of course, inverts a recent and guilt-producing hierarchy. But contrary to the century-long and English-speaking program to demarcate Science from the rest of the culture—a strange program, when you think about it—science is, after all, a matter of arguing. The ancient categories of argument are going to apply.[14]

As the economists Argo Klamer and Don Lavoie have pointed out, applying rhetorical thinking to economics leads one to an "interpretive economics." Interpretive economics would not be antiquantitative or antimathematical. To swing back against formal methods is to adopt another dichotomy of modernism, if only from the other side. The symbiotic relationship between rationalism and its alleged opposite, irrationalism, is captured nicely in this fact: The Rand Corporation, that bastion of rationalism, is located in Santa Monica, that bastion of irrationalism.

Economics can do better than choose up sides between feeling and thought, between the Humanities (note the capitalization again) and the Sciences. Since Adam Smith, economists have been both analyzing action and analyzing behavior, understanding the reasonableness of what people do down in the ruck of the market and seeing them also "from the eighth floor," as a sociologist once put it. To do economics otherwise is to be a few bricks short of a load.

It is easy to see the academic field of economics in rhetorical terms. No wonder: Academics are arguers. A scientific text can be analyzed like a poem, to see how it achieves its purposes through metaphors and ethos, implied readers and ruling stories.[15]

Maybe one can see the economy itself in rhetorical terms, too. If it proved possible—that is, if it resulted in empirical programs of research that explained more of what we see—an interpretive economics would reunite the sentence and the equation. For instance, business people spend a great deal of time persuading each other, and the fact might well figure in a wider economics. David Lodge describes a businessman, in his novel *Nice Work*, through the eyes of Robyn Penrose:

It did strike [her] that Vic Wilcox stood to his subordinates in the relation of teacher to pupils. . . . [S]he could see that he was trying to *teach* the other men, to coax and persuade them to look at the factory's operations in a new way. He would have been surprised to be told it, but he used the Socratic method: he prompted the other directors and middle managers and even the foremen to identify the problems themselves and to reach by their own reasoning the solutions he had himself already determined upon. It was so deftly done that she had sometimes to temper her admiration by reminding herself that it was all directed by the profit-motive. (p. 219)

The interpretive economists have been trying recently to formulate a theory of the entrepreneur as a rhetorician, a persuader of bankers and workers.

It is early days yet for interpretive economics. But an economics brought back into the conversation of humankind has already a few things to whisper across the disciplinary walls. Allow me to sell you a couple.

First, if economics is a good imitation of physics, as it is supposed to be if it is a Science, then it should predict.[16] But if you're so smart, oh predictor of human events, why ain't you rich? The question is the American Question, natural to economics.

The question cuts deeper than most intellectuals and experts care to admit. The test of riches is a perfectly fair one if the expertise claims to deliver actual riches, in gold or in glory. The American Question embarrasses anyone claiming profitable expertise who cannot show a profit, the historian second-guessing generals or the critic propounding a formula for art. He who is so smart claims a Faustian knowledge, "Whose deepness doth entice such forward wits / To practice more than heavenly power permits."

Start with economics. Take it as an axiom of human behavior that people pick up $500 bills left on the sidewalk. The Axiom of Modest Greed involves no close calculation of advantage or large willingness to take a risk. The average person sees a quarter and sidles over to it (it has been found experimentally that Manhattanites will stoop for a quarter); he sees a $500 bill and jumps for it. The axiom is not controversial. All economists subscribe to it, whether or not they "believe in the market" (as the shorthand test for ideology goes), and so should you.

Yet the Axiom of Modest Greed has a distressing outcome, a dismal commonplace of adult life, a sad little $500 Bill Theorem:

If the Axiom of Modest Greed applies, then today there exists no sidewalk in the neighborhood of your house on which a $500 bill remains.

PROOF. By contradiction, if there had been a $500 bill lying there at time $T - N$, then, according to the axiom, someone would have picked it up before T, before today.

From this advanced scientific reasoning, it is a short step to common sense. If a man offers advice on how to find a $500 bill on the sidewalk, for which he asks merely a nominal fee, the prudent adult declines the offer. If there really were a $500 bill lying there, the confidence man would pick it up himself. "A tout," said Damon Runyon, who knew the score on the economics of prediction, "is a guy who goes around a race track giving out tips on the races, if he can find anybody who will listen to his tips, especially suckers, and a tout is nearly always broke. If he is not broke, he is by no means a tout, but a handicapper, and is respected by one and all."

The payment need not be monetary if money is not what the seer desires. Prestige in the local saloon would be cheaply acquired if the American Question did not also cast doubt on predictions of sporting events. But it does. The lineaments of the sporting future apparent to the average guy will be reflected in the sporting odds. Only fresh details give profits above average, measured in money or prestige. Fresh details are hard to come by. Information, like steel and haircuts, is costly to produce.

The upshot is that American Question and the $500 Bill Theorem radically limit what economists and calculators can know about the future. No economist watches the TV program "Wall Street Week," which claims to predict the future, without a vague sense that he is betraying his science. He should be pleased. His science proves its robustness by asserting confidently that the science cannot profitably predict; indeed, that no science of humankind can profitably predict, even the science of stockbrokers. The economic theorem is so powerful that it applies to economists.

An economist looking at the business world is like a critic looking at the art world. Economists and other human scientists can reflect intelligently on present conditions and can tell useful stories about the past. These produce wisdom, which permits broad, conditional "predictions." Some are obvious; some require an economist. But none is a machine for achieving fame or riches. The study of the human sciences can produce wisdom; but it cannot produce prediction and control.

To become an effective manager or college dean, the consistent modernist must unlearn his modernism—the notion that Procedure will tell all. If it were easy to organize "correctly," then people would do it, which is what is wrong with the journalistic notion that it is easy for business to choose the Swedish Way or the Japanese Way or whatever Way is currently on their minds (note that the Swedish Way is now in disrepute, as the Japanese Way will be by the year 2000). The hubris of social engineering is the same as the hubris of facile social criticism.

No one is justly subject to the American Question who retains a proper modesty about what observation and recording and storytelling can do. We can observe the history of economies or the history of painting and, in retrospect, tell a story about how security of commercial property or the analysis of vanishing points made for good things. An expert, such as an economist, is an expert on the past and about the future that can be known without divine and profitable possession. Human scientists and critics of human arts, in other words, write history, not prophecy.

As Harry Truman once said, the expert as expert, a bookish sort consulting what is already known, cannot by his nature learn anything new, "because then he wouldn't be an expert." He would be an entrepreneur, a statesman, or an Artist with a capital *A*. The expert critic can make these nonexpert entrepreneurs more wise, perhaps, by telling them about the past. But he must settle for low wages. Smartness of the expert's sort cannot proceed to riches.

Economics teaches this, the limit on social engineering. It teaches that we can be wise and good but not foresighted in detail.

So that's one thing economics can tell other disciplines when it gets back into the conversation, that the disciplines are not magic. The other one is that the disciplines must trade. American and other academic life is thoroughly departmental. We know that in a century the disciplines will be organized differently, yet most institutions of higher learning are arranged to keep the inevitable from happening. Not all the change in the next century, but a lot of it (he says wisely, on the basis of looking backward), will come from between the disciplines—thus biochemistry and biophysics, thus comparative literature, thus history renewed by drawing on the social sciences, thus economics remaking itself between philosophy and engineering.

You will hear from deans—I hear it from some of my own—the tired argument that what we need is more specialization, building on strength; that what is wrong with letting the interdisciplines flourish is that they have no Standards, these nondepartmental things. And what are the Standards? Ah, well: the departmental. Something, you see, is fishy.

What is fishy is the economics involved. Specialization is an economic idea. But it is grossly misused by academic planners (and even by some economists when they become academic planners) to justify what could be described in economic terms as autarchic protectionism. The key economic point is this: *Specialization itself is not good.* In fact, Adam Smith himself (not to speak of Marx, you see) was eloquent on the damage that specialization does to the human spirit. What is good is specialization *and then trade*. As Adam Smith remarked famously, "Consumption is the sole end and purpose of all production; and the interest of the producer ought to be attended to, only so far as it may be necessary for promoting that of the consumer." There is no point in a shoemaker piling up shoes in the backyard unless he is going to sell them some day in order to consume the fruits of other people's specialization.

The trade in intellectual life is precisely the use of other people's work for one's own: It is what goes on in interdisciplinary activity, if the activity is something more than polite acknowledgment of the other's expertise, insulated carefully from disturbing one's own. If we actually read each other's work and let it affect our own, we are well and truly following the economic model of free trade. If we do what most academics do—never crack a book outside of their subdiscipline—then we are following the economic model of old Albania, specializing in ox carts and moldy wheat. Modern academic life has whole departments of ox carts.

Understand, the argument is not against specialization but against the failure at last to trade. It will be sweet work for psychologists, say, to talk long and hard about observable behavior, temporarily setting aside arguments from introspection. There is nothing hostile to systematic work in my argument. No one would wish to stop systematic specialization.

The problem comes when the narrow, temporary agreement hardens into a methodological doctrine for all time. Then the shoes start piling up, unsold, in the backyard. If the psychologists make the methodological rule permanent, throwing introspection into a nonspecific outer darkness forever and ever on merely epistemological grounds, they fall into absurdities. Speaking of psychology in the late 1930s, Jerome Bruner remarks, "For reasons that now seem bizarre, you *had* to convert contested issues into rat terms in order to enter the 'in' debates."[17] Two strictly behaviorist psychologists make love. One says to the other, "*You* enjoyed that. Did I?"

The failure of specializing modernism in psychology, economics, and elsewhere to achieve their inflated promises does not say they were bad ideas to try. And it certainly does not say that we should now abandon fact and logic, surface and cube, and surrender to the Celtic curve and the irrational. We are all very glad to keep whatever we have learned from the Bauhaus or the Vienna Circle or the running of rats. It says merely that we should now turn back to the work at hand, equipped with the full tetrad of fact, logic, metaphor, and story.

The anthropologist Roy D'Andrade put it well recently: "One cannot expect to improve upon Freud by observing less about human beings than he did."[18] It is economics again: We will do better with fewer arguments ruled out. That entails less sneering in academic life, less ignoring of chemists by physicists or of sociologists by economists or of statisticians by mathematicians. Considering that other scholars read different books and lead different lives, it would be economically remarkable, a violation of economic principles, if nothing could be learned from trading with them. The notion that something can be learned from trading with others merely applies consistently the economics of intellectual life. Just as differences in taste or endowment are grounds for trade, disagreements about the causes of crime or the nature of capitalism are grounds for serious conversation.

One can arrive at the same result against arrogant specialization through a philosophical/linguistic argument, too. A Maxim of Presumed Seriousness would assert that we, as serious scholars, must presume, until sound evidence contradicts it, that others are serious, too. The official rhetoric of scholarship presupposes the maxim. In linguistic terms, the maxim is a "conversational implicature," which is to say, a rule for making sense of what another scholar says. We are contradicting our own pragmatics of scholarship if we decide on poor evidence that sociologists are flat-earthers beside the Scientific majesty of economics.

The rhetoric in this is that languages are used to exclude people. When you walk into a pub in the Outer Hebrides, the men will switch from English to Gaelic. We do that a lot in academic life. The language in economics nowadays (wait a few years) is game theory. People have told me that their papers have been sent back by journals to be translated into game theoretic terms, although everyone knows that there is not always a point in doing so.

The two propositions in metaeconomics, then, are the Theorem of Intellectual Modesty and the Theorem of Intellectual Exchange. It would be nice if economists themselves would learn them.

Notice that nothing here is particularly French. I mention this because anything that smacks of reflexive criticism these days is liable to be attacked as "deconstruction" or some other foul-smelling French concoction, and then related to fascism, communism, and the decline of the West. What I am relying on here is plain old English-speaking, Scottish-invented economics, with a dash of American pragmatism and a half cup of ancient rhetoric. The American Question and the Principle of Toleration are not French.

If you want my opinion, I regard deconstruction and postmodernism as a jokey end game to modernism. But I regard them, too, as necessary: End games are not optional. I am not going to indulge in the violent sneering against them that many other English-speaking intellectuals of conservative leanings favor. I do not believe that deconstruction foretells a new dark age; or that people I cannot understand are crypto-fascists or crypto-communists. My only problem with deconstruction is that it seems to be ancient rhetoric made into a founding theory. Rhetoric is ill-suited to founding theories. Notably, the French fathers of deconstruction were all trained in rhetoric, as no Briton and few Americans are. Ancient rhetoric is about how language achieves its ends, about what the linguists call pragmatics, and, as the linguist Stephen Levison remarks:

> There is a fundamental way in which a full account of the communicative power of language can never be reduced to a set of conventions for the use of language. The reason is that wherever some convention or expectation about the use of language arises, there will also therewith arise the possibility of the non-conventional exploitation of that convention or expectation. It follows that a purely . . . rule-based account of natural language usage can never be complete.[19]

But that is merely the wisdom of if-you're-so-smart, and is derivable from economics and ancient rhetoric as much as from po-mo playfulness.

The way to inaugurate the intellectual trade and intellectual modesty that will, I hope, characterize the world after modernism is to focus on rhetoric. It is an antiepistemological epistemology that breaks down the walls dividing disciplines. How do I know? Because we have done it at Iowa over the past ten years, in 250 meetings involving hundreds of faculty in departments ranging from mechanical engineering to English, discussing the speaker's work in the line-by-line style of the Writers' Workshop. Our Project on Rhetoric of Inquiry has resulted in now dozens of books and scores of articles. Some day the Coasties will recognize that they do not have to betake themselves to Paris or Frankfurt for their criticism, merely to Iowa.

The common ground is argument. We have discovered at Iowa that what professors have in common is not some subject or social problem but the art of argument. It is not epistemology or chaos theory or international relations that can create real conversations across disciplines. It is a focus on the very words. A professor of Spanish cannot give her colleague in mathematics any advice on the substance of his paper; but she can point out to him that the form is part of the substance, and can remind him that the appeals to authority (so important in mathematics) can be found in seventeenth-century Spanish plays. From this would come a revitalized science, rehumanized—without giving up even one of the gains from our long experiment in suppressing a part of our humanity.

The problem has always been trying to vault into a higher realm, asking whether such-and-such a methodology will lead ultimately to the end of the conversation, to the final Truth about economics or philosophy. This is the question asked by Plato and reiterated by Descartes and Bacon and confidently answered by the men of the nineteenth century, the Kelvins sneering at the possibility of radioactivity and predicting that physics was nearly complete, who gave us Scientism. The modesty of the sophist Protagoras, who said that *man* is the measure of all things, was not pleasing to Plato, Descartes, and Bacon.

> For it is a false assertion that the sense of man is the measure of all things. On the contrary, all perceptions as well as of the sense as of the mind are according to the measure of the individual and not according to the measure of the universe. And the human understanding is like a false mirror, which, receiving rays irregularly, distorts and discolors the nature of things by mangling its own nature with it.[20] [Bacon, *The Great Instauration*, 1620, XVI]

The "measure of the universe," however, cannot be taken direct; it can only be taken from the sublunary mirrors we have. Questions such as What will economics look like once it is finished? are not answerable on this side of the Last Judgment. Wolfgang Pauli used an economic metaphor to scold his fellow physicists for anticipating the physics that would arise once judgment was ended, claiming "credits for the future." Economists, with their dismal jokes that lunches are not free and $500 bills do not lie about unclaimed, should have no trouble seeing that little can be hoped for from pre-science in such matters. The problem is that pre-science is precisely pre-science, knowing before knowing. We can be wise, if we trade intellectually. But we cannot be social engineers independent of society, for if we were, in fact, so smart, we would be rich.

Notes

1. Parts of the argument are pursued at greater length in D. N. McCloskey, *If You're So Smart: The Narrative Of Economic Expertise* (Chicago: University of Chicago Press, 1990).

2. Randall Collins, *Sociological Insight: An Introduction to Non-Obvious Sociology* (New York: Oxford University Press, 1982).

3. There is a genre in economics of "Everything You Thought You Knew About the Economy That Is In Fact Wrong." See, for example, Douglass C. North and Roger L. Miller, *The Economics of Public Issues*, 6th ed. (New York: Harper Collins, 1983); and A. Smith, *The Nature and Causes of the Wealth of Nations* (1776).

4. An article in *Science* (Robert Pool, "Strange Bedfellows," *Science* 245 (18 August 1989): 700-3) describes the amazement of the physicists collaborating with economists at the new Sante Fe Institute (formed to do economic science properly) at how much mathematics the economists used—far more than the physicists themselves thought useful.

5. The conclusion has become a cliché among scientists. To name three eminent scientists who make the point: Michael Polanyi (crystallography) in *Personal Knowledge* (Chicago: University of Chicago Press, 1958); Ludwik Fleck (bacteriology) in *Genesis and Development of a Scientific Fact* (Chicago: University of Chicago Press, 1979; originally published in German in 1935); and Steven Weinberg (theoretical physics) in "Beautiful Theories," Revision of the Second Annual Gordon Mills Lecture on Science and the Humanities (University of Texas, 5 April 1983).

6. The two books that a decade ago did most to reorient epistemology were, of course, Paul Feyerabend, *Against Method: Outline of an Anarchistic Theory of Knowledge* (London: Verso, 1978); and Richard Rorty, *Philosophy of the Mirror of Nature* (Princeton: Princeton University Press, 1979). An extension of this line, making full use of the British sociologists of science such as Bloor, Collins, Pinch, Barnes, and Mulkay, is Steve Fuller, *Social Epistemology* (Bloomington: Indiana University Press, 1988); Steve Fuller, *Philosophy of Science and Its Discontents* (Boulder: Westview Press, 1989); and Fuller's new journal, *Social Epistemology.* See also Gary B. Madison, *Understanding: A Phenomenological-Pragmatic Analysis* (Westport, CT: Greenwood, 1982); and Maurice A. Finocchiaro, *Galileo and the Art of Reasoning: Rhetorical Foundations of Logic and Scientific Method* (Dordrecht, Holland: Reidel, 1980).

7. A colleague at Iowa in hydraulic engineering, Enzo Macagno, is writing a book on Leonardo's drawings of water, chaos theory before the name.

8. See, for example, Mary Hesse, *Models and Analogies in Science* (South Bend: University of Notre Dame Press, 1963); and D. N. McCloskey, *If You're So Smart.*

9. Cf. Wayne Booth, *Modern Dogma and the Rhetoric of Assent* (Chicago: University of Chicago Press, 1974), who makes this point about Russell in persuasive detail.

10. George Santayana, *Persons and Places: Fragments of Autobiography*, ed. W. G. Holzberger and H. J. Saatkamp Jr. (Cambridge: MIT Press, 1987), 441.

11. When a conference was organized a few years ago to discuss the "rhetoric of economics," the organizers expected the journalists invited from *Newsweek*, the *New York Times*, and the *Boston Globe* to be the most canny of the guests. But, in fact, the science journalists could not grasp why the 3 × 5 card definition of scientific method was inadequate. The working economic scientists had no problem understanding it; the working journalists were uncomprehending and scandalized. See David Warsh's piece in Arjo Klamer, D. N. McCloskey, and R. M. Solow, eds., *The Consequences of Economic Rhetoric* (Cambridge: Cambridge University Press, 1988). Science journalists are puzzled at how to cover non-normal science or the criticism of science. They know how to cover astounding new findings that will make us wise and rich but not the finding that the findings are not astounding and will not make us wise or rich. They impose a naive metastory on science.

12. *The Origin of Species* (London: Penguin, 1968 [1859]), 65. In his *Autobiography*, Darwin asserts that he "worked on true Baconian principles, and without any theory collected facts on a wholesale scale" (quoted in John Angus Campbell, "Charles Darwin: Rhetorician of Science," in *The Rhetoric of the Human Sciences*, ed. John S. Nelson, D. N. McCloskey, and Allan Megill (Madison: University of Wisconsin Press, 1987), 73.

13. Quoted in Campbell, "Charles Darwin," 74.

14. For which see, among others in the revival of rhetoric, Chaim Perelman and Lucy Olbrechts-Tyteca, *The New Rhetoric: A Treatise on Argumentation*, trans. J. Wilkinson and P. Weaver (Notre Dame: University of Notre Dame Press, 1969); Wayne C. Booth, *Modern Dogma*; Brian Vickers, *In Defense of Rhetoric* (Oxford: Clarendon Press, 1988); Richard McKeon, *Rhetoric: Essays in Invention and Discovery* (Woodbridge, CT: Ox Bow Press, 1987); and the best short introduction to the techniques in practice, George A. Kennedy, *New Testament Interpretation through Rhetorical Criticism* (Chapel Hill: University of North Carolina Press, 1984). In particular fields (mathematics, anthropology, history, political science), see Nelson, Megill, and McCloskey, eds., *Rhetoric of the Human Sciences*; and other books in the Wisconsin University Press series The Rhetoric of the Human Sciences.

15. D. N. McCloskey, *The Rhetoric of Economics* (Wisconsin: University of Wisconsin Press, 1985); Arjo Klamer, *Conversations with Economists* (Totowa, NJ: Rowman and Allanheld, 1984).

16. See Stephen G. Brush, "Prediction and Theory Evaluation: The Case of Light Bending," *Science* 240 (1 December 1989): 1124-29. The prestige of prediction (as against postdiction, history) probably arises from the "discredited empiricist conception of science" (p. 1127) still dominant in the minds of nonscientists.

17. Jerome Bruner, *In Search of Mind: Essays in Autobiography* (New York: Harper & Row, 1983), 29.

18. Roy D'Andrade, "Three Scientific World Views and the Covering Law Model," in *Metatheory in Social Science*, ed. D. W. Fiske and R. A. Shweder (Chicago: University of Chicago Press, 1986), 39.

19. Stephen C. Levison, *Pragmatics* (Cambridge: Cambridge University Press, 1983), 112.

20. Francis Bacon, *The New Organon* and *The Great Instauration [Instauratio Magnal]*, in *Francis Bacon: A Selection of His Works*, ed. S. Warhaft (Indianapolis: Bobbs-Merrill, 1965).

2

The Truth/Value of Judgments[1]

Barbara Herrnstein Smith

The slash in my title, between "truth" and "value," marks an opposition and a proposed exchange: *value* as opposed to *truth*, value gained for truth lost. What would be lost would be a theoretical conception of truth that has become, in any case, quite problematic. What would be gained would be a way of thinking about the social operation of value judgments—and, in fact, of all utterances, including scientific statements—that accounts for their value in actual verbal transactions. In my own cognitive economy and, I think, that of many others concerned with these questions, there would be a net profit in such an exchange. Those quite heavily invested in that problematic conception of truth are, of course, likely to calculate it otherwise.

To clarify this, I must say a few words about the larger study from which these remarks are drawn. The focus of that study is a reconceptualization of value as radically contingent: that is, what we speak of as "*the* value" of some entity is seen as neither a fixed nor intrinsic property of that entity in itself but, rather, as a variable product of various heterogeneous conditions, including the states, interests, and perspectives—or, as I usually refer to them, the "economies"—of some subject or set of subjects. By "contingent," then, I mean not merely provisional, and not at all unconstrained or personally whimsical, but, precisely, *conditional*; and I say "radically" contingent not to ally myself with any specific political or theoretical radicalism (at least not here), but to stress that the conditionality of value is thorough—"all the way down," as it is sometimes said—and also without exceptions. The formulation applies, in other words, to value of all kinds: aesthetic, moral, and—this being my specific topic on the present occasion—epistemic.

Two corollaries of the conception of value just outlined are of particular interest here. The first is that a verbal judgment of "*the* value" of some entity—for example, a painting, a literary work, a moral action, or

any other object, event, practice, text, or utterance—cannot be a judgment of some independently determinate (or, as it is said, "objective")
property of that entity. What it can be, however—and, I would say,
typically *is*—is a judgment of that entity's contingent value: that is, the
speaker's observation or estimate of how that entity does or will figure
in the economy of some more or less limited population of subjects
under some more or less limited set of conditions.

The second corollary is that no value judgment can have truth-
value in the usual sense. That usual sense, however, is no longer all
that usual. When it is interpreted in accord with some version of the traditional telegraphic model of discourse—in which communication is
seen as the duplicative transmission of a message from one consciousness to another—truth-value is seen as a measure of the correspondence between such a message (or, as it might be said, "proposition")
and some independently determinate fact, reality, or state of affairs.
That model of discourse, along with the entire structure of conceptions,
epistemological and other, in which it is embedded, is now felt in many
places to be theoretically unworkable. It has not, however, been
replaced by any other widely appropriated model. There have been, of
course, throughout the century, sophisticated demonstrations of precisely that unworkability; and there have also been attempts, some of
them quite painstaking, to rehabilitate the key terms, concepts, and
conceptual syntax of the traditional model.[2] What appears to be needed,
and is perhaps emerging, is a thorough and appropriately elaborated
reformulation—in particular, one in which the various fundamentally
problematic explanatory structures involving duplicative transmission,
correspondence, equivalence, and recovery are replaced by an account
of the dynamics of various types of *consequential interaction*.

With respect to its epistemological component (or what is traditionally referred to as "perception," "knowledge," "belief," and so forth)
this would be an account of how the structures, mechanisms, and
behaviors through which subjects interact with—and, accordingly, constitute—their environments are modified by those very interactions.[3]
With respect to what we call "communication," it would be an account
of the dynamics of the differentially constrained behaviors of subjects
who interact with, and thereby act *upon*, each other, for better and for
worse. I return to this latter suggestion below, but, for the moment, it is
enough to observe that, whatever its emergent shape (or, more likely,
shapes), an alternate account of our commerce with the universe and
our commerce with each other is not yet available.

In the meantime, the telegraphic model of communication, along
with its associated conception of truth as correspondence to an inde-

pendently determinate reality, continues to dominate theoretical discourse, and the theoretical interest of the term "truth" itself continues to be reinforced by its numerous—and, it must be emphasized here, irreducibly *various*—idiomatic and technical uses. Indeed, the term appears to be irreplaceable and, economically speaking, priceless: for its rhetorical power in political discourse alone—and there is perhaps no other kind of discourse—would seem to be too great to risk losing or even compromising. Nevertheless, as already indicated, the theoretical value of the concept of truth-value has already been compromised. Indeed, the value of truth and of truth-value seem to be as contingent—as conditional, as historically and locally variable—as the value of anything else.

One more preliminary observation, to anticipate certain anxieties. To question the idea of a reality with independently determinate features is not to say that we cannot describe the features of our world on the basis of our interactions with it. It is to say, rather, that the world with which we *can* interact depends on the kinds of creatures we are (our perceptual and cognitive capacities, for example), and that however we *do* describe the features of our world must always be a function of our particular—historically and otherwise variable—ways of conceiving it. To speak of our *conceiving* the world requires that there be "something" other than itself—something "out there," if you like—other than the process of conceiving-the-world. I am not, in short, offering a solipsistic or "idealist" epistemology. But I cannot conceive of a single other thing to say or way to think about that "something"—not a single feature to predicate of it, or any way to describe, analyze, or manipulate any of its properties—that would be altogether *independent* of that process.

So much for preliminaries. I turn now to the first part of these remarks, which is concerned with the general value—or, we might say, social economics—of value judgments.

The Value of Value Judgments

Value judgments may be considered not as a class of "propositions" identified through certain *formal* features but, rather, as a type of communicative behavior responding to, and constrained by, certain social conditions. The latter sort of analysis avoids, but makes apparent, the theoretical impoverishment as well as fundamentally problematic dualism of more traditional approaches. For, as will be seen, the classic dichotomies typically invoked and perpetuated by these approaches (dualisms such as personal *vs.* impersonal, expressing subjective pref-

VJ = comm. behavior w/in social conditions

1) solipsism: theory holding that the self can know nothing but its own modifications — that the self is the only existent thing; extreme egocentrism

erences *vs.* making objective judgments, speaking for oneself alone *vs.* claiming universal validity, and so forth) have obscured the range, variety, richness, and modulation of individual value judgments, the crucially relevant continuities between value judgments and other types of discourse, and, perhaps most significantly, the social dynamics through which *all* utterances—evaluative and otherwise, including scientific statements—acquire their value.

VJ= fund. form   Value judgments appear to be among the most fundamental forms
of soc. comm of social communication and also among the most primitive benefits
benefit of of social interaction. Insects and birds, for example, as well as mam-
soc. intern mals, signal to other members of their group, by some form of specialized overt behavior, not only the location but also the "quality" of a food supply or territory. And, creatures such as we are, we, too, not only produce but also eagerly solicit from each other both, as it might be said, "expressions of personal sentiment" (How do you like it?) and "objective judgments of value" (Is it any good?). We solicit them because, although neither will (for nothing can) give us knowledge of any (supposed) independently determinate value of an object, both may let us know (or—and this will be significant here—at least *appear* to let us know) other things that we could find interesting and useful.

It is evident, for example, that other people's reports of how well certain things have gratified them, though "mere expressions of their subjective likes and dislikes," will nevertheless be interesting to us if we ourselves—as artists, say, or manufacturers or cooks—have produced those objects, or if—as parents, say, or potential associates—we have an independently motivated interest in the current states of *those people* or in the general structure of *their* tastes and preferences. Also, no matter how magisterially delivered and with what attendant claims or convictions of universality, unconditionality, impersonality, or objectivity, any assertion of "*the* value" of some object can always be unpacked by the listener as a judgment of its *contingent* value and appropriated accordingly; that is, as that speaker's observation and/or estimate of how well that object, compared to others of the same (implicitly defined) type, has performed and/or is likely to perform some particular (even though unstated) desired/able functions[4] for some particular (even though only implicitly defined) subject or set of subjects under some particular (even though not specified) set or range of conditions. Any evaluation, then, no matter what its manifest syntactic form, ostensible validity claim, and putative propositional status, may be of *social* value in the sense of being appropriable by other people. It remains the case, however, that the value of a particular evaluation will itself be contingent, for it will be a function of, among other things, the particu-

evaluation is social
any eval. it is appropriable

lar perspective from which that value is being figured.

Consider a critic's verbal evaluation of an art work: "Brava, brava," for example, or the following, which I cite from an actual set of comments on a painting: "The work is physically small—eighteen by thirteen inches—but massive and disturbingly expressive in impact." This is, by the way, an interesting combination of what would traditionally be seen as a hard-facts "objective" description (you could check it with a measuring rod) and a vague "subjective" judgment ("disturbingly expressive in impact"—hmm, I see . . . but is that good or bad?). The point that I want to emphasize here, however, is that the value of the judgment just cited would be figured *differently* by each of the various people who might be involved: these would include *(a)* the critic himself, who could be anyone from the artist's teacher, brother, or agent to some casual gallery visitor, a Warburg Institute art historian, or a member of a Committee for the Preservation of Cultural Standards and Ideological Purity; *(b)* the artist, whose interest in the critic's comment would be different from that of the critic himself but would still depend on the latter's identity and/or institutional role; and *(c)* any of various specifically addressed listeners or bystanders or eavesdroppers—for example, a potential patron, a gallery-going reader of *Art News*, a fellow art student, or someone who just likes to know what's going on and what other people think is going on. My point is that, for each of these people, the critic's evaluation of the painting would itself be registered as good, bad, or middling in relation to a different configuration of interests: interests that might be quite personal but might also be more or less shared by other—perhaps many other—people.

The social value of value judgments is illustrated most concretely, perhaps, by the most obviously commercial of them, that is, the sorts of assessments and recommendations issued by professional evaluators: film and book reviewers, commissioned art connoisseurs, and those who prepare consumer guides, travel guides, restaurant guides, racetrack tipsheets, and so forth. Such evaluations are not only regularly produced but also regularly sought and bought by the citizens of late capitalist society who live in what is, in effect, a vast supermarket, open twenty-four hours a day, with an array of possible goods that is not only enormous but that constantly increases and changes and, moreover, does so at a pace that constantly outstrips our ability to obtain current information about them and thus to calculate how they might figure in our personal economies. Indeed, if we were the optimizing "rational consumers" so beloved by economists—that is, consumers who, given total information about market conditions, always buy the best for their money—we would have to spend so much of our time acquiring that information that there would be little time left to buy, much less to consume, anything at all.[5]

The supermarket described here is, to be sure, a flagrant feature of contemporary Western society. It is not, however, as recent or as culturally unique as is sometimes suggested. For we always live in a market, always have limited resources—including limited time, energy, and occasion to locate and sample for ourselves the entire array of possible goods in it—and therefore always find it economical to pay others to locate and sample some of those goods for us. Professional evaluations—reviews, ratings, guides, tips, and so forth—are only highly specialized and commoditized versions of the sorts of observations and estimates of contingent value commonly exchanged more informally among associates in any culture; and, though we do not always pay each other for them in hard coin, we commonly do pay for them in coin of some sort, such as gratitude and good will, redeemable for return favors and future services.

It appears, then, that evaluations—of art works along with anything else consumable, and what isn't?—are themselves *commodities* of considerable value, and this in spite of what is sometimes alleged to be their tenuous cognitive substance and suspect propositional status as compared with other kinds of utterances: factual descriptions, for example, or empirical scientific reports. Of course, the cognitive substance and propositional validity of aesthetic judgments have been strenuously defended. Indeed, the dominant tradition in post-Kantian aesthetic axiology has characteristically offered to demonstrate that such judgments *do* have truth-value, or at least that they can properly claim to have it under the right conditions—which, however, always turn out to be rather excruciating ones to meet and also rather difficult, or perhaps impossible, to certify as having *been* met. I am, however, approaching the issue here from a different—in fact, reverse—direction, my procedure and objective being not to demonstrate that aesthetic judgments have as much claim to truth-value as factual or descriptive statements but, rather, to suggest that just as aesthetic judgments do not have but also do not *need* truth-value in the traditional sense, neither, it seems, do any of those other traditionally epistemically privileged forms of discourse.

There is, of course, no way for us to be *certain* that our associates' reports of their personal likes and dislikes are sincere or that the ratings and rankings produced by professional connoisseurs and local men and women of taste are, as we might say, "honest" and "objective." Indeed, we may grant more generally that any judgment, aesthetic or otherwise, will be shaped by the speaker's own interests, both as a party to the verbal transaction in which the judgment figures and in other ways as well. It may also be granted that, since value is especially subject-variable for certain classes of objects, among them art works, the appropriability of value judgments of such objects may be correspondingly highly subject-variable. For these reasons—that is, because we do tend to learn that there's no such thing as an honest opinion and that one man's meat is another's poison—we typically supplement and discount the value judgments we are offered "in the light," as we say, of knowledge we have from other sources: knowledge, for example, of the reviewer's personal and perhaps idiosyncratic preferences, or the connoisseur's special interests or obligations and thus suspect or clearly compromised motives.

Or, rather, knowledge we *think* we have. For there is, of course, no way for us to be sure of the accuracy, adequacy, or validity of this *supplementary* knowledge either, and we may therefore seek yet further supplementary information from yet other sources: some trustworthy guide to travel guides, perhaps, or a reliable review of the reliability of film reviewers, or an inside tip on what tipsheet to buy. It is clear, however, that there can be no end to this theoretically infinite regress of supplementing the supplements and evaluating the evaluations, just as there is none to that of justifying the justifications of judgments, or grounding the grounds of knowledge of any kind—though, in practice, we do the best we can, all things considered . . . at least as far as we know those things, or think we know them. We need not linger over the epistemological regress here. What is more pertinent to observe is that, *in all the respects mentioned*, value judgments are not essentially different from "descriptive" or "factual" statements, and that their reliability and objectivity are no more compromised by these possibilities—or, for that matter, any *less* compromised by them—than the reliability or objectivity of any other type of utterance, from a pathetic plea of a headache to the solemn communication of the measurement of a scientific instrument.[6]

Not *essentially* different: there are, however, *relative* differences of various kinds. That is, these various types of discourse (evaluative, descriptive; personal, impersonal; informal, scientific) may be seen not as absolutely distinct by virtue of their radically opposed claims to truth or objective validity, but as occupying different positions along a number of relevant continua. Thus, although the value of *all* objects is to some extent subject-variable, the value of *some* objects will be *relatively more uniform* than others among the members of some community—as will be, accordingly, the judgments concerning their value exchanged within that community. Similarly, although the conditions under which a particular judgment or report can be appropriated by other people are *always* to some extent limited, they will be *relatively broader* for *some* judgments and reports than for others. And although fraud, exploitation, and idiosyncrasy are possibilities—and perhaps to some extent inevitabilities—in *any* verbal utterance, their occurrence in *certain* types of utterance will be *relatively better controlled* by social and institutional constraints than in other types. Indeed, the familiar distinctions and contrasts among types of discourse that are at issue here (that is, between "merely subjective" and "truly objective" judgments, or between "mere" value judgments and "genuine" factual descriptions, or between statements that can and cannot claim truth-value) are no doubt continuously reinforced by the undeniability of just such *relative* differences—which, however, in accord with certain conceptual operations perhaps endemic to human thought, are typically *binarized, polarized*, and *absolutized*.

We may take note here of the recurrent anxiety/charge/claim—I refer to it as the Egalitarian Fallacy—that, unless one judgment can be said or shown to be more valid than another, then all judgments must be equal or equally valid. While the present account does imply that no value judgment can be more "valid" than another *in the sense of* an "objectively truer statement" of "the objective value of an object" (for these latter concepts are seen here as fundamentally problematic), it does not follow that all value judgments are equally valid. On the contrary, what does follow is that the concept of "validity" *in that sense* is unavailable as a parameter by which to measure or compare judgments, whether as better or worse *or* as "equal." Value judgments can, however, still be compared and still be seen and said to be "better" or "worse" than each other. The point, of course, is that their value—"goodness" or "badness"—must be understood and compared *otherwise*, that is, as something other than their "truth-value" or "validity" in the traditional objectivist sense. What feeds the Egalitarian Fallacy is the widespread conviction that validity in an objectivist sense is the only possible measure of the value of utterances.[7] What the present account suggests is that there are other gradient parameters by which the value—goodness or badness—of judgments and all other utterances can be conceived and, accordingly, measured and compared.[8]

As I noted above, value judgments may themselves be considered commodities. What I would add here, glancing at the issue of the alleged equality of their validity under this account, is that some judgments are evidently worth more than others in the relevant markets. For example, the Michelin guides to Italian hotels, restaurants, and altar paintings have, we might say, a well-attested reputation for objectivity and reliability, at least among certain classes of travellers. This is not because there is, after all, just a little bit of objective—or universal sub-jective—validity to which the Michelin ratings can properly lay claim. On the contrary, their good reputation among those classes of travellers may be seen as a consequence of precisely those "compromising" con-ditions that I described above and summed up in the lesson that there is no such thing as an honest opinion: no verbal judgment, that is, that is not conditioned by the contingent circumstances of its own produc-tion, including the (assumed) interests and desires of its (assumed) audience—or, we could say (because it cuts both ways), no judgment that is altogether unresponsive to those interests and desires. For if we do not regard them as the regrettable effects of fallen human nature or as noise in the channels of communication or (in the terms of Jürgen Habermas's account) as "distortions" of the ideal conditions "presup-posed" by all genuine speech-acts,[9] then we may be better able to see them as the conditions under which all verbal transactions take place and which *give* them—or are, precisely, the *conditions of possibility* for—whatever value they do have for those actually involved in them.

The Economics of Verbal Transactions

That which we call "communication" is a historically conditioned social interaction, in many respects also an economic one and, like other or perhaps all economic transactions, a political one as well. It is his-torically conditioned in that the effectiveness of any particular interac-tion depends on the differential consequences of the agents' (speakers and listeners) prior verbal acts and interactions with other members of a particular verbal community. It is an economic interaction—and thus, one could say, transaction—to the extent that its dynamics operate on, out of, and through disparities of resources (or "goods," e.g., material property, information, skills, influence, position, etc.) between/among the agents and involve risks, gains, and/or losses on either or all sides. Communication is also a political interaction, not only in that its dynam-ics may operate through differences of power between the agents but also in that the interaction may put those differences at stake, threaten-ing or promising (again, it must cut both ways) either to confirm and maintain them or to subvert or otherwise change them.

Not all the implications of this conception of communication can be spelled out here.[10] What is significant for our present concerns is that *all* discourse—descriptive and factual as well as evaluative—operates through social economics and that, under *certain* conditions, speakers are constrained (so that it is, we could say, "in their own interest") to serve the interests of their assumed listeners in the ways we commonly characterize as "objectivity" and "reliability."

Thus, to return to the example given above, certain conditions relevant to the publishing industry (the need for the Michelin guides or *Art News* to secure a minimum number of regular readers and subscribers, the actual or potential competition from other such guides, reviews, or individual evaluators, etc.) will make it *more* profitable for professional raters and reviewers to produce evaluations appropriable by a relatively large but still relatively specific set of people and, accordingly, *less* profitable for them to accept bribes for favorable ratings or to play out idiosyncratic or inappropriately specialized personal preferences. We recall the familiar disclaimer commonly attached to such judgments (here an obviously somewhat, but not altogether, disingenuous one):

> Note that we have no ties to manufacturers or retailers, we accept no advertising, and we're not interested in selling products. The sole purpose of this book is to help you make intelligent purchases at the best prices.[11]

To increase the likelihood that the review or rating of a particular object (e.g., a new film showing in Los Angeles or an altar painting to be seen in Palermo) will be appropriable by that group of readers, the evaluator will, of course, typically sample it for himself or herself, operating as a stand-in for those subjects or, we might say, as their metonymic representative, and, to that end, will typically be attentive to the particular contingencies of which the value of objects of that kind appear to be a function for people of that kind. To do this reliably over a period of time, the evaluator will also be attentive to the shifts and fluctuations of those contingencies: that is, to the current states of the personal economies of those readers, to what can be discovered or surmised concerning their relevant needs, interests, and resources, to the availability of comparable and competitive objects, and so forth.[12]

As this suggests, competent and effective critics and evaluators—those who know their business and stay in business (and, of course, there are always many who don't do either)—operate in some ways very much like market analysts. But professional market analysis is itself only a highly specialized and commoditized version of the sorts of informal or intuitive research, sampling, and calculating necessarily performed by any evaluator. If we are inclined to reserve particular loathing for professional market analysts as compared to professional critics, it is no doubt because the latter typically operate to serve our interests as consumers whereas the former typically operate to serve the interests of our marketplace adversaries: those who seek to predict, control, and thereby profit from our actions and choices, that is, producers and sellers. But it must be remembered that *some* of us—or, indeed, *all* of us, some of the time—are producers and sellers, too, a point to which I will return below.

Given the general conditions and dynamics described above, professional critics and evaluators will typically seek to secure as large a group of clients as possible. The size of that group will always be limited, however, for, given also that one man's meat is the other's poison, the more responsive a judgment is to the needs, resources, desires, tastes, and so forth of *one* client, the less appropriable it will be by *another*. It is desirable all around, then, that verbal judgments, professional or amateur, be (as they usually, in fact, seem to be) more or less explicitly "tailored" and "targeted" to particular people or sets of people rather than offering or claiming to be appropriable by "everybody" or, in the terms of classic axiology, "universally valid."

- Validity in Science and the Value of "Beauty"

The market conditions that constrain evaluators to produce what we call objective and reliable judgments have their counterpart in social and institutional conditions that characteristically constrain scientists' behavior to comparable ends. Western disciplinary science has been able to pursue so successfully its defining communal mission—which we might characterize here as the generation of verbal/conceptual structures[13] appropriable by the members of some relevant community under the broadest possible range of conditions—because it has developed institutional mechanisms and practices, including incentives or systems of reward and punishment, that effectively constrain the individual scientist to serve that particular mission in the conduct and reporting of his or her research.[14]

Physicists and other scientists often recall that, in the course of their pursuit, production, and testing of alternate models or theories, they were drawn to what turned out to be the "right" one by their sense of its "beauty" or "aesthetic" appeal. Attempts to account for this phenomenon commonly focus on what are seen as the formal and hence aesthetic properties of the model or theory itself (for example, its "simplicity" or "elegance") or on what is seen as its correspondence to or conformity with comparable aesthetic features in nature (for example, the latter's "order," "pattern," or "regularity").[15] What makes such explanations questionable, however—that is, their ignoring of the historical, social, and institutional conditions under which

1) language is shaped by a community
2) s/he represents a community - is metonymic
34   *Barbara Herrnstein Smith*

scientific constructs are produced and appropriated, and their assumption of a "nature" with independently determinate features— suggests an alternate explanation more pertinent to our present concerns.

scientist is social

No matter how insulated his laboratory or how solitary his research, the scientist always operates as a *social* being in two fundamental respects. First, the language or symbolic mode of his conceptualizations—both its lexicon and syntax: that is, the tokens, chains, routes, and networks of his conceptual moves—has been acquired and shaped, like any other language, through his social interactions in a particular verbal community, here the community of scientists in that discipline or field. Second, in the very process of exploring and assessing the "rightness" or "adequacy" of alternate models, the scientist, too, like professional critics and other public evaluators, characteristically operates as a metonymic representative of the community for whom his product is designed and whose possible appropriation of it is part of the motive and reward for his own activity. In this respect, the scientist also operates as does any other *producer* of consumer goods, including, significantly enough here, the artist. For a significant aspect of the "creative" process is the artist's pre-figuring of the shifting economies of her assumed and imagined audiences, including audiences who do not yet exist and who are in many respects altogether unimaginable but whose emergent interests, variable conditions of encounter, and rival sources of gratification she will nevertheless intuitively surmise and to which, among other things, her sense of the *fittingness* and *fitness* of her creative/productive decisions will be responsive.

The point here is that the process of testing the "adequacy" of a scientific model or theory is never only—and sometimes not at all—a measuring of its fit with what we call "the data," "the evidence," or "the facts," all of which are, in any case, themselves the products of comparable conceptual and evaluative activities already appropriated to one degree or another by the relevant community. It is also a testing, sampling, and, in effect, *tasting* in advance of the ways in which the product will taste to other members of that community—which is to say also a calculating in advance of how it will figure for them in relation to their personal economies, including (though not necessarily confined to) those aspects of their personal economies that we call "intellectual" or "cognitive." Thus, what is commonly called "elegance" in a theory or model is often a matter of how sparing it is in its introduction of novel conceptual structures (novel, that is, relative to conceptualizations current in the community), in which case its beauty would indeed be a matter of its economy for its consumers: In effect, minimal cognitive processing and hence expenditure would be required for its effective appropriation, application, or "consumption." The sense of beauty or aesthetic appeal that draws the scientist in one direction rather than another may indeed, then, be a proleptic glimpse of its fit, fittingness, or rightness: not, however, in the sense of its correspondence with or conformity to an independently determinate reality but, rather, in the sense of its suitability for eventual communal appropriation.[16]

I have not specified any of the numerous and quite diverse ways in which a scientific construct *could* "figure" for the members of some relevant community. Consideration of such matters would be excessively digressive here, but one further point relating to the social economics of validity should be emphasized. Insofar as the development of a theory, model, or hypothesis has been directed toward the solution of some relatively specific set of technological and/or conceptual problems, its structure will have been produced and shaped in accord with the scientist's sense—perhaps largely intuitive—of its fitness or potential utility to that specific end, and its appropriability and hence social value will be largely a matter of the extent to which that surmised or intuited utility is actually realized. Or, it might be said, its validity will be tested by "how well it works" and will consist, in effect, in its working well. Pragmatist conceptions of validity, however, are not much of an improvement over static essentialist or positivist ones if they obliterate the historically and otherwise complex processes that would be involved in the *multiple and inevitably diverse* appropriation of any verbal/conceptual construct—or, to appropriate Jacques Derrida's useful term and concept here, its dissemination. Pragmatist reconceptualizations of scientific validity, then, must give due recognition to the fact that theories and models that work very badly or not at all—or no longer work—in the implementation of specific projects or the solution of specific problems may nevertheless "work" and acquire social value in other ways. They may, for example, come to figure as especially fertile metaphoric structures, evoking the production and elaboration of other verbal and conceptual structures in relation to a broad variety of interests and projects under quite diverse historical and intellectual conditions. One may think here of Marxist economics, psychoanalytic theory, and various ancient and modern cosmological models, including more or less "mystical," "metaphysical," and "primitive" ones—all of these, we might note, also classic examples of "nonfalsifiability" and/or nonscientificity in positivist philosophies of science.

[handwritten margin note: pragmatist validity (?)]

[handwritten footnote: 1) prolepsis: anticipation; the repre'n or assumption of a future act or dev't as if presently existing or accomplished;]

"Self-Refutation"

I anticipate here two questions—or, rather, two versions of the same question/objection—that the foregoing account frequently elicits. The first asks: If there is no truth-value to what anyone says, then why are you bothering to tell us all of this and why should anyone listen? The second, a quite classic taunt, goes as follows: But are you not making truth-claims in the very act of presenting these views, and isn't your account, then, self-refuting?

I would, by way of reply, make two points. The first is that, since these questions and objections appeal to the very network of concepts that are at issue, they beg the question. Thus, when someone (an objectivist, for example) says that I necessarily "make truth-claims" when I speak, she merely registers her inability to entertain any alternate conception of verbal value or what she calls "truth." It is equivalent to her saying that I can *speak* only under *her* (objectivist) description of language. Thus M. R. Burnyeat reformulates and reaffirms Plato's supposed demonstration that Protagoras's "man is the measure of all things" is self-refuting:

> No amount of maneuvering with his relativising qualifiers will extricate Protagoras from the commitment to truth absolute which is bound up with the very act of assertion. To assert is to assert that *p*—[i.e.,] that something is the case—and if *p*, indeed if and only if *p*, then *p* is true (period) [*sic*]. This principle, which relativism attempts to circumvent, must be acknowledged by any speaker.[17]

What I have offered here, however, is neither an "assertion" of some "*p*" nor a "circumvent[ion]" of assertion-in-itself or truth-in-itself, but an *alternate account* of what Burnyeat describes as "assertion" and "truth." Moreover, my alternate account, under its *own* description of language, as opposed to Burnyeat's, is not self-refuting but self-*exemplifying*.[18]

Accordingly, the second part of my reply to the charge of self-refutation consists of not merely "acknowledging" but *insisting* that everything I have already said here about *saying* applies to my own saying of it. Having designed this verbal/conceptual construct to be of value—interest, use, and perhaps even beauty—to the members of a certain community, I exhibit it here for possible appropriation, hoping that some members of this audience will, as we say, buy it, but by no means expecting all of them to do so. For, as the account itself indicates and as I very well recognize, each listener enters such a transaction with only so much coin and with other investments to secure: most significantly, prior cognitive investments, but also, perhaps, other (for example, professional or specifically religious) ones. My hope and expectation is that this account, or a piece of it, will find some buyers and, among those who cannot afford any of it, at least some admirers and, among those who do not admire it, at least some who are nevertheless affected by it. For it is thus—in part anyway, and in this respect like both the scientist and the artist—that I am, in effect, paid. As the account indicates, however, and as I also recognize, I cannot, in spite of my efforts to do so, predict or control either the fact or the manner of its consumption, now or henceforth, for both are as radically contingent as the value of the account itself. These conditions apply, it appears, to all those doing business in a market of this kind: Such are the constraints, such are the risks, such are the possible rewards.

Notes

1. Adapted, with revisions, from Barbara Herrnstein Smith, *Contingencies of Value: Alternative Perspectives for Critical Theory* (Cambridge: Harvard University Press, 1988). Permission to reprint is gratefully acknowledged.

2. Among the most recent of those—of course quite diversely produced, articulated, and circulated—demonstrations (and critiques of those attempted rehabilitations) are Jacques Derrida, *Of Grammatology*, trans. Gayatri C. Spivak (Baltimore & London: John Hopkins University Press, 1974); Jacques Derrida, *Margins of Philosophy*, trans. Alan Bass (Chicago: University of Chicago Press, 1982); Nelson Goodman, *Ways of Worldmaking* (Indianapolis: Hackett, 1978); Richard Rorty, *Philosophy and the Mirror of Nature* (Princeton: Princeton University Press, 1979); Richard Rorty, *The Consequences of Pragmatism* (Minneapolis: University of Minnesota Press, 1982); and David Bloor, *Wittgenstein: A Social Theory of Knowledge* (New York: Columbia University Press, 1983).

3. For further elaboration of this suggestion, see Barbara Herrnstein Smith, "Belief and Resistance: A Symmetrical Account," *Critical Inquiry* 18.1 (Autumn 1991): 125-39.

4. Having particular desired/able *effects* rather than performing particular desired/able functions is, in many cases, a more suitable unpacking.

5. As a current rating service puts it: "CONSUMER GUIDE knows what a challenge it is to pick the 'best buy' that meets your requirements . . . so we call in the experts to do the comparison shopping for you" (*Consumer Buying Guide*, Skokie, IL, 1987, 4).

6. The relation of scientific practice to evaluation is examined more extensively below, but the following summary of why, contrary to standard views of scientific method, the *replication* of a "finding" does not constitute a test of truth in science is especially relevant here: "The problem is that, since experimentation is a matter of skillful practice, it can never be clear whether a second experiment has been done sufficiently well to count as a check on the first. Some further test is needed to test the quality of the experiment—and so forth. . . . The failure of these 'tests of tests' to resolve the difficulty demonstrates the need for further 'tests of tests of tests' and so on—a true regress" (H. M. Collins, *Changing Order: Replication and Induction in Scientific Practice* (London, Beverly Hills, New Delhi: Sage Pub., 1985, 2).

7. For further discussion of the Egalitarian Fallacy in relation to the supposedly disabling effects of "relativism" in ethics and political theory, see Barbara Herrnstein Smith, "The Unquiet Judge: Activism Without Objectivism in Law and Politics," *Annals of Scholarship* 9.1-2 (1992): 111-33.

8. The force of J. .L. Austin's insight that there are other measures of verbal value, e.g., "felicity," has been all but lost in the objectivist appropriation of his work in so called "speech act theory." It may be noted as well that Austin appreciated, though he did not pursue his own emphasis of it, the radical contingency of truth: "It is essential to realize that 'true' and 'false' . . . do not stand for anything simple at all; but only for a general dimension of being a right or proper thing to say as opposed to a wrong thing, in these circumstances, to this audience, for these purposes and with these intentions" *How to Do Things with Words* (New York: Oxford University Press, 1962, 144).

9. Jürgen Habermas, "What Is Universal Pragmatics?", in *Communication and the Evolution of Society*, trans. Thomas McCarthy (Boston & London: Beacon Press, 1979). For further discussion of Habermans's problematic conception of communication, see Smith, *Contingencies of Value*, 110-12.

10. For further elaboration, see Barbara Herrnstein Smith, *On the Margins of Discourse* (Chicago: University of Chicago Press, 1978), 77-106; and Smith, *Contingencies of Value*, 107-10. Other accounts along these lines include Erving Goffman, *Strategic Interaction* (Philadelphia: University of Pennsylvania Press, 1969); Erving Goffman, *Relations in Public* (New York: Basic Books, 1971); and Morse Peckham, *Explanation and Power: The Control of Human Behavior* (New York: Seabury Pubs., 1979). Pierre Bourdieu develops a somewhat different but compatible sociological analysis of "the linguistic marketplace" in "The Economics of Linguistic Exchange," *Social Science Information* 16 (1977): 645-88.

11. *Consumer Buying Guide*, 4.

12. Thus, readers of the *Consumer Buying Guide* are assured: "Our experts are also careful to match the products to the changing needs of consumers, including, for instance, downsized appliances for small households" (4).

13. The mission of disciplinary science is also the production of appropriable *technical skills*, and the two may not always be separable; but, in connection with questions of verbal communication and the value of "propositions," our focus here is on its verbal/conceptual products: reports, statements, writings, theories, measurements, models, and so forth.

14. For recent discussions of the structure and operation of social and institutional constraints in disciplinary science, see David Bloor, *Knowledge and Social Imagery*, 2d ed. Chicago: University of Chicago Press, 1991); Bruno Latour and Steve Woolgar, *Laboratory Life: The Construction of Scientific Facts* (Princeton: Princeton University Press, 1986); Karin D. Knorr-Cetina, *The Manufacture of Knowledge; An Essay on the Constructivist and Contextual Nature of Science* (Oxford: Pergamon, 1981); Andrew Pickering, *Constructing Quarks: A Sociological History of Particle Physics* (Chicago: University of Chicago Press, 1984); and Bruno Latour, *Science in Action: How to Follow Scientists and Engineers through Society* (Cambridge: 1987).

15. For a recent attempt to analyze the good-true-beautiful relation in modern theoretical physics, see Paul Davies, *Superforce: The Search for a Grand Unified Theory of Nature* (New York: 1984), Simon & Schuster, 50-69.

16. The account here shares many elements with the analysis by Paul Davies in *Superforce*. Davies points out, for example, that the "rightness" of certain highly abstract features of a theory cannot be a matter of their validation "by concrete experience," that "beauty in physics is a value judgment involving professional intuitions," and that, with regard to theories, "better" means not truer (he does not, in fact, use the term) but more "useful," "more economical," "smoother," "more suggestive," and so on (66-69). He nevertheless moves repeatedly towards gratuitously objectifying formulations (e.g., "Nature *is* beautiful" and "Nevertheless the aesthetic quality *is there* sure enough" [68, 69]) that obscure the significance of the relationship, here emphasized, between the scientist's intuitive sense of the beauty of a theory and its suitability for appropriation by the members of a relevant community.

17. M. R. Burnyeat, "Protagoras and Self-Refutation in Plato's *Theaetetus*," *Philosophical Review* 85.2 (April 1976): 195.

18. For further analysis of the circular logic, rhetoric, and psychology of the charge of self-refutation, see Barbara Herrnstein Smith "Unloading the Self-Refutation Charge," *Common Knowledge* 2.2 (Fall 1993): 81-95. For a witty discussion and reflexive exemplification of self-exemplification, see Malcolm Ashmore, *The Reflexive Thesis: Wrighting Sociology of Scientific Knowledge* (Chicago: University of Chicago Press, 1989).

(handwritten annotations at top of page:)

(organization)
3 part structure to schema paradigm.

method   epistemic result   ontology
   structure   Content known   states-of-
   system   affairs
   form   the things
                                   themselves

3

Is There a Problem in Explaining Cognitive Progress?

Aaron Ben-Ze'ev

Introduction

The possibility of explaining cognitive progress is related to the assumed model of the mind in general and the cognitive system in particular. In a simplistic container paradigm, there is no problem of cognitive progress, since such progress merely consists of a quantitative increase in the amount of information the system possesses. This paradigm is, however, inadequate in describing the cognitive system. An alternative is a schema paradigm in which the cognitive system is of a dynamic and constructive nature. The system is dynamic in the sense that its own structure undergoes constant changes—some of which are qualitative; it is constructive in the sense that the cognitive system influences the cognitive content to a certain degree. This nature of the cognitive system precludes a simple positive answer to the question of whether or not there is cognitive progress. Admitting the problematic nature of such progress is not identical with identifying the very possibility of such progress; it implies, however, that such progress will not be that of a linear, forward march toward truth.

The container paradigm is clearly expressed by Locke: "the understanding is not much unlike a closet wholly shut from light, with only some little openings left, to let in external visible resemblances, or ideas of things without; would the picture coming into such a dark room but stay there, and lie so orderly as to be found upon occasion, it would very much resemble the understanding of a man" (1959, 2.11.17). Although Locke's formulation is simplistic, its assumptions can be found in current theories, particularly those influenced by Cartesian thought. Thus, Fodor argues that the prevailing representational theory of mind is, in fact, the good old theory to which "both Locke and Descartes (among many others) would certainly have subscribed. . . .

(handwritten annotations in right margin:) container paradigm   schema paradigm

Much of cognitive science is philosophy rediscovered—and, I think, vindicated" (1981, 26; see also 214, 217). In this view, the mind is an internal container, and cognitive progress is a quantitative increase in the amount of internal representations. In such a mechanistic paradigm, the cognitive system remains more or less stable, the only difference being that its empty shelves are gradually filled with more information. Cognitive progress is attained by adding a certain part to an existing system. When this mechanistic picture is applied to the realm of scientific knowledge, science is conceived as essentially taking pictures of the external world; the more pictures a science has, the more adequate the science is. Hence, there is always a linear cognitive progress. Both the individual person and science as a whole are constantly marching toward a better understanding of their surroundings. There is no problem of comparing performances of a cognitive system in various periods, because the cognitive system is hardly changed during the acquisition of knowledge. What is changed is merely the quantity of the information possessed. The nonproblematic nature of cognitive progress is achieved by describing a simplistic and inadequate picture of the cognitive system.

In the schema paradigm, which I advocate, the mind is not an internal container but a dynamic system of capacities and states. Mental properties are states of a whole system, not internal entities within a particular system. In this paradigm, the cognitive system is complex and dynamic; new information changes the system itself. An increase in the incoming information involves a gradual development of the cognitive system itself. Novel information is not stored in a separate warehouse, but is ingrained in the constitution of the cognitive system in the form of certain cognitive structures (or schemas). Since in this paradigm there are qualitative changes in the cognitive system, we cannot assume that all changes necessarily involve a better understanding of our surroundings; in consequence, the issue of cognitive progress becomes problematic. In this regard I make the following assumptions:

1. The cognitive system is essentially constitutive: Its structure is expressed in its content.
2. The basic cognitive structures are not permanent.
3. Knowledge is not certain.
4. Knowledge is not arbitrary—there is room for cognitive progress.

The first assumption is at the center of Kant's view; Kant, however, rejects the second one and, hence, the third assumption, which derives from the first two. The first two assumptions pose difficulties in comparing claims belonging to different cognitive systems; hence the uncertain nature of knowledge. The problem is how to maintain (4) despite (3).

I begin the discussion of the two paradigms by considering their stands concerning personal cognitive progress as expressed in memory and learning.

Personal Cognitive Progress

The prevailing metaphors for memory and learning, which are associated with the container paradigm, are essentially mechanistic: Memory is usually conceived as a kind of storehouse, and learning is often described as adding an external part to an internal system. Both metaphors are inadequate.

In keeping with the container approach, Locke described memory as "the storehouse of our ideas" (1959, 2.10.2). Versions of this idea, which seems to be in accord with the commonsense conception of memory, are quite common. The basic elements of the container approach are entities (things) and a storage place. The natural predicates for describing the relations between these elements are essentially mechanical: The entities are stored in the storage area and are then brought to the center of the mental stage. Locke argues that the ideas "are lodged in the memory." In remembering, the mind "sets itself on work in search of some hidden idea, and turns as it were the eye of the soul upon it." Sometimes the ideas offer themselves to the understanding, and sometimes they "are roused and tumbled out of their dark cells into open daylight, by . . . passions; our affections bringing ideas to our memory, which had otherwise lain quiet and unregarded" (1959, 2.10.7). Memory, in this view, consists of permanently stored entities which remain stable throughout the agent's life. There is no real development of the mental (or cognitive) system here.

Several thinkers oppose the simplistic container view of the mind in general, but only few of them draw the necessary implications concerning memory. Among those few opposing the storehouse metaphor, we may mention Reid (1967), Ryle (1949), Wittgenstein (1980) and Arnold (1984). Pribram also opposes this metaphor, arguing that "images and other mental contents as such are not stored, nor are they 'localized' in the brain. . . . Images and mental events emerge and are reconstructed" (1986, 514). The advocates of connectionism make a similar point. They reject the view that knowledge is stored as a static copy of a pattern, and propose instead that what is stored is the connection strengths between units that allow this pattern to be re-created (see, e.g., Rumelhart and McClelland 1986).

[margin note: mechanistic metaphors for memory + learning]

In light of such opposition, an alternative to the container view of memory may be proposed. In this alternative, which may be termed "the schema paradigm," the mind is thought to consist of capacities and states. Memory, in this view, is the capacity of the organism to arrive at states similar to its previous states of awareness while preserving a knowledge of their past origin. Remembering is a state of awareness directed at events that have taken place or were learned in the past. Here the metaphor of internal storage is inadequate, because the basic elements in this paradigm, capacities and states, are not stored. The capacity to play the piano and the state of being beautiful are *retained* but not *stored*. Similarly, capacities are not brought out of storage but are realized or actualized. The state of a car in motion is not stored in its engine when the car is stationary; rather the car has the capacity to repeat its state of being in motion. And by the same token, when a squeaky toy does not actually squeak, it retains (rather than stores) its capacity to squeak (Malcolm 1977, 197; Squires 1969).

Storing and retaining are two different forms of keeping something. A storage place is usually conceived as a passive container for holding something. This is the way we store furniture and books. The ideal conditions for such a storage are those entailing minimal external influence on the items being stored. We keep an item "on ice," as it were, so that it should remain unchanged until we want to use it again. A storage place is where you put things away in the expectation of finding them again in exactly the same condition as when you put them away (Bartlett 1932, 201). Retention is an active capacity for preserving something. Certain activities must be performed in order for a capacity or state to be retained. Retention of the ability to play the piano, speak a foreign language, or tell jokes require their use. One cannot expect to lay them away somewhere for a number of years and then to pick them up again in the same condition as when one left them. Concerning most capacities, we either use them or lose them. The same goes for states, such as being healthy or beautiful: Their preservation requires certain activities on our part.

Things that are stored are separate from the storage itself. On the other hand, although what is retained may be conceptually distinguished from the form of retention, it is not actually separate from this form. Taking the same tack, Skinner makes the point that we "put electricity into a battery and take it out when needed, but there is no electricity in the battery. When we 'put electricity in,' we charge the battery, and it is a charged battery that 'puts out electricity' when tapped" (1985, 295). Similarly, Skinner argues that organisms do not store away their

acquired traits inside themselves as though these were a kind of possession. Rather, organisms are changed in a way that enables them to
exhibit their traits. Storing, therefore, is not the only way to hold on to
something for a long time.

I believe that the schema paradigm is more adequate than the
storage model for explaining memory. I sustain this belief on three
bases: (1) the difficulties of the container paradigm; (2) the importance
of organization and relations in memory is more compatible with the
schema paradigm; (3) the schema paradigm gives a better account of
learning and forgetting.

why the schema paradigm?

1. Difficulties of the container paradigm

I will point out three major difficulties: *(a)* the problem of duplication, *(b)* the necessity of assuming a homunculus, and *(c)* the problem
of the individuation of memories (see also Ben-Ze'ev 1993).

a. The problem of duplication. Our knowledge of the past is
explained in the container paradigm by assuming an internal mental
entity (idea) which represents the past event. The difficulty here is obvious. The postulation of an entity which represents the object does not
solve the problem of the relationship between the agent and the remembered object; it merely relocates the problematic relation inside the agent
by shifting it to the relation between the homunculus and that entity. If
we cannot know something without being in possession of an internal
entity, how can one know the internal entity itself? There is here duplication without explanation. Two senses of duplication in the container
paradigm are *(a)* the external world is duplicated into internal mental
pictures, and *(b)* the conscious realm is duplicated into the unconscious
one. Both types of duplication are without real explanatory power.
Duplicating something does not explain it.

duplication w/o explanation

b. The necessity of assuming a homunculus. Another obvious difficulty of the container paradigm is the crucial explanatory role assigned
to the homunculus, who must be postulated in this paradigm. If the
conscious mental realm is duplicated into the unconscious one, we
should assume a homunculus who performed the various unconscious
activities such as looking at the internal pictures.

assumption of homunculus

c. The problem of the individuation of memories. Does a mental image
replicate a whole occasion in one picture, or merely parts of it? And
what are the temporal boundaries of an occasion? When did it begin
and end? This problem arises because the storage devices proposed by
the container paradigm are discrete pictures or images, whereas the

individuation of memories

1) homunculus: a little man; a miniature adult that in the
theory of preformation is held to inhabit the
germ cell — to produce a mature individual
merely by an increase in size

remembered events are continuous rather than discrete. Unlike internal images, schemas can easily accommodate continuous events because they represent rules of organizing such events.

2. The importance of organization and relations in memory

The conceptual categories of the schema paradigm are better suited for describing most phenomena of memory. In a storehouse, it makes very little difference how the items are disposed or organized. Something may be stored at the right or left side of the storehouse without being affected. However, in the schema paradigm, organization is an essential property, not a later addition. The importance of organization and relations in memory can, for instance, explain that it is much harder to recall the months of the year in alphabetical order than in their chronological sequence. A junkyard or tape recorder model of memory is feasible and even natural in the container paradigm, whereas the schema paradigm stresses the importance of the relations and organization among the various items. Many phenomena indicating the sensitivity of memory to organization attest to the greater suitability of the schema than the container paradigm for memory.

In the schema paradigm, an agent's knowledge of the past is explained by assuming the capacity to arrive at certain states of awareness. Here we actually speak not of representation but of re-presentation—of redoing what we have done before. We are doing, or are aware of, something which is similar in its significant aspects to something we have done, or were aware of, in the past. Remembering does not need internal entities which represent the remembered events any more than perceptual awareness does. Similarly, a diagram of the birthrate in the United States represents for some people the birthrate itself, without an internal entity having to be assumed.

3. The schema paradigm gives a better account of learning
   and forgetting

The container paradigm assumes a simplistic model of learning which is not compatible with many learning phenomena. Since, in this view, the cognitive system is hardly changed by its various activities, the system might be quite developed in the first place. (In this paradigm, there are other reasons for assuming a developed cognitive system right from the beginning; these are largely connected with the assumed internal nature of mind and with the impoverished data concerning the external world that the mind receives [see Ben-Ze'ev 1992, 1993].) In light of the developed nature of the cognitive system, learning is merely filling the empty shelves in the system with more information.

In the container paradigm, the agent's knowledge is stored in a separate, static warehouse, and no real development of the cognitive system occurs during the acquisition of knowledge, because the very complicated reasoning mechanisms, assumed to exist from early infancy, do not improve with use.

The alternative schema paradigm abolishes the artificial separation of the cognitive system from the information it receives. In this view, learning something new involves a dynamic change in the structure of the cognitive system. Accordingly, we can assume a gradual development of the cognitive system along with an increase in the incoming information. Information is embodied in the structure of the cognitive system, and there is no separation between the system and the newly acquired information. Past experience and other personal characteristics are not stored in a separate warehouse; rather, they are ingrained in the constitution of the cognitive system in the form of certain cognitive structures. In this view, learning, adaptation, and readiness are expressed as changes in the sensitivity of the cognitive system and not as changes in stored propositional information. Learning is a dynamic change of the whole system, not an addition of a discrete part; it involves the continuous updating of the schematic rules. In this sense, history is embodied in the schemas (Ben-Ze'ev 1992).

learning

The dispute over the nature of forgetting is revealing for clarifying the differences between the two paradigms. There are two major views of forgetting: *(a)* Forgetting is only the loss of access to memory, and hence nothing is ever lost from storage, and *(b)* forgetting is a true loss of information, and hence memory is not completely preserved. If memory is a kind of a storehouse, then, indeed, there is no reason why something should be destroyed within this warehouse. However, in a schema paradigm, in which learning is expressed in acquiring certain schemas and remembering consists of reactivating these schemas, there is no reason why experience should not strengthen certain schemas while weakening, and even destroying, others. There is no empirical evidence to support the view that true forgetting does not occur. On the contrary, there is some evidence that true forgetting does occur and forgetting is not merely a loss of accessibility (Squire 1987). Both learning and forgetting change the structure of memory, and both are constantly taking place in our everyday experience. Learning leads to the reorganization of memory; such reorganization includes the strengthening of certain structures and the weakening (even to the extent of destroying) other structures.

forgetting

relat. b/t learning + forgetting

The schematic account of memory clearly insists on the constitutive (or constructive) nature of the cognitive system involved in memory. The cognitive system is not a passive container but a dynamic system whose structure both influences the remembered content and is influenced by the incoming information. An example that would seem to indicate that remembering is a constitutive rather than a duplicative process is the familiar case of people reporting their recollection of a particular event in slightly different versions at different times, although they are convinced on each occasion that they are giving an accurate account of their recollection of the very same event. The container view would have difficulties in accounting for situations of this sort, because there is no apparent reason why the event should not be described in precisely the same way on each occasion; after all, the same image is supposed to be retrieved from storage each time (Coulter 1983, 79). This presents no problem for the schema paradigm, because remembering resembles other varieties of awareness in being influenced by the context in which it takes place. Whereas memory-images are more or less stable in the way that entities generally are, schemas contain flexible features that are responsive to circumstances and are, therefore, amenable to changes. Remembering is not comparable to a videotape replay of the original event; rather, it is an experience which is in certain respects similar to, although not identical with, an experience we have had before.

What are the implications of the two paradigms for the issue of personal cognitive progress? In the mechanistic paradigm, where learning is an addition of discrete elements, there is always a linear growth of personal knowledge. Adult knowledge is clearly more adequate than the knowledge of children, and in principle there is no problem in determining the adequacy of the knowledge of two different persons. There is no problem in such comparison, since the only difference between them is quantitative. In the schema paradigm, any type of comparison is more complex. Cognitive progress is not merely a quantitative change; it is also a qualitative change in the schematic structure of cognition. We can assume that this change usually involves more adequate and useful ways of cognition—otherwise there will be no evolutionary sense in such changes. But evolution does not always march forward; there may be cases in which previous cognitive structures may have been more useful. And in any event, even if the new cognitive structure is, generally speaking, a more adequate cognitive tool, the old structure may have some advantages over the new one concerning certain local issues. In comparison with knowledge of children, adult knowledge is more adequate knowledge overall, but children may know certain things better than adults. The same goes for the comparison between an artist and a scientist. The former is not always in an inferior cognitive position.

Scientific Progress

The difficulties in comparing various cognitive structures after a qualitative cognitive change are even more evident regarding scientific progress. In discussing this issue we will also find the container and the schema paradigms. Again, the container paradigm will offer a nonproblematic notion of scientific progress, but, like the case of personal cognitive progress, this paradigm is too simplistic. In the more complex schema paradigm, the issue of scientific progress is quite problematic.

When applying the container paradigm of memory to science as a whole, we receive the same mechanistic picture involving a basically passive cognitive system. The main features of this picture are the following:

1. Scientific knowledge consists of pictures (representations) of the external world.
2. The cognitive system is hardly changed.
3. The cognitive system is not constitutive—it does not leave traces upon the final cognitive products.

(margin note: container paradigm of scient. progress)

Just as personal memory is conceived as a storehouse, scientific knowledge is often thought of as a type of storehouse whose history involves a linear increase in true information about the world. To know something, in this view, is to take pictures of it; scientific progress is an increase in the accuracy and quantity of these pictures. The scientific system is passive in two important senses—(2) and (3); its basic structure (including the truth criterion) does not change, and this structure has no influence on the content of scientific theories.

The schema paradigm describes the scientific enterprise differently. Its main assumptions are the following:

1. Scientific knowledge consists of various projections of the world.
2. The cognitive system is constantly changed (including qualitative changes in the truth criterion).
3. The cognitive system is constitutive (or constructive) in the sense that it determines, to a certain extent, the cognitive content.

(margin note: schema paradigm of scient. progress)

In the container paradigm, scientific progress is nonproblematic in two basic senses: (*a*) There is no problem in likening the agent's knowledge to the world's properties, and (*b*) there is no problem in likening a particular item of knowledge to other instances of knowledge. These

(margin note: 2 assumpt. of the cont. para.)

two contentions are challenged by the schema paradigm.

The most serious challenge to the first assumption comes from Kant, who argued that the knower somehow organizes or constitutes what is known. His view assumes the relational nature of cognition: The meaning and validity of a claim is not simply determined by the world but is also related to the agent's conceptual schema. The adequacy of a claim is not a simple two-term relation between claims and states of affairs but, at the very least, a three-term relation among claims, states of affairs, and conceptual schemas. The conceptual schema is a parameter in determining the meaning and validity of a cognitive claim. If this parameter is not constant (as Kant believes it is), we have a problem concerning scientific progress.

It is important not to confuse (as often occurs) the epistemological dispute of whether cognition is constructive with the ontological dispute about the independent existence of known objects. The epistemological dispute questions whether cognition (or knowledge) is loaded with the agent's contributions. The two positions on this issue may be termed "constructivism" and "nonconstructivism" (or the "naive" paradigm). The ontological dispute questions whether the known objects exist independently of the knower. The two opposing positions with respect to this issue may be termed "realism" and "idealism." There appear to be three possible positions in this regard: (a) naive realism, according to which the agent has neither an epistemic nor an ontological influence on the known world; (b) constructive realism, according to which the agent has an epistemic but not an ontological influence, that is, knowledge is constructive in nature, but the existence of the world does not depend on the existence of an agent; and (c) constructive idealism, according to which the agent has both an epistemic and an ontological influence on the known world. From a purely logical point of view, naive idealism represents still another possible position. But such a view, which assumes ontological but not epistemic dependency, is implausible, since ontological dependency is the stronger and seems to entail epistemic dependency. I cannot analyze here in detail each of the above three views, but I will briefly comment on each of them (Ben-Ze'ev 1993).

Naive realism assumes that the known world exists independently of the knower and is not affected by cognitive processes. Realism is an ontological view assuming the existence of entities which are independent of the agent; and "naive" is an epistemic term referring to the cognitive passivity of the knower. In this view, any influence of personal and social characteristics (such as memory, belief, desire, emotion, expectations, social and cultural background, etc.) on the cognitive content is taken to be an interference with valid cognition. Cognition does not change the properties of the known objects, but merely reveals them as they exist independently, outside the agent. There is an identity here between the cognitive content and the properties of the external world. Naive realism has its own charm. It is the position with which we start before reflecting upon the nature of cognition. It is also close to common sense. The question is whether naive realism can explain the complexity of cognition. I believe it cannot. There is considerable empirical evidence for the active epistemic role of the agent. The cognitive content is constitutive in nature; personal and social characteristics exert an influence on the cognitive content. Thus, the agent's perception, memory, and thinking are influenced by the agent's experience, expectations, motivations, emotions, values, and so forth. The question is whether scientific knowledge can be purified of similar constitutive elements. To a certain extent, adequate scientific knowledge overcomes personal biases stemming from the specific personal and social background of the particular scientist. But this does not mean that there are no other, more fundamental constitutive elements which stem from the very nature of cognition. I will return to this issue later on.

It is quite clear that the agent is active at least from an epistemological viewpoint. Hence, any kind of a naive view of cognition is wrong. It remains to be seen whether the epistemic constructive nature implies an ontological constructive nature as well, namely, whether the agent's cognitive activity implies an ontological dependency of the known objects.

Constructive idealism is similar to naive realism in disposing of the difficulties involved in the agent-object relation by denying the very existence of one side of the problematic relation. In its extreme form, which is a version of extreme idealism or solipsism, constructive idealism is a bizarre view which I doubt is seriously held by anyone outside the classroom. After all, an independent world had existed long before any agent evolved. I will enlarge no further on this version of idealism (or solipsism), but turn instead to a consideration of the more moderate views deriving from the constructive nature of cognition.

Constructive realism seems to be the most promising position. It admits a significant cognitive activity of the agent, but assumes an ontological independence of the external world. Among the various forms of constructive realism, I advocate that which may be termed "constitutive realism." The unique feature of this version is that the subject's contributions are not separate additions to the existing cognitive content but structural constituents of this content. For the purpose of our discussion, however, constituent realism is similar to constructive realism (indeed, it is a type of constructive realism).

Constitutive realism seems to be adequate in regard to the physical sciences. The description of the physical world, like that of other realms, is constitutive: It is described from a particular cognitive perspective which determines the content, to a certain extent. However, the descriptive framework in physics is directed at a world that exists independently of the cognitive system. Scientific physical theories describe an independent world. The description, but not the existence of the physical world, is relational. My realistic position in the ontological dispute concerning the independent existence of physical entities does not imply a naive position in the epistemological dispute concerning whether the entities described by modern physics are independent of the physical cognitive framework. To believe that there are entities independent of any cognitive system, one need not believe that cognition is simply picking up these entities and transferring them into the head. The claim that describing X depends upon a certain cognitive perspective does not necessarily imply that the existence of X depends upon that perspective. Knowing X from a certain cognitive perspective does not deny the independent existence of X (Lewis 1929, ch. 6).

Is the same true of social sciences? Social sciences are also constitutive from an epistemological viewpoint; theories in social sciences are formulated from a particular cognitive perspective which determines, to a certain extent, the content. Social reality is essentially independent of the particular scientist investigating it. Accordingly, personal biases can be detected and rejected in the social sciences as they are detected and rejected in the physical sciences. Since the social realm presupposes the existence of social beings, its existence is relational in this sense. This does not undermine the possibility of comparing and determining the adequacy of various social theories. The relational existence of the social realm does not make social sciences less "objective"; social scientists just have to take into account the ontological flexibility of their subject matter. Generally, I believe that the problems discussed here are of equal importance to both the physical and the social sciences. There is no essential difference between the two types of science in this regard.

There is no sense in speaking of scientific progress while assuming constructive idealism. Such progress is possible in naive realism. The only trouble with naive realism is that it is false. Naive realism cannot explain the complexity of the cognitive system; in fact, it hardly assumes any role for such a system. (There is nothing wrong in being naive; actually, there is a certain attraction in such an attitude, but one should not expect much from it.) Scientific progress is possible, although somewhat problematic, in constitutive realism. To clarify this issue, I refer

map → ship of the
metaphors system
cognitive

now to two metaphors of the cognitive system: the map metaphor (as I've heard it in lectures by Michael Strauss) and the ship metaphor (first suggested to me in the work of Nevrath; also see Campbell 1988).

map metaphor

The function of a map is to copy the globe, and cognition supposedly should copy reality. While the map has only two dimensions, the globe has three. An exact copy can be achieved only between similar surfaces; there is no plane that can copy the globe exactly. There must always be some distortion—we can have perfect superimposition only when we copy onto other global surfaces. Several basic methods of drawing maps are available: One is true for shape, another for area, and a third for distance; there are some projections which are true for two elements, but none is true for all three elements. Because the map cannot be an exact copy of the globe, we must choose the distortion we want least, or the adequacy we want most. The adequacy of a map depends not only on the globe but also on the method of projection. In Mercator's projection, Greenland is bigger than Australia, but on the globe, the situation is the opposite. The meaning and truth of a map is not a two-term relation between the map's content and the globe but a three-term relation among the map's content, the globe, and the method of projection.

The difficulties found in the transition from the three-dimensional surface of the globe to the two-dimensional surface of the map should be magnified in the transition from, say, the physical realm to the conceptual one. In the first case, both that which copies and that which is copied belong to the physical realm; in the second case, the copying is between two realms with enormous differences. For example, physical objects are in space, they have energy and mass, and they are measured in a quantitative manner. Cognition lacks these properties. As in the case of the map, we should expect some distortion in the cognitive content. This content is determined not only by the state of affairs of the world but also by the agent's conceptual schema. The meaning (and truth) of the agent's cognition is not a two-term relation between the agent's claims and states of affairs, but is (at least) a three-term relation among claims, state of affairs, and conceptual schemas.

The map comparison, if adequate, clearly expresses the dynamic and problematic nature of cognition, and in particular the problematic notion of scientific progress. The difficulties in the latter stem from two basic assumptions: (a) The agent's conceptual schema has a constitutive role in cognition, and (b) there may be more than one possible conceptual schema. As mentioned, Kant accepted the first assumption but denied the second. Hence, his view has no difficulty accounting for scientific progress and assuming certainty in scientific knowledge.

However, if we accept the second assumption and assume a qualitative change in the cognitive system and in its truth criterion, the problem of comparing the new and old schemas arises. If cognition is not merely copying the external world, but also involves constructive elements, the notion of truth is in jeopardy and it is hard to compare the truth value of various scientific theories.

ship metaphor

To deal with this problem, let us turn to the ship metaphor. Scientists are like sailors who must repair a rotting ship at sea. They rely on the great bulk of the timbers while replacing a particularly weak one; each of the timbers may, in its turn, be replaced. There are some planks which are more fundamental than other planks and hence will be replaced less often. Although all planks may be replaced, the proportion at any time of planks being replaced to all planks must always be small. This metaphor, too, suggests that the relational nature of cognition (the ship) is related to, and determined by, the system's assumptions (the planks). But this metaphor can explain conceptual (or cognitive) changes. It is possible that all planks will be replaced without an abrupt, unexplained change. Even after a basic change in the cognitive system, most old scientific facts remain valid. Different perspectives do not necessarily imply a complete separation of worldview. Wearing different-colored eyeglasses results in seeing different colors of the objects but not different shapes or sizes. Therefore, individuals with different conceptual schemas, or perspectives, can have common understanding and meaningful communication. Self-knowledge concerning one's unique perspective is essential for such communication. Having to know everything from a certain perspective (as the map metaphor suggests) may limit our knowledge, but it does not make our knowledge invalid. Being able to see and know things from various perspectives may reduce the limitations of our present knowledge (Lewis 1929, 174). Scientific knowledge is closer than other types of knowledge to the non-constitutive "view from nowhere" (to use Nagel's phrase). Scientific knowledge expresses the ability to describe objects not as they are seen from a momentary perspective but as they exist independently of such a perspective.

Cognitive changes are not an all-or-nothing affair; rather, they are a complex process involving both gradual and radical changes (Campbell 1988; Toulmin 1972). The diversity and complexity of factors in the scientific enterprise reduce the weight and, with it, the problematic nature of each factor. It is not the case that one single factor carries all the burden of explaining a conceptual change; in its own way, each factor influences the whole process of conceptual change. The assumption that cognitive content and truth criteria are determined not merely by the agent's conceptual schema denies the arbitrary nature of cognition, not its constitutive nature. It is likely that personal, sociological, and other contextual factors, which may hinder scientific progress, have greater weight in the short run than in the long run. Consequently, we are less certain about scientific progress in the short run than in the long run.

We may assume that (a) the knower somehow organizes (or even constitutes) what is known and (b) there is no uniquely correct way of doing so; however, we can still hold that (c) there is an order of preference of doing so. Although there are various ways of knowing things, none of which is the only correct one, some ways are more truthful (or adequate) than others. The myth viewpoint may have correct insights absent in modern science, but, all in all, modern science is closer to truth than the myth viewpoint. Scientific progress is put in doubt when we assume the constitutive nature of cognition and the change in the basic conceptual schemas. However, a number of circumstances can be cited that might reduce, though not abolish, the difficulties resulting from the change in our basic conceptual schemas. First, there are some features which are common to different schemas. Second, comparing different schemas can usually be done by referring to a more general schema. Third, in many cases, there are objective constraints which indicate the success of different schemas. In this manner, the success of most scientific theories is being constantly examined. Though these and other considerations do not make our claims certain, they certainly make them more reliable.

To return to our initial problem, there are models of mind and the cognitive system in which cognitive progress is not a real problem. These models are simplistic and insufficient. In alternative models, which describe more adequately the cognitive process, such a problem exists and its implications should be known. The presence of a problem, however, does not imply denying the existence of such progress; it merely implies the complexity of its explanation. The attraction of the mechanistic paradigm is its simplicity; this, however, is an inadequate paradigm, because it fails to explain various relevant phenomena. Although the complex schema paradigm does not offer clear-cut solutions, it offers more adequate explanations.

References

Arnold, M. B. 1984. *Memory and the Brain*. Hillsdale, NJ: Lawrence Erlbaum.

Bartlett, F. C. 1932. *Remembering*. Cambridge: Cambridge University Press.

Ben-Ze'ev, A. 1992. "Cognitive Development: Two Paradigms." In *Cognition, Information Processing and Psychophysics: Basic Issues*, ed. H. G. Geissler, S. W. Link, and J. T. Townsend, 67-90. Hillsdale, NJ: Lawrence Erlbaum.

————. 1993. *The Perceptual System: A Philosophical and Psychological Perspective.* New York: Peter Lang.

Campbell, D. T. 1978. "Descriptive Epistemology: Psychological, Sociological, and Evolutionary." In *Methodology and Epistemology for Social Science*, 435-86. Chicago: University of Chicago Press.

Coulter, J. 1983. *Rethinking Cognitive Theory.* New York: St. Martins Press.

Fodor, J. 1981. *Representation.* Cambridge: MIT Press.

Lewis, C. I. 1929. *Mind and the World Order.* [1956.] New York: Dover.

Locke, J. 1959. *An Essay Concerning Human Understanding.* [1690.] New York: Dover.

Malcolm, N. 1977. *Memory and Mind.* Ithaca, NY: Cornell University Press.

Pribram, K. H. 1986. "The Cognitive Revolution and Mind/Body Issues." *American Psychologist* 41: 507-20.

Reid, T. 1967. "Essays in the Intellectual Powers of Man." [1785.] In *Thomas Reid Philosophical Works*, vol. I, ed. W. Hamilton. Hildersheim: George Olms.

Rumelhart, D. E., and J. L. McClelland. 1986. *Parallel Distributed Processing*, vol. I. Cambridge: MIT Press.

Ryle, G. 1949. *The Concept of Mind.* London: Hutchinson.

Skinner, B. F. 1985. "Cognitive Science and Behaviourism." *British Journal of Psychology* 76: 291-301.

Squire, L. R. 1987. *Memory and Brain.* New York: Oxford University Press.

Squires, R. 1969. "Memory Unchained." *Philosophical Review* 78: 178-96.

Toulmin, S. 1972. *Human Understanding.* Princeton: Princeton University Press.

Wittgenstein, L. 1980. *Remarks on the Philosophy of Psychology*, vol. I. Chicago: University of Chicago Press.

4

The Dialogical Self

Charles Taylor

In a sense, "the self" is a modern phenomenon. Only in modern Western culture have we begun to speak of the human person as "the self" and of people as having and being selves. But this is not to propound the absurd thesis that earlier ages had no sense of reflexivity. Of course, they did. Moreover, reflexive pronouns exist in all sorts of languages (for all I know, in all languages). So what is special about "the self" in modern times?

The first thing to note is that we only begin to use this expression in modern times. That is, we put an article (definite or indefinite) in front of the reflexive pronoun, or we pluralize it. What does this signify? I want to argue that it reflects a description of something which has become a crucial feature of the human person for us, viz., certain powers of reflexivity.

We sometimes speak of the human person as "a self," where our ancestors might have said "soul." The shift reflects a change in our understanding of what is essential. We have developed practices of radical reflexivity in the modern world. By "radical reflexivity" I mean the focus not only on oneself but also on one's own subjective experience. To be interested in my own health or wealth is to be reflexively oriented, but not radically. But when I examine my own experience, or scrutinize by own thinking, reflexivity takes a radical turn.

The post-Cartesian ideal of clear, self-responsible thinking is the source of one set of disciplines of reflexivity, one in which the subject disengages himself from embodied and social thinking, from prejudices and authority, and is able to think for himself in a disengaged fashion. At the same time, the post-Romantic ideal of self-sounding and self-expression has launched us in another whole range of practices of reflexivity which bring into play the creative imagination.

The ideal subject of either or both of these practices cannot easily identify himself with some substantive description, particularly one with the metaphysical overtones of the "soul." What he essentially is is rather just this subject of reflexivity—that is, "a self."

What I am suggesting is that we see ourselves as selves, because our morally important self-descriptions push us in this direction; or, alternatively, because we identify ourselves with this kind of description.[1]

But this definition of what is peculiar to our age suggests a description of what is perennial in human life. There is one recurrent dimension of reflexivity which consists in the fact that humans devise or accept or have thrust upon them descriptions of themselves, and these descriptions help to make them what they are. Further, these self-descriptions, that is, descriptions which situate us relative to some goods, or standards of excellence, or obligations, we cannot just repudiate. A human being exists inescapably in a space of ethical questions; she cannot avoid assessing herself in relation to some standards. To escape all standards would not be a liberation but a terrifying lapse into total disorientation. It would be to suffer the ultimate crisis of identity.

What do we mean by "identity" when we speak of people defining their identity, suffering a crisis of identity, and the like? The notion of identity is linked to that of "who" we are. I sometimes answer the question "who" I am by telling my function ("I am the professor for 231D") or sometimes by stating my relationship ("I am X's brother-in-law"). In this way, I tell who I am by situating myself in some sort of social space, professional, familial. But the kind of identity which is crucial to having a coherent sense of self is one which relates us to ethical space. To have an identity is to know "where you are coming from" when it comes to questions of value or issues of importance. Your identity defines the background against which you know where you stand on such matters. To have that called into question, or to fall into uncertainty, is not to know how to react, and this is to cease to know who you are in this ultimately relevant sense.

With this in mind, we can hazard the following claims: Human beings always have a sense of self, in the sense that they situate themselves somewhere in ethical space. Their sense of who they are is defined partly by some identification of what are truly important issues, standards, goods, or demands; and correlative to this, by some sense of where they stand relative to these and/or measure up on them.[2] The sense of self so defined is something more than the bare reflexive awareness that they are a continuing subject discussed, for instance, by classical empiricists such as Hume, and raised again in recent discussion by Derek Parfit.[3] This latter awareness is quite independent of ethical assessment. That the issue of identity should have been raised in connection with this bare self-awareness, as against the richer sense of moral situation, is itself a product of the disengaged perspective which has helped to shape the modern self. I want to return to this below.

But first, I cannot try to state the relation between what is perennial and what is ever changing in human life. Humans always have a sense of self that situates them in ethical space. But the terms that define this space, and that situate us within it, vary in striking fashion. As we look through history, even at cultures more or less familiar to us, we can see a range of ethical spaces which are so different as to be often incommensurable. When we try to compare the sense of the good which goes along with the recognition of a universe of Forms—each of which defines its own telos and excellence—on one hand, with the sense of the right which goes with the standard of law which for purely procedural reason gives to itself, on the other, we find it impossible to define a common set of terms in which both these radically different outlooks could be undistortively stated. And these belong, after all, to the same civilization, if not the same age; neither of them is equivalent to the space of Dharma, or of Tao. Anthropologists will have no difficulty multiplying the examples.

My claim in the opening lines above was about the particular ethical space of us moderns, one in which the excellences of radical reflexivity bulk so large, that we are tempted to define ourselves as "selves." This peculiar use of the reflexive pronoun belongs to our particular language. In one sense, humans always have a sense of self; but we see ourselves as having or being "a self," and that is something new.

Among the practices which have helped to create this modern sense are those which discipline our thought to disengagement from embodied agency and social embedding. Each of us is called upon to become a responsible, thinking mind, self-reliant for her judgments (this, at least, is the standard). But this ideal, however admirable in some respects, has tended to blind us to important facets of the human condition. There is a tendency in our intellectual tradition to read it less as an ideal than as something which is already established in our constitution. This reification of the disengaged first-person-singular self is already evident in the founding figures of the modern epistemological tradition—for instance, in Descartes and Locke.

It means that we easily tend to see the human agent as primarily a subject of representations: representations first about the world outside; and second, depictions of ends desired or feared. This subject is a monological one. She is in contact with an "outside" world, including other agents, the objects she and they deal with, her own and others' bodies, but this contact is through the representations she has "within." The subject is first of all an "inner" space—a "mind," to use the old terminology, or a mechanism capable of processing representations, if we follow the more fashionable computer-inspired models of today. Other people may form the content of my representations. They may also be causally responsible for some of these representations. But what "I" am, as a being capable of having such representations, the inner space itself, is definable independently of body or other. It is a center of monological consciousness.

It is this stripped-down view of the subject that motivates the discussion of identity in terms of bare self-awareness which I mentioned above. But this is a rather arcane consequence, of interest only to (some) philosophers. Of greater moment is the fact that this view of the subject has made deep inroads into social sciences, breeding the various forms of methodological individualism, including the most recent and virulent variant, the current vogue for rational choice theory. It stands in the way of a richer and more adequate understanding of what the human sense of self is really like and, hence, of a proper understanding of the real variety of human culture and, hence, of a knowledge of human beings. (the trad. view of self)

This is perhaps the most inappropriate audience to make this point, because anthropology, of all the social sciences, has been founded on the recognition of deep cultural difference. But perhaps even here a critique of monological consciousness might arouse some interest.

What this kind of consciousness leaves out is the body and the other. I want to make a brief sketch of what is involved in bringing them back in.

A number of philosophical currents in the last two centuries have tried to get out of the cul de sac of monological consciousness. Prominent in this century are the works of Heidegger, Merleau-Ponty, Wittgenstein.[4] What all these have in common is that they see the agent not primarily as the locus of representations but as engaged in practices, as a being who acts in and on a world.

Of course, no one has failed to notice that human beings act. The crucial difference is that these philosophers set the primary locus of the agent's understanding in practice. On the mainline epistemological view, what distinguishes the agent from inanimate entities which can also affect their surroundings is the former's capacity for inner representations, whether these are placed in the "mind" or in the brain understood as a computer. What we have which animate beings don't—

Handwritten margin notes:

monological consciousness

identity as bare self-awareness — see pg 59

the trad. view of self

important of practice

1) arcane: known or knowable only to the initiate
2) virulent: marked by a rapid, severe, & destructive course; ~~able to overcome~~ markedly pathogenic; objectionably harsh or strong

understanding—was identified with representations and the operations we effect on them.

To situate our understanding in practices is to see it as implicit in our activity and, hence, as going well beyond what we manage to frame representations of. We do frame representations: We explicitly formulate what our world is like, what we aim at, what we are doing. But much of our intelligent action in the world, sensitive as it usually is to our situation and goals, is carried on unformulated. It flows from an understanding which is largely inarticulate.

(margin: practical theory… EM)

This understanding is more fundamental in two ways: (1) It is always there, whereas we sometimes frame representations and sometimes do not, and (2) the representations we do make are only comprehensible against the background provided by this inarticulate understanding. It provides the context within which alone they make the sense they do. Rather than representations being the primary locus of understanding, they are just islands in the sea of our unformulated practical grasp on the world.

Seeing that our understanding resides first of all in our practices involves attributing an inescapable role to the background. The connection figures, in different ways, in virtually all the philosophies of the contemporary countercurrent to epistemology, and famously, for example, in Heidegger and Wittgenstein.

But this puts the role of the body in a new light. The body is not just the executant of the goals we frame nor just the locus of causal factors shaping our representations. Our understanding itself is embodied. That is, our bodily know-how, and the way we act and move, can encode components of our understanding of self and world. I know my way around a familiar environment in being able to get from one place to another with ease and assurance. I may be at a loss when asked to draw a map or even give explicit directions to a stranger. I know how to manipulate and use the familiar instruments in my world, usually in the same inarticulate fashion.

But it is not only my grasp of the inanimate environment which is thus embodied. My sense of myself, of the footing I am on with others, also are, in large part. The deference I owe you is carried in the distance I stand from you, in the way I fall silent when you start to speak, in the way I hold myself in your presence. Or alternatively, the sense I have of my own importance is carried in the way I swagger. Indeed, some of the most pervasive features of my attitude toward the world and others is encoded in the way I carry myself and project in public space: whether I am macho or timid, eager to please or calm and unflappable.

(handwritten: understanding itself is embodied so is my sense of self)

In all these cases, the person concerned may not even possess the appropriate descriptive term. For instance, when I stand respectfully and defer to you, I may not have the word *deference* in my vocabulary. Very often, words are coined by (more sophisticated) others to describe important features of people's stance in the world. (Needless to say, these others are often social scientists). This understanding is not, or is only imperfectly, captured in our representations. It is carried in patterns of appropriate action, that is, action which conforms with a sense of what is fitting and right. An agent with this kind of understanding recognizes when they or others "have put a foot wrong." Their actions are responsive throughout to this sense of rightness, but the "norms" may be quite unformulated, or only in fragmentary fashion.

In recent years, Pierre Bourdieu has coined a term to capture this level of social understanding: the "habitus."[5]

But then one can see right away how the other also figures. Some of these practices which encode understanding are not carried out in acts of a single agent. The example of my deference above can often be a case in point. Deferent and deferred-to play out their social distance in a conversation, often with heavily ritualized elements. And, indeed, conversations in general rely on small, usually focally unnoticed rituals.

But perhaps I should say a word first about this distinction I am drawing between acts of a single agent (let's call them "monological" acts) and those of more than one ("dialogical" acts). From the standpoint of the old epistemology, all acts were monological, although often the agent coordinates his actions with those of others. But this notion of coordination fails to capture the way in which some actions require and sustain an integrated agent. Think of two people sawing a log with a two-handed saw, or a couple dancing. A very important feature of human action is rhythming, cadence. Every apt, coordinated gesture has a certain flow. When one loses this, as occasionally happens, one falls into confusion, one's action becomes inept and uncoordinated. Similarly, the mastery of a new kind of skilled action goes along with the ability to give one's gestures the appropriate rhythm.

Now, in cases like the sawing of the log and ballroom dancing, it is crucial to their rhythming that it be shared. These only come off when we can place ourselves in a common rhythm, in which our component action is taken up. This is a different experience from coordinating my action with yours, for instance, when I run to the spot on the field where I know you are going to pass the ball.

Sawing and dancing are paradigm cases of dialogical actions. But there is frequently a dialogical level to actions that are otherwise merely coordinated. A conversation is a good example. Conversations with some degree of ease and intimacy move beyond mere coordination, and have a common rhythm. The interlocutor not only listens but participates with head-nodding and "uh-huh" and the like, and at a certain point the "semantic turn" passes over to him by a common movement. The appropriate moment is felt by both partners together in virtue of the common rhythm. The bore, the compulsive talker, thin the atmosphere of conviviality because they are impervious to this. There is a continuity between ordinary, convivial conversation and more ritualized exchanges such as litanies, or alternate chanting, which we see in many earlier societies.[6]

I have taken actions with a common rhythming as paradigm cases of the dialogical, but they are, in fact, only one form of these. An action is dialogical, in the sense I am using it here, when it is effected by an integrated, nonindividual agent. This means that, for those involved in it, its identity as this kind of action essentially depends on the agency being shared. These actions are constituted as such by a shared understanding among those who make up the common agent. Integration into a common rhythm can be one form this shared understanding can take. But it can also come to be outside the situation of a face-to-face encounter. In a different form it can also constitute, for instance, a political or religious movement whose members may be widely scattered but are animated together by a sense of common purpose—such as linked, for example, the students in Tienanmen Square and their colleagues back on the campuses and, indeed, a great part of the population of Beijing. And this kind of action exists in a host of other forms, and on a great many other levels as well.

The importance of dialogical action in human life shows the utter inadequacy of the monological subject of representations which emerges from the epistemological tradition. We can't understand human life merely in terms of individual subjects, who frame representations about and respond to others, because a great deal of human action only happens insofar as the agent understands and constitutes himself as integrally part of a "we."

Much of our understanding of self, society, and world is carried in practices which consist in dialogical action. I would like to argue, in fact, that language itself serves to set up spaces of common action, on a number of levels, intimate and public.[7] This means that our identity is never simply defined in terms of our individual properties. It also places us in some social space. We define ourselves partly in terms of what we come to accept as our appropriate place within dialogical actions. In the case that I really identify myself with my deferential attitude toward wiser people such as you, then this conversational stance becomes a

identity as dialogical & social

1)convivial: relating to, occupied with, or fond of feasting, drinking, & good company constituent of my identity. This social reference figures even more clearly in the identity of the dedicated revolutionary.

At this point, the name of George Herbert Mead tends to be invoked in discussions among social scientists. But it is important to see that the dialogical view I am propounding here is quite different from Mead's. He allows that I develop a self when I adopt the stance of the other toward myself. A person "becomes a self insofar as he can take [the] attitude of another and act towards himself as others act."[8] In the very impoverished behaviorist ontology which Mead allowed himself, this seemed to be a brilliant way to make room for something like reflexivity while remaining within the austere bounds of a scientific approach. But what we have here is something like a theory of introjection. My self is socially constituted, through the attitudes of others, as the "me." Mead also recognizes that this cannot be the whole story, that something in me must be capable of resisting or conforming, will be in tension or harmony with what I internalize from my social world. We can't be simple functions of external demands. So Mead allows for the "I" as well. But Mead's "I" has no content of its own. It is a sort of principle of originality and self-assertion which can lead at times to impulsive conduct, or to resistance to the demands of society,[9] but doesn't have an articulated nature that I can grasp prior to action. It is our previously unarticulated response to the demands of the community. We don't know what it's about until after it has acted. "The 'I' appears in our experience in memory."[10] It is obviously more closely related to the Kantian "I" than to Erikson's "identity." This latter has to be found in the "me."

What this fails to capture is the way in which the "I" is constituted as an articulate identity defined by its position in the space of dialogical action. Being able to take the attitude of another is an important part of growing up, of overcoming what Piaget calls "egocentricity," but it is not what gives us a self in the first place. The self does not preexist all conversation, as in the old monological view; it arises within conversation, because this kind of dialogical action by its very nature marks a place for the new interlocutor who is being inducted into it.

Of course, our first definitions of ourselves are given by our parents and elders, because our first scenarios of dialogical action are provided by them. In this way, we are initially shaped by our surroundings. So why object to Mead's theory of the self constituted as a "me," which, after all, might just be intended to do justice to our initial passivity? But my objection is not that Mead's theory overstates the initial dependence of the child but that it fails to capture perspicuously what happens after. The conversation between the "I" and the "me," or between one's own self-generated transformations of the offered scenarios and their original form, is not between an introjected identity and some unformed principle of spontaneity. It is more a matter of gradually finding one's own voice as an interlocutor, realizing a possibility which was inscribed in the original situation of dependence in virtue of its dialogical form. This is not to say that this process may not be accompanied by oppression and force; clearly it often is. It is just that the image of introjection distorts the process, whether smooth or conflictual.

This image becomes necessary for Mead, because he doesn't have a place in his scheme for dialogical action, and he can't have this because the impoverished behavioral ontology only allows for organisms reacting to environments. But this pushes toward a monological conception. Taking the stance of the other is another monological act, one that is causally influenced by—or, at best, coordinated with—the other but still thoroughly mine. The only way to get the other into this behaviorist act is to introject him, and so that's what Mead does. One needs a richer concept of action and the self to come to grips with the formation of identity.

Introjective models abound in the human sciences, because of the hold of the monological perspective. Freud is another source of them. Conscience as superego is the introjected voice of the parent. Once again, this image makes it difficult to understand what it might mean to develop a mature, autonomous moral outlook—except, in the form of a disengaged inner freedom from all this introjected matter, the cool distance of the scientific spirit from the messy battlefield of human emotions, an ideal which not surprisingly seems to have moved Freud.

Children plainly need recognition, confirmation, and love in order to grow and be inducted into adult life, at the limit even to survive. But this can be conceived as a monological need, a comfort that they have to receive from others as they depend on others for food but which only contingently comes through conversation. Or it can be seen as a need which is essentially fulfilled in a certain form of conversation itself. The latter understanding places dialogue at the very center of our understanding of human life, an indispensable key to its comprehension, and requires a transformed understanding of language. In order to follow up this line of thinking, we need not Mead and his like but, rather, Bakhtin. Human beings are constituted in conversation; and hence what gets internalized in the mature subject is not the reaction of the other but the whole conversation, with the interanimation of its voices. Only a theory of this kind can do justice to the dialogical nature of the self.

Notes

1. I have discussed this at greater length in "The Moral Topography of the Self," in *Hermeneutics and Psychological Theory*, ed. Stanley Messer, Louis Sass, and Robert Woofolk (New Brunswick: Rutgers University Press, 1988), pp. 298-320.

2. I have gone into this further in *Sources of the Self* (Cambridge: Harvard University Press, 1989), ch. 2.

3. See Derek Parfit, *Reasons and Persons* (Oxford: Oxford University Press, 1984).

4. Martin Heidegger, *Sein und Zeit* (Tubingen: Niemeyer, 1927); Maurice Merleau-Ponty, *La Phenomenolgie de la perception* (Paris: Gallimard, 1945); Ludwig Wittgenstein, *Philosophical Investigations* (Oxford: Blackwell, 1953).

5. Pierre Bourdieu, *Outline of a Theory of Practice* (Cambridge: Cambridge University Press, 1977); and Pierre Bourdieu, *Le Sense pratique* (Paris: Miniut, 1980).

6. See the work of Greg Urban, from whom I have drawn much of this analysis; for example, "Ceremonial Dialogues in South America," *American Anthropologist* 88 (1986): 371-86.

7. I have tried to argue this in "Theories of Meaning," in *Human Agency and Language* (Cambridge: Cambridge University Press, 1985).

8. George Herbert Mead, *Mind, Self, and Society* (Chicago: Chicago University Press, 1934), 171.

9. Ibid., 198-99, 210.

10. Ibid., 196.

II

Reorientations in Social Science Inquiry

5

Causality and Causal Inference in the Study of Organizations

Donald A. Schon

Introduction: Causality and Causal Inference in Social Science and Social Practice

Causality and causal inference are subjects of longstanding and sometimes contentious interest among social scientists. Over the past twenty years, some researchers have tried to emulate a certain view of the methodology of the physical sciences, while others have opposed this positivist conception in the name of doctrines such as symbolic interactionism, hermeneutics, critical theory, or ethnography. In social psychology, for example, Harre and Secord's 1972 book, *The Explanation of Social Behavior*, proposed, in opposition to an "Old Paradigm" based on a Humean conception of causality and a positivist view of science, a "New Paradigm," according to which "the idea of men as conscious social actors, capable of controlling their performances and commenting intelligently upon them, is more scientific than the traditional conception of the human "automaton."[1] And as recently as 1989, R. B. Zajonc defended the traditional experimental methods of social psychology, with their reliance on standard experimental environments, by analogy with physics where, he argued, "the basic laws of motion are also studied in standard environments."[2]

But causality and causal inference are also critically important to the everyday practice of people in the social world, including those—to address the special interest of this paper—who live and work in organizations. In everyday organizational life, people are continually trying to search out the causes of events in order to figure out what to do about them. They inquire, for example, into the causes of systems failures, unexpected successes, and deviations from ordinary routines. And they are continually devising new structures, policies, practices, and procedures in order to reach their goals or correct the errors they have detected, all in the belief that such actions will *produce* their intended effects. In the design of new strategies of action, as in the explanation of past events, there is an unavoidable dependence on some concept of causality and some method of causal inference.

But how are the social science conceptions of cause and causal inference like or unlike their analogues in everyday practice? What guidance can and should social science offer to people who try in their everyday lives to make things happen and discover why things happened? These are the questions I shall take up in this paper. Although they are broadly applicable to all social science and all social practice, I shall concentrate, for reasons of personal interest and experience, on a narrower version of them: the relations between organizational practice and the social science of organizations. What is true of the narrower field is also true of the broader one, I suspect, but I shall not try to argue that case here.

Causality and Causal Inference in Normal Social Science

The still-dominant view of the relationship between social science and social practice goes back to nineteenth-century ideas that lie at the origin of both the social sciences and the modern research university. These ideas pivot on a particular epistemology of practice, which I call "technical rationality,"[3] according to which practical knowledge consists in instrumental know-how and becomes "professional" when it is grounded in systematic, preferably scientific, knowledge. By "science," I mean a particular *view* of science, which I shall call "normal science." Technical rationality holds that it is the function of normal social science to provide general causal knowledge from which professional practitioners can derive particular local judgments, plans, and policies.

Technical rationality leads to a dilemma of rigor or relevance. If researchers tilt toward rigor, according to the standards of normal social science, they risk becoming irrelevant to practitioners' demands for knowledge that is usable under the pressured and often confusing conditions of everyday practice; if they tilt toward relevance, on the other hand, they tend by the same standards to become unrigorous. Why I believe this to be so I shall briefly state in the remainder of this section.[4]

The concepts of causality and causal inference are complementary: Different views of causality carry different conceptions of the methods by which valid causal inferences are made. So it is with normal social science. The normal social science view of causality depends, to begin with, on a particular *ontology* according to which the complexity of observed phenomena is reduced to a collocation of simple *variables*. Variables are understood as named attributes extracted from the complexity of observed phenomena, and they are treated as essentially the same in whatever local contexts they occur. It is this presumed constancy that allows normal scientists to speak of *variations* in the local values and relationships of variables, and it is because of the generality and constancy of meaning inherent in the idea of a variable that the findings of normal social science can be couched in terms of general covering laws.[5]

In normal social science, a causal relation is taken to be a function of an effect-variable (y) on one or more cause-variables (x's), and has the form $y = f(x)$. Such a function is, to use Herbert Simon's term, "self-contained";[6] that is, there is one and only one value of y associated with each value of x, and the values of y are determined completely by the values of x. Here are two examples of causal relations that normal social scientists have at one time or another proposed: (1) "The occurrence of aggressive behavior always presupposes the existence of frustration and, contrariwise, . . . the existence of frustration always leads to some form of aggression."[7] (2) "State anxiety, defined as 'subjective, consciously perceived feelings of tension, apprehension and nervousness,' is caused by perceptions of role overload."[8]

In the field of organizational behavior, normal social scientists have advanced causal propositions of this kind in such areas as motivation, leadership, group performance, control, authority, participation, and the effects of centralization or decentralization.

Under the normal science view of causality as a self-contained function of the form $y = f(x)$, researchers who want to assert a causal relation are obliged to present evidence that given the values of x and the knowledge that x has occurred, the values of y can be determined exactly and with high probability, independent of any other features of the contexts in which x and y occur. Evidence of this kind should consist in quantitative data representing values of x and y across a wide range of variance, and may be provided by either of two methods of experimentation. In a "contrived experiment," as I shall call it, the researcher creates an experimental environment removed from the practice setting. In such an environment, he seeks to apply Mill's methods of causal inference,[9] creating for this purpose experimental and control groups. He tests whether y is regularly accompanied by x (method of agreement); whether y occurs in the absence of x (method of difference); or whether variations in the value of y are accompanied by corresponding variations in the value of x (method of concomitant variations). In a contrived experiment, the research setting is protected from the constraints and confusions of the practice setting, although conclusions drawn from the former are held to be transferrable to the latter—a leap whose difficulties normal scientists sometimes overlook.

In the method of "natural experiment," or "quasi-experiment" (to use Donald Campbell's phrase),[10] the researcher observes a number of practice settings, identifying and measuring in each case the values of the relevant cause- and effect-variables. Observations are distributed across many local contexts, so that the researcher can avoid being misled by the peculiarities of any particular one. As in the case of contrived experiment, the researcher analyzes the resulting data to test whether values of the effect-variables are uniquely determined by values of the cause-variables.

In both types of experiments, normal social scientists treat practitioners as subjects rather than as co-researchers and avoid any attempt to make research findings immediately useful to them. This "research distance" is held to be necessary lest the researchers become affected by practitioners' biases and lose their status as neutral, objective observers. Similarly, normal scientists seek to avoid referring to their subjects' intentions—the meanings and reasons by which individuals design their actions—because these tend to be seen as subjective, idiosyncratic, and qualitative—unsuited to the objectivity, generality, and quantitative measurability essential to normal science.

Chris Argyris and I believe that the results of normal social science research fail, even in the long term, to provide knowledge usable by practitioners in the everyday world of organizations. The reasons for this failure are inherent in the normal science conception of causality and causal inference, and they are as follows:

1. Representations of Knowledge

The functional relationships of variables that result from normal science research tend to be precise, quantitative, probabilistic, abstract, and complex, in the sense of involving many variables. All of these attributes of research results follow from the normal scientist's efforts to show that values of y are uniquely determined by values of x. But these very attributes tend to make it difficult for practitioners to form images of research results that can be connected to the peculiar features of a local context.

2. The Gap of Valid Application

How does a practitioner know that general causal relationships among variables, established in a research context, will hold at a particular time in a particular practice setting? In order to gain such knowledge, practitioners will have to recreate in the practice context the conditions under which the research results were created in the first place. This means that they will have to construct operational definitions of the key terms and show that observers who do not know the propositions to be tested can use these definitions to make reliable observations of the relevant phenomena across a suitable range of variance. Moreover, the practitioners will need to minimize threats to internal and external validity through the use of suitable controls—including keeping the experimental strategy secret from subjects lest their awareness of it confound its results. Under the pressure, confusion, and time constraints of real practice conditions, such actions are difficult to carry out. Moreover, when implemented, they are not neutral. As Argyris has shown,[11] actions of this kind imply an approach to management that is reminiscent of the managerial climate of hierarchical organizations. Such an approach places subordinates in a submissive, dependent role that is very likely to create strong feelings of ambivalence or outright hostility.

3. The Gap Between Discovery and Production

Argyris and I have been impressed, as a result of our research, with the step-function difference between what happens when people discover problems and invent strategies of action, and what happens when they actually try to produce their inventions under everyday conditions of real time and pressure—especially when it comes to situations of embarrassment or threat. Under these conditions, individuals frequently produce actions contrary to their inventions and are unaware of the discrepancy. To take one instance, a manager may want to persuade her subordinates (middle managers) to stop withholding negative information in their evaluations of their workers. But she may actually employ, unawares, the very strategies she wants her subordinates to give up. In order to avoid upsetting her subordinates, for example, she may smooth over her negative attributions. And her unawareness in such a case is likely to be due not so much to ignorance as to skillful adherence to theories-in-use learned early in life.[12]

In ordinary organizational practice, phenomena like these are the rule rather than the exception. Yet it is a rare normal scientist who takes them into account or focuses on the skills practitioners would actually need in order to produce inventions based on the results of normal science research. Hence, normal scientists are unlikely to generate research results that are usable in the sense that practitioners can actually produce inventions derived from them.

Causality and Causal Inference in Organizational Practice

In their revolt against the mechanistic, positivistic conception of social science, some academic researchers have sought to deemphasize the issues of validity and rigor in causal inference, or to avoid them altogether by declaring them out of place in interpretive social research. In one recent treatise on ethnographic method, for example, the author asserts that the criteria of validity and disconfirmability have been given far too much importance, to the detriment of the more significant criterion of "verisimilitude."[13]

But just as causality and causal inference are essential to the everyday world of organizational practice, so, too, are conceptions of validity and rigor. People in organizations who engage in causal inquiry usually try to get their inferences right. They try to avoid error, and when it occurs nonetheless, they often try to learn from it so as to avoid reproducing similar errors in the future. In organizational life, it is not unusual to find distinctions made between skillful and less skillful causal inquirers. And many organizations attempt through training, supervision, and coaching to help their members become more skillful.

What is more, organizational insiders are not the only ones to take a lively interest in the quality of organizational inquiry into causes. Outsiders affected by the activities of a given organization may also have such an interest; one need only think of the public interest in the quality of investigation into the causes of disasters or near-disasters in the management of nuclear facilities.

From at least two perspectives, then, there is a manifest interest in enhancing the quality of causal inquiry in everyday organizational practice—an interest in the rigorous production of valid causal inferences. However, the meanings of "validity" and "rigor" appropriate to organizational inquiry may be different from the meanings assigned to these terms in normal social science.

In order to address the dilemma of rigor or relevance, therefore, we must clarify what *should* be meant by "validity" and "rigor" in everyday organization practice. We will then be in a better position to explore (1) how such inquiry might be enhanced so as to increase the likelihood of producing usable causal knowledge in an appropriately rigorous way, and (2) what a social science devoted to *that* purpose would be like.

Causal Inquiry in Everyday Practice

Let us consider a few examples of situations in which individuals who occupy roles in an organization carry out inquiries into the causes of organizational phenomena. By "organizational phenomena" I mean phenomena that occur within the organization, or phenomena that are seen as affecting the life of the organization, or for which the organization may be partly responsible.

Systems Failures. A human or technological or sociotechnical system for which an organization is responsible has gone wrong. People in the organization try to discover what has caused it to go wrong. They may do so in the midst of the event itself, in order to prevent or mitigate the systems failure; or they may conduct their investigation after the fact, in order to prevent a recurrence of the failure.

A very recent example of such a failure occurred when large portions of a telecommunications network went down. Immediately, numbers of technical staff worked furiously, first to discover what had gone wrong and then to get the network up and running again. Subsequently, the telecommunication company in question created a corporate task force to determine the more fundamental causes of the failure and recommend long-term preventive measures.

A more famous example was the nuclear accident—an exposure of the fuel rods and a near meltdown—at Unit II of the Three Mile Island nuclear facility in rural Pennsylvania, on 28 March 1979. Here, too, there was the on-the-spot thinking and acting of operators and managers who tried to diagnose and respond to alarming signals during the crisis period, and there were retrospective reconstructions of events and conditions that caused the accident. The latter was undertaken by the Kemeny Commission, the Congressional committee investigating the incident, and other groups.

Disturbing or Surprising Patterns of Organizational Behavior. Here, people in an organization, operating at various levels and roles, identify a pattern of behavior which they find disturbing or surprising. They try to discover the causes of that pattern in order to learn how to change it. For example, the chief executive officer of a well-known high technology firm instituted a "pay for performance" system—a system of worker compensation aimed at rewarding and encouraging superior performance—only to discover, through a recent companywide survey, that his employees believed very good performance was not rewarded under the new system while average or mediocre performance was overrewarded. The CEO then set up a project team, composed of outside consultants and inside staff, to learn why the system had produced these unintended effects.

To take a very different kind of example, a professor of mathematics at a large West Coast university was curious and concerned, some ten years ago, to learn that black freshmen who had done well in math and science in their high schools, and who had relatively high SAT scores in math, tended nevertheless to flunk freshman calculus. He took on himself the task of inquiring into this phenomenon, spending months interviewing black freshmen, following them around the campus with a video camera strapped to his back. He also interviewed and followed Asian students, who tended to do well in freshman calculus. What he learned he built into the design of a program widely believed to have been successful in helping minority students to do well in math and science.

Notable Organizational Events. Here, an event occurs in the life of an organization, an event judged by members of the organization to be significant as an example of "successful" or "unsuccessful" performance, or as a puzzle that requires explanation. For example, many firms conduct reviews to determine what caused the firm to win or lose a large contract; they aim to discover which practices should be cultivated for future replication and which should be modified.

In the architectural field, over the past twenty or so years, a practice of "postoccupancy evaluation" has grown up. Its purpose is to inform future design practice by assessing how well or badly buildings perform in use. In one particularly instructive case, a postoccupancy evaluation was conducted in a large correctional facility in California. The researcher discovered, to his surprise, that in a recreation room of the facility, an arrangement similar to a "panopticon" had been created: a raised, enclosed tower from which guards, themselves unseen, could observe inmates all over the recreation room and in adjacent cells. This had happened despite the announced intention of correctional managers and their designers to produce a more "open," "communitylike" facility in which guards and inmates could mingle. The researcher set out, together with participants from the facility, to discover how such a result could have been produced when no one had apparently intended or wanted it.[14]

These few examples are enough to indicate something of the variety and frequency of causal inquiry in organizational life. It is clear that the types of precipitating situations I have identified are by no means exhaustive and not necessarily mutually exclusive.

Let me now sketch some of the causal accounts that resulted from these inquiries. In each of these cases, I have had some involvement with the organization in question, or have had access to the results of studies conducted by others. I shall give very brief resumes of these accounts at first. My purpose is to identify some very broad features of the meaning of "causality" and the nature of causal inquiry in organizational practice. Later on, I shall consider some of the accounts in greater detail.

Network Failure. In the year prior to the network failure, the telecommunications company instituted a changeover of some major segments of its long-distance network. As a part of this shift, new software was introduced into the switching system in order to provide more efficient and reliable service under conditions of increasing demand. Such software is extraordinarily complex; it may involve many thousands, or even millions, of lines of code. The debugging of software of this complexity is, in any case, a very tricky business. Bugs may remain undetected for long periods of time, lying in the system as potential time bombs of sorts, awaiting the precise set of network conditions that will trigger their expression.

The telecommunications company maintains strict standards of software reliability and requires that new software undergo a series of highly demanding reliability checks. At the time of the network changeover, however, staff charged with the task were under a great deal of pressure to effect rapid installation. (It should be noted that this was only one strand of causal explanation resulting from the company's investigations, albeit an important one.) Some of this pressure was attributable to the perceived need to respond to the challenges of competitive suppliers of long-distance service. Without the knowledge of upper management, and in order to speed up installation, technical staff chose to bypass certain reliability checks. Unknowingly, they introduced a bug into the new system. That bug remained dormant, however, until the right network conditions for its expression occurred.

Pay for Performance. The new pay-for-performance system instituted by top management called for line supervisors to make yearly reviews of workers' performances and to give them rankings that would be directly reflected in salary increases. The task group of researchers discovered, however, that when supervisors were faced with the need to make a judgment which they felt a subordinate would take in a negative way, they tended to avoid making the negative evaluation explicit, or they softened it. They did these things, they said, in order to avoid upsetting the workers, violating the norms of a caring and just company (important elements of management policy), or creating grievances that might take up scarce executive time.

These action strategies produced several first-order consequences. There was an inflation of performance scores and a wage bill larger than the one planned by compensation specialists, who had envisioned a normal curve. At the same time, there was an appearance of calm; very few complaints surfaced. Mediocre performance was protected. Very good performers resented being underpaid, but they also realized that this was in line with company norms of "caring" and "equal treatment." Only the very poor performers complained, claiming that their low raises violated norms of caring and equal treatment.

The company maintained a review board to deal with employee grievances, but its reports often upset lower-level supervisors. These individuals usually felt that their negative evaluations of workers were well justified. Nevertheless, they had learned to smooth them over because their bosses would communicate, overtly or covertly, "Let's not make a federal case out of this; the last thing I need is a grievance." Such messages upset the lower-level supervisors because they belied the company's espoused policy that local managers were "key" and "in charge." This discrepancy led lower-level managers to mistrust their superiors, who often expressed *their* mistrust by complaining that their lower-level managers had made a very poor case for their negative judgments. As a result of all this, lower-level supervisors became less willing to coach their employees in successful job performance lest the employees use the coaching as evidence that management thought they had a bright future.

The cumulative effect of these outcomes was polarization around issues of pay-for-performance and general acceptance of the idea that mediocre performance was to be protected.[15]

Academic Performance of Minorities. As a result of his investigations, the math professor discovered what he believed to be a profound difference between the black and the Asian students he observed on campus. He found that the typical black students had been "loners" in high school. They had done well by setting themselves apart from their fellows, achieving academic success by "going it alone," and they continued into their freshman year at the university the pattern that had worked for them in high school. Here, however, and especially in freshman calculus, the "loner" pattern no longer worked. The black students suffered from the lack of support, information, and collaboration that study groups can provide. Among Asian students, however, the pattern was reversed. These students, almost always high achievers, had typically established a pattern of collaborative group work in high school, where it had been associated with academic success. They continued the pattern into their freshman year at the university, where it continued to work. As the professor put it, informal study groups enable their members "not only to share mathematical knowledge but also to check out their understanding of what was being required of them by their professors and, more generally, by the university."

The professor also investigated what happened in the various remedial programs the university had established to help minority students who were having difficulties in math and science courses. He found that these programs did not encourage the formation of informal study groups and that their remedial aura created a sense of stigma that adversely affected students' performance.

Enlightened by these discoveries, the professor set about designing a new program. He believed that minority students who succeeded in gaining admission to the university had enough of the skills and all of the desire necessary to do well at the university level. What he believed they needed, though, was a sense of "academic community" and the support necessary to raise their performance. He proceeded to create a program based on what he called an "honors/group study" approach. It was a tutorial program open to all students who aspired to honors-level work, and it depended critically on the formation of small study groups. When this program was put in place, its results were impressive. In six years, the average grades of black participants in first-term calculus went from C– to B–. Almost all the students passed the class, and one-half of them received grades of A or B. University graduation rates also reflected these results. Minority students graduating from the program went on to graduate from the university at the rate of 64 percent, roughly the same as the campus average of 65 percent, and in contrast to a 41 percent graduation rate for students who had not gone through the program.[16]

The Panopticon. The research team discovered that the original architect's design of the prison recreation room had called for an open guards' booth to be located in one corner of the large, rectangular space. However, when the booth was installed, the guards complained that in the summer months the room became hot and stuffy. They asked for air conditioning. The facilities manager, mindful of the importance of maintaining good relationships with the guards' union, wanted to comply with their request. Nevertheless, because he was under budget constraints, he was unwilling to provide air conditioning for the entire recreation space. An acceptable solution seemed to consist in enclosing the guards' booth so that it could be air conditioned independently. But, because the manager feared that such an enclosure would also obstruct the guards' view of their surroundings, he decided to raise up the booth by several feet. When the guards were presented with this design, they complained that they would feel uncomfortably exposed.

The manager decided, then, to fit out the booth with one-way glass, which would allow the guards to see out of the booth while remaining unobserved. Thus, the full conditions of the "panopticon" were realized.

Meanings of "Causality" in These Examples

Each of the sketches outlined above I call a "causal story." Beginning with a puzzle to be explained—the network failure, the disappointing results of the pay-for-performance system, bright and hardworking students flunking freshman calculus, or the unexpected and unwanted emergence of the "panopticon"—each sketch presents a set of initial conditions combined with a series of chronological events in such a way as to make the generation of the phenomenon in question seem "natural." Each narrative says, in effect, "There were initial conditions; and then, when certain things were done, certain other consequences followed; and, behold, there naturally resulted the phenomenon we had found so puzzling."

What can we say about the nature of the causality involved in these stories?

We may notice, first of all, that the stories refer to two different types of simple causes which they combine in more complex patterns of causal explanation.

The first of these types I call "design causality." It is the causal relation that connects an actor's intention to the actions he designs in order to realize that intention. To explain the cause of an action, in this sense, one describes the intention one believes the actor was trying to achieve by means of the action. In other words, one describes the reasoning that led up to the action (*not*, it must be noted, the reasoning by which that action might be justified after the fact). Olafson (1979) calls this type of causality "cause by reason"[27] and Von Hayek (1979) calls it "sufficient reason."

In everyday organizational life, individuals continually exhibit design causality, formulating intentions and striving to achieve whatever consequences they intend. So, for example, the causal stories sketched above make reference to supervisors who smoothed over their evaluations for fear of upsetting the workers, technical staff who bypassed reliability checks in order to respond to pressures for fast installation of the network, and students who continued to operate as "loners" because that strategy had worked for them in high school.

The second type of simple causality Von Hayek (referring indirectly to Aristotle) calls "efficient causality"; the causal connection between an action and its intended or unintended consequences, or

going from actions to consequences

between such first-order consequences and the further consequences to which they may lead. So, for example, the network failure story tells how the bypassing of reliability checks caused a software bug to go undetected and how that bug triggered a network failure when network conditions favorable to its expression occurred. In the pay-for-performance story, collective grade inflation is said to result when each supervisor smooths over his negative evaluations of workers' performance, and a higher wage bill is said to result when inflated grades are translated into salary raises. The math professor's story tells how black students' decisions to work as "loners" resulted in their being deprived of the benefits of participation in informal study groups, and goes on to identify that deprivation as a partial cause of their poor grades. Finally, the panopticon story describes the initial enclosure of the guards' booth as resulting in the obstruction of their view of the inmates, and then presents the raising up of the booth as a cause of the guards' feelings of uncomfortable exposure.

In each of these causal stories, instances of design and efficient causality are treated as components of more complex patterns of causal explanation. Such models of *pattern causality* have a recognizable structure: There is an organizational setting which is subject to certain governing conditions. Under these conditions, individuals habitually design their behavior (design causality) through the use of characteristic action strategies. These yield, by efficient causality, certain first-order consequences, which lead, in turn, through various combinations of design and efficient causality, to higher-order consequences. The entire pattern makes up a complex system of organizational behavior.

So, for example, under conditions that include an espoused company policy of pay-for-performance *and* norms of being a just and caring company, first-level supervisors smooth over their negative evaluations of workers' performance, with the result that workers' grades are collectively inflated, and with the further result that wage bills are also inflated and that mediocre performance is protected. Once such systems have been created, they tend to maintain themselves through feedback loops that influence how individuals carry out the further design of their behavior in the organization. For example, the precedent of grade inflation makes it more difficult for supervisors to give workers negative evaluations.[18]

In the pay-for-performance and calculus stories, such a model is advanced to explain the persistence of a continuing pattern of organizational behavior. In the network failure and panopticon stories, it serves to explain a single event. This distinction may be an artifact of what the storyteller has *chosen* to explain, however. Both the network failure and the panopticon stories may be (and, I suspect, are) examples of recurrent patterns of organizational behavior.

Causal stories based on models of pattern causality are likely to be usable by practitioners; indeed, they are the sorts of stories practitioners generate for themselves. Their language is close to the language of everyday organizational life. They tend not to contain operational definitions whose precision is an obstacle to communication with ordinary people who occupy roles in organizations. They tend to be relatively simple in the sense that they do not contain an unmanageable number of variables (a point to which I shall return). Because they are derived from particular organizational settings, rather than from cross-cutting research on multiple settings or from contrived experiments, they do not present what I have earlier described as gaps of valid application. For all of these reasons, their *relevance* to organizational practice is not in question.

But what of their rigor?

Clearly, these stories do not meet normal social science criteria for rigorous causal inference. They contain no clearly identified, quantitatively measurable variables. No causal function of the $y = f(x)$ form is readily abstractable from them, nor do they demonstrate that values of y are uniquely determined by values of x. Let us consider the sorts of causal inquiry that typically produce stories of this kind, in order to see in what sense, if any, their causal inferences may be said to be "valid" and "rigorously made."

Causal Inquiry in Organizational Practice

I use the term "inquiry" in John Dewey's sense, to mean thinking and acting that originates in and aims at resolving a situation of uncertainty, doubt, or puzzlement.[19] Deweyan inquiry includes the framing of questions or problems as well as the attempt to answer or solve them. It includes the gathering as well as the interpretation of data. Causal inference that moves from considering evidence to asserting a causal relation is a part—but only a part—of causal inquiry. Causal inquiry also includes *actions* that function as "intervention experiments," serving both to test the validity of the story in question and to try out (in some instances) a way of remedying the problem whose causes the story explains—a point that has important implications, as we shall see, for the logic of experimentation in organizational practice.

Organizational inquirers tend to begin by exploring phenomena they find puzzling, and then go on to suggest ways of explaining these phenomena by the gradual construction of a causal story that contains (often implicitly) a model of pattern causality.[20] We can distinguish in this process two kinds of tasks: (1) tracing component causes and (2) constructing a larger causal pattern. Although the two are distinguishable, they are also complementary. We cannot know what component causes to trace unless we have some intimation of the larger causal pattern into which they may fit, and we cannot articulate a larger causal pattern unless we have some sense of the components that make it up. Moreover, both kinds of tasks have certain features in common: modeling, reliance on background knowledge, and the conduct of on-the-spot experiments.

How does such a process work when it works well?

It is not unlike the kind of detective work that a good auto mechanic, plumber, or physician does. When a plumber traces a leak to its source, for example, there are two senses in which he works back from the leak. He literally works back from the leak to its feeder channels in the system of pipes; in the metaphorical sense, he also "works back" from the leak through a chain of possible causes. But these two senses of "working back" are coordinated: each possible cause has a different location in the system.

The plumber forms hypotheses about proximate causes of the leak—considering as possible culprits, for example, a bad valve or a rusted pipe—on the basis of a *background knowledge* of the system which is commonplace and largely tacit. He is also likely to make use of experiences he has in situations that he sees as more or less similar to the present one. When he has formed a hypothesis about a proximate cause of the leak, he may test it by an on-the-spot experiment. For example, he may close and then reopen a valve, checking to see what happens to the leak.

Causal tracing in organizations proceeds in a roughly similar way, but the organizational system is not accessible to the inquirer in quite the same way as the system of pipes is to the plumber. So the organizational inquirer is more dependent on an ability to build and indirectly test mental models of causal linkages. But the sources of these models are not unlike the plumber's background knowledge of the system and prototypes of previously experienced causal relations and patterns which are projected onto the present system. Like the plumber, again, the organizational inquirer tests his causal tracings in a preliminary way by experiments conducted on the spot: Can he find actual evidence of the phenomena that correspond to design or efficient causes in his mental model? Can he discover naturally occurring variations in these phenomena? Or can he produce such variations? And does he then detect corresponding variations in the phenomena whose causes he seeks to explain?

In the pay-for-performance case, for example, the researchers traced the unexpectedly high wage bill to grade inflation. And the discovery of grade inflation led to a search for *its* causes. The researchers interviewed first-level supervisors, to take one instance, and asked, "What led you to give him a '5' when you thought he deserved a '3'?" Such questions produced information the researchers interpreted as meaning that supervisors tended to smooth over their negative evaluations of the workers' performance. And this finding was traced, through further questioning, to a further (design) cause: "for fear of upsetting the workers."

In the calculus case, the professor began by exploring the study habits of black and Asian undergraduates, a choice of topic that already suggests a rudimentary experiment. The professor learned that black students tended to work as loners and Asian students as members of informal study groups. Already suspecting that this difference in habits might make a difference in academic performance (perhaps by virtue of the influence of his own youthful experience in study groups), the professor sought to trace its (design) causes. He learned, through further questioning, that the two groups of students were continuing the habits that had worked for each of them in high school.

In examples like these, the inquirer selectively attends to features of the situation that seem like promising candidates for the role of proximate cause of the puzzling phenomenon to be explained. These phenomena he traces back to *their* proximate causes, continuing the process until he has assembled what, again, seems like a promising causal pattern. His judgments of "seems like" are guided, at least in part, by his background knowledge of the way things work in the system he is exploring. For example, researchers in the pay-for-performance case knew (that is, had ready access to a model of) how supervisors' evaluations of workers were translated into salary decisions and how these, in turn, were translated into paychecks. On the basis of such a model, the researchers could infer that the unexpected rise in wage levels *had* to be traceable to the supervisors' grading of the workers. Similarly, the investigators in the telecommunications case, with their understanding of the software development process, were bound to probe the debugging process and to ask, among other things, what happened to the usual reliability checks. Knowing how the system was supposed to work, they could zone in on the subprocesses that were likely to have gone wrong.

Background knowledge of this kind suggests where to look for proximate causes; it may suggest the identity of the proximate causes themselves; and finally, as Cohen and Lindblom[21] pointed out long ago, it may serve as a check on the plausibility of a new and unfamiliar line of causal reasoning. In all of these ways, background knowledge provides an indispensable basis for causal tracing. Of course, it may occasionally turn out to be mistaken. But in any particular case, the possibility of such a mistake must be weighed against longer-term track records of reliability. And, as Cohen and Lindblom also showed, even the correction of a piece of everyday knowledge depends on everyday knowledge of a different variety.

Background knowledge is necessary but not sufficient. The organizational inquirer's detective work depends, in addition, on an ability to generate *ad hoc* hypotheses in the form of models of causal relations in the situation at hand—for example, the models suggested by statements such as "The network failure may have been caused by a hitherto unexpressed software bug" or "The panopticon may have been generated piecemeal by a series of independent local decisions." Such models guide the search for further evidence, leading the inquirer, for example, to seek out a hidden bug in the network software or to try to locate a sequence of local decisions that could have accumulated to produce the panopticon.

The inquirer tends to construct such hypothetical models of component and pattern causality by drawing from a repertoire of familiar causal stories. He or she *sees* the present situation *as* a version of the familiar prototype, often before being able to say "similar with respect to what?"[22] The ensuing process tends to be transactional: the inquirer who adjusts the prototype to fit the situation may also adjust her perception of the situation in the light of the prototype.

But when she has constructed such a promising model, and has partially tested it by finding some of its elements and relations in the situation, she still faces the issue of the model's validity.

The Meaning of "Validity"

Although we may colloquially refer to the "validity" of statements, models, or experiments, this term has a narrower and more precise usage in logic and the philosophy of science, where it refers specifically to *inferences* in which a conclusion is said to follow logically from a premise or premises. Accordingly, I shall limit myself here to a discussion of the validity of *causal inferences*, where a conclusion asserting a causal relationship is said to follow logically from a set of premises asserting evidence for that relationship. I believe that the "validity of causal inference" has approximately the same meaning in organizational practice as in normal social science. In both cases, Karl Popper's[23] treatment of validity seems to me to be appropriate.

Popper distinguishes validity from plausibility, arguing that a causal inference has *plausibility* when it is shown that *y* occurred, *x* was present, and the occurrence of *y* can be inferred from *x*'s presence—always conditional, of course, on a non-numerable set of assumptions drawn from background knowledge of situations like the one in which *x* and *y* occur. The *validity* of a causal inference depends, however, on reference to alternate causal explanations of *y*. According to Popper, one can never confirm the validity of a causal inference; one can only disconfirm it, by adducing evidence incompatible with it. In the pursuit of validity, Popper argues, the best one can achieve is *competitive resistance* to refutation and one achieves this by showing that the preferred causal story explains evidence that alternates to it cannot explain. Of course, since one can never be sure of having come to the end of plausible alternates, a judgment of competitive resistance to refutation is never final.

Popper's distinction between validity and plausibility, and his analysis of validity in terms of competitive resistance to refutation, hold for causal inquiry in everyday organizational practice as well as for normal social science. An important difference between the two contexts comes to light, however, when we consider the kinds of *experimentation* by which evidence may be generated for the plausibility or the disconfirmation of a causal inference.

Experimentation in Causal Inquiry

An experiment, in the broadest sense of the term, is an action taken in order to generate information, an action guided by the question, "What if . . . ?" In organizational practice, I distinguish three kinds of experiments, each with its own distinctive logic, that is, its distinctive conditions for success or failure. An *exploratory experiment* probes a situation in order to stimulate discovery; it "succeeds" when discovery ensues and "fails" when it does not. A *hypothesis-testing experiment* generates evidence relevant to the plausibility or validity of a hypothesis; it succeeds in creating a presumption of validity when it produces information consistent with the hypothesis to be tested and inconsistent with its alternates. An *intervention experiment* is an action undertaken in order to change a situation "for the better." It succeeds, from the perspective of a given inquirer, when two conditions are met: the intended consequences are brought about *and* the unintended consequences are acceptable or desirable; in other words, the inquirer "gets what she wants and likes what she gets."

From the point of view of the logic of experiment, the context of organizational inquiry differs from that of normal social science because the inquirer here is not only a researcher but an actor in the situation—in Geoffrey Vickers's phrase, an "agent-experient."[24] The organizational inquirer investigates puzzling phenomena in order to figure out what to *do* about them, and when she takes action in order to fix what a causal story says has gone wrong or capitalize on what it says has gone right, she subjects that story to a critically important test. In organizational practice, therefore, the very same actions tend to function *at the same time* as exploratory, intervention, and hypothesis-testing experiments. This has significant implications for the logic of experimentation in organizational practice.

In the case of the math professor, for example, the causal story about the differential academic performance of black and Asian students is critically tested by the design and implementation of a supplementary teaching program based on that story. When the "honors/group study" program succeeds in producing a significant rise in black students' calculus scores and graduation rates, the search for alternate causal explanations comes to a stop. The validity of the causal story is taken to be sufficiently demonstrated by the success of an intervention experiment derived from it. This is, in effect, the "stopping rule" that brings to a close the process of generating and testing alternate causal accounts. (We should note, however, that such an inquiry might be reopened later on if new surprises or puzzles presented themselves—if for example, the honors/study group program gradually loses its impact on black students' calculus scores or if a different group of minority students emerged who seemed resistant to such an approach.)

In the normal social science context, in contrast, there is, at least in principle, no end to the search for alternate causal stories and no end to their attempted disconfirmation. The process may continue indefinitely, as long as some members of the community of social scientists choose to keep on challenging the dominant contenders. And when a community of researchers does converge on a settled explanation of some phenomenon, this seems to be more nearly a function of convenience, fatigue, or social solidarity than because the process of establishing competitive resistance to refutation has been definitely concluded. As William James remarked, disagreements in science are never finally settled; it is, rather, that scientists lose interest in pursuing them.[25]

The centrality of intervention experiments in organizational inquiry also has a bearing on what might be called the "radical incompleteness" of the range of causal stories entertained by organizational practitioners. It is significant, for example, that the math professor felt no need to enter into the scientific, or pseudoscientific, controversy over the possible genetic basis for differential academic performance. It was obvious to him that he should search out causal patterns about which he could possibly *do* something. More generally, the causal stories entertained by organizational inquirers tend to be designed in the first place with an eye to intervention: Inquirers select out patterns of phenomena that seem to lend themselves to possible future action.[26]

Finally, it is important to notice one more consequence of the fact that organizational inquirers are agents-experient: In the course of their causal tracings, they may discover opportunities to invent and test causal hypotheses in the situation itself. Such on-the-spot experiments may be interventions aimed at changing the situation for the better, but they need not be. For example, just as the plumber in our earlier example might open and close a valve in order to observe its effect on a leak, so the researchers in the pay-for-performance case might look for variations in the supervisors' approaches to evaluation of the workers. To take one instance, they might seek out an exceptional supervisor who did *not* smooth over his negative evaluations. They might ask, then, "How did this supervisor's practice affect his 'grading'?" With what consequences for the triggering of grievance procedures and for the supervisor's relations with upper management? Similarly, researchers in the telecommunications case might try subjecting the network software installed at the time of the changeover to the reliability checks that had originally been bypassed: Were these checking procedures capable of detecting software bugs that had previously gone undetected? Discoveries made in the course of on-the-spot experiments like these may suggest new causal stories, which may lend themselves, in turn, to testing by new on-the-spot experiments.

Among normal social science researchers, in contrast, the practice of improvising experiments in the situation tends to be taboo. For these researchers, norms of objectivity and neutrality require avoiding "interference with the situation," lest experiments be confounded, and require remaining at arm's length from the organization, lest the researchers become contaminated by the biases of its inhabitants. In this sense, normal social science researchers are at a disadvantage. On the other hand, on-the-spot experimentation carries its own peculiar vulnerabilities to error, to which we shall shortly turn.

External Validity

So far, we have considered only the internal validity of a causal inference, that is, the validity of a causal inference applied to the particular organizational context in which a causal inquiry has been conducted. What can we say about external validity, the validity of causal generalizations drawn from a limited experimental context?

Normal social science and organizational inquiry yield different types of generalizations, and employ different strategies of generalization.

A certain potential for externally valid causal inference is built into the methodology of normal social science. As we have already observed, the normal scientist constructs causal formulae, of the $y = f(x)$ type, where x and y are chosen to stand for variables abstracted from the local contexts of their occurrence; and normal science experiments are designed in such a way as to produce many values of x and y across a wide range of variance in order to test whether the values of y are uniquely determined by the values of x. For this purpose, quasi experiments must include observations of multiple settings; and contrived experiments, multiple runs. Along with their conformity to such methodological strictures, normal scientists tend to select their very questions with an eye to the production of theoretically based causal generalizations. A social psychologist recently observed about the pay-for-performance case, for example, that its motivating question—Why do compensation programs aimed at rewarding superior performance end up by giving equal rewards to mediocre performance?—is not one that most normal scientists would ask, mostly because, as he said, "It does not contain any theoretical basis." Normal scientists would prefer, he believed, to ask a question such as, What is the specific psychological effect of rewarding superior and mediocre performance at the same rate?

Normal social scientists strive to design their questions and experiments so as to produce valid *covering laws*—general causal propositions instantiated by a wide range of instances of the occurrence of x and y. I have already noted how these strivings tend to undermine the usability of research results: Distortions are introduced when individual variables are extracted from the local contexts in which they occur, and a gap of application arises when one tries to apply normal science generalizations to particular organizational settings.

In the causal inquiry of organizational practice, on the other hand, the setting is typically that of a particular organization at a particular time. From a normal social science perspective, the assertion that such an inquiry can yield externally valid results must seem paradoxical. Yet there is a kind of generality built into causal stories like the ones I have sketched earlier. These stories present causal patterns in such a way as to lend plausibility to the claim that, *in any such case*, similar conditions and events would combine to produce similar results. They represent prototypes of causal patterns that might be transferred to other organizational situations in which similar phenomena occurred.

So, for example, the pay-for-performance story presents a prototypical model of a causal pattern that explains how a compensation scheme designed to reward superior performance ends up reinforcing mediocre performance, and it does so by showing how the kinds of reasoning and the action strategies brought by individuals to the task of evaluating subordinates' performance combine with corporate structure and ideology to produce grade inflation and a rising wage bill, and how, in turn, this pattern feeds back to reinforce individuals' action strategies.

Here, a causal pattern detected in a particular organizational system is described in a way that lends itself to generalization, even though it does not have the characteristic form of a covering law. Such a generalized causal story can be carried over to a new organizational situation in which a compensation scheme designed to reward superior performance ends up reinforcing mediocre performance, suggesting how the unintended consequences of the scheme might be explained in this case as it was in the earlier one. But the validity of such an inference would have to be tested in the new case, just as it was in the old one, by a combination of causal tracings, predictions, and experiments.

The generalization of such a model is better understood as a process of *reflective transfer*—"transfer," because the model is carried over from one organizational situation to another by the process I have called "seeing-as"; "reflective," because the inquirer should attend critically to analogies and disanalogies between the familiar situation and the new one. In reflective transfer, causal stories play roles similar to the roles of legal precedents in judicial decision making, or precedents in architectural design.[27] The utility of the prototype lies in its ability to generate explanation and experimentation in a new situation. When it is carried over to a new situation, its validity must be established *there* by a new round of inquiry, through which it is very likely to be modified. And the modified prototype that results from such a new round of inquiry may serve, in turn, as a basis for reflective transfer to a new situation.

It may be argued that generalizations of this kind are inferior to the covering laws produced by normal social science. It seems to me, however, that the value of a strategy of generalization ought to be judged according to its intended use. If the purpose of generalization is to contribute to psychological theory, for example, covering laws may be superior to generalizable prototypes (though even here, there is, I think, a danger of underestimating the potential fruitfulness of prototypical causal stories). If, on the other hand, the purpose of generalization is applicability to organizational practice, then we should remember that the covering laws of normal social science must be tested, in any case, in each new practice context in which one attempts to put them to use. And, as I have argued earlier, normal social science generalizations are strikingly ill-suited to testing in a practice context.

The Enhancement of Organizational Inquiry

In this section, I shall turn to the question of the meaning of "appropriate rigor" in the causal inquiry of everyday organizational practice. I shall describe some of the ways in which this sort of inquiry is vulnerable to error, focusing especially on the tracing of design causality and on the construction and testing of complex causal patterns. What does it mean for practitioners to cope well with these sorts of vulnerabilities? What would be the nature of a social science that tried to help them to do so?

Tracing Design Causality

There is a long tradition of debate in social psychology over the trustworthiness of our everyday intuitions into the reasoning—the intentions, thoughts, and feelings—that motivate other people's actions. Zajonc raises this question and concludes, in opposition to Harre, that although our own experience "can be a rich source of ideas and a source of hypotheses . . . everything we know from the systematic study of social perception indicates that we should be very distrustful of our so-called intuitions."[28] He cites in support of this position the large number of studies that have revealed "a substantial self-serving bias in estimating probabilities of causal events."

Even if we take a much more sanguine view of the reliability of our everyday intuitions into human reasoning and intention, it is certainly clear that we sometimes find them to be mistaken. A reasonably competent organizational inquirer—one who exhibited appropriate rigor—would certainly try to test such intuitions, especially those that played important roles in his construction of a causal story. Consider, for example, the notion that supervisors in the pay-for-performance case smoothed over their negative evaluations in order to avoid upsetting the workers, or that technical staff in the telecommunications company bypassed software reliability checks in order to respond to management's pressure for fast installation. How might such inferences be tested? Certainly one of the principal tests consists in a very familiar form of on-the-spot experiment, namely, asking for information.

However, this form of experimentation is also vulnerable to error, and for several different sorts of reasons. Consider a situation in which one person asks another, "What led you to do this?", receives an answer to the question, and infers from it an interpretation of the actor's intentions. First of all, the informant may not be able to make an accurate reconstruction of the before-the-fact reasoning that led to her action. She may not remember it, or, in accordance with the widespread tendency to engage in instant historical revisionism, she may reconstruct it more or less unconsciously to suit her *present* thinking, interests, or inclinations. Such distortions might be corrected, perhaps by inducing the informant to make a careful reconstruction of the incident in which she was involved or (when this is possible) by comparing the responses of several different informants.

But remedial measures such as these are vulnerable to a second source of error—one that also affects any attempt to inquire directly into reasons for action. An inquiry into an actor's reasons for acting in a certain way is itself an intervention, and when it takes place in an organizational setting, it is also an intervention into the life of the organization. Both of these factors can and usually do have powerful effects on the ways in which both parties—inquirer and informant—construe the meaning of their interaction, interpret each other's messages, act toward each other, and perceive each other's actions. These effects can complicate and, not infrequently, subvert the inquirer's quest for valid information.

One of the reasons for this is that the individual who finds herself in the role of informant is also an inquirer. She seeks, for example, to discover the meanings of the situation in which she is involved, and she acts on the basis of the meanings she constructs. For example, she may answer questions in the light of what she believes the inquirer expects of her. She may construe the situation as one that calls for putting the best possible face on her prior actions. Her interaction with the interviewer may be designed, more or less consciously, as a form of image management.[29] To the extent that she feels threatened or distrustful in the interview, she may deliberately withhold information she feels might be taken in a negative way.

All such interactions are also affected by what George Devereaux once described (borrowing from quantum physics) as "complementarity."[30] The interviewer's questions and his responses, verbal and nonverbal, are also intrusions into the interpersonal situation, affecting the informant's constructions of meanings and her willingness to give valid information. The act of inquiry influences the situation inquired into. So, for example, an investigator into the network failure may convey a threatening, judgmental attitude that makes his informants even more defensive than they would otherwise be.

And what is true of the informant is also true of the inquirer. *His* interpretation of the messages he receives are also affected by the more or less conscious meanings he constructs for his interaction with the informant, his attributions of meanings to her, his intimations of the way in which she perceives him. If he perceives her as likely to withhold negative information, for example, he may interpret her answers in the light of his suspicions about the information he believes her to be withholding.

These interaction effects are by no means peculiar to causal inquiry in organizations. They are also characteristic of the experimental environments of normal social science, where they are equally capable of foiling the researcher's quest for valid information. As Harre and Secord have noted, "Social psychological experiments are also social episodes."[31] Indeed, the very controls by which social psychologists strive to make their contrived experiments rigorous are likely, as observed earlier in this paper, to introduce systematic distortions into their research results.

In organizational inquiry, however, all such interaction effects may be exacerbated by certain peculiarities of the organizational context. Organizational inquiry is almost inevitably a political process in which individuals consider—whether or not they choose to be decisively influenced by such considerations—how the inquiry may affect their standing, or their reference group's standing, within an organizational world of competition and contention. The attempt to uncover the causes of a systems failure is inevitably, whatever else it may also be, a perceived test of loyalty to one's subgroup and an opportunity to allocate blame or credit. Such an inquiry is likely to trigger familiar organizational games—for example, allocation of blame and avoidance of blame, exercise of control and avoidance of control, winning credit and preventing others from winning credit. And within such games, strategies of deception, preemptive blame, "stone-walling," "fogging," and camouflage—including camouflage of these very strategies—frequently inhibit inquiry into the causes of organizational events and the reasoning of the actors involved in them. Argyris and I have described such phenomena from the point of view of what we call "limited organizational learning systems."[32]

Given these effects—the personal, interactive, and organizational phenomena that can inhibit the quest for valid information about design causality—how ought one to carry out organizational inquiry so as to increase the likelihood of producing valid information? This global question sets a critically important direction for a possible social science that might take seriously the problem of enhancing organizational inquiry. It has at least two main parts. First, How can we build more accurate and usable accounts of the personal, interpersonal and organizational patterns that inhibit causal inquiry in organizations? And second, from the point of view of the process of inquiry itself, What strategies, values, and underlying assumptions—what theories of action—are most likely to enable an inquirer to elicit information, interpret it, and test interpretations so as to form valid inferences about design causality?

These questions form the basis of an approach that Argyris and I have pursued, along with our colleagues, under the title of "the theory of action perspective" or "action science."[33] Our approach is a development of the one initiated many years ago by Kurt Lewin. It focuses on the problem of creating conditions for collaborative inquiry, in which people in organizations function as co-researchers rather than only as "subjects"; and it does this on the assumption that people are more likely to provide valid information about their own intentions and reasons for action when they share control of the process of generating, interpreting, testing, and using information. It posits the existence of a "behavioral world" created by the parties to an interaction, and identifies the characteristics of behavioral worlds that may inhibit or encourage valid inquiry. It explores the features of theories-in-use that are conducive to the exchange of valid information in behavioral worlds of interpersonal inquiry, emphasizing the importance of making private attributions public, treating these attributions as disconfirmable, and subjecting them to public test. It operates from the assumption—for which we think there is considerable evidence—that theories-in-use tend to exert a "contagion" or "mirroring" effect. We believe that individuals become more effective inquirers when *they* employ theories-in-use which, if "mirrored" by their informants and co-researchers, would be likely to produce valid information.

It is not my purpose here to expand on the theory of action perspective; Argyris and I have done this elsewhere, as noted above. My purpose, rather, is to argue that the *questions* we have addressed—the questions stated above—are central to any social science that takes the enhancement of organizational inquiry as its objective.

Building Models of Pattern Causality

In the causal inquiry undertaken by organizational practitioners, the tracing of design causes and efficient causes feeds into the construction of larger, more complex models of pattern causality like the ones sketched in the four cases described earlier in this paper. These models tend to constitute usable knowledge because they are framed in language already familiar to organizational practitioners, because they are of manageable complexity, and because they are selectively designed in such a way as to lend themselves to the invention of enactable policies. For these very reasons, however, such models may be limited or distorted in a way that makes them vulnerable to error. And the detection and correction of these vulnerabilities suggest a further direction in which social science might enhance organizational inquiry.

For example, organizational practitioners may bring their inquiry to a close when they arrive at a causal pattern that seems both to account for the puzzling phenomenon that triggered their inquiry and to open up a promising approach to intervention. But they may not go on to explore what factors *have kept that causal pattern in being*, factors that might also reintroduce themselves in such a way as undermine the remedial intervention they have in mind. In the pay-for-performance case, for example, the investigators may choose not to examine the complex system of organizational incentives that has shaped supervisors' learning to avoid upsetting the workers. In the network failure case, the inquirers may not try to get behind the private choices made by technical staff to respond to perceived management pressure for fast installation by circumventing the usual reliability checks. What was the nature of the learning that shaped such perceptions and responses? What, for example, were the causal patterns that led technical staff in the telecommunications company to keep their choices private rather than to test them publicly with upper management?

More generally, it seems to me that managers, who tend to be the ones to lead organizational inquiries into causal patterns, are often selectively inattentive to their own contributions to the phenomena in question. They are relatively unlikely to ask themselves, How has our behavior contributed to the patterns we have uncovered?

There is also a tendency for organizational inquirers, who are usually charged with very specific objectives and heavily constrained by time and resources, to limit the scope of their explorations to a rather narrow slice of historical time and to a rather narrow zone of the larger map of organizational behavior. They may not ask, for example, How did we get to the kind of situation in which this pattern holds— how may our decisions, or failures to decide, have cumulatively shaped this pattern over time? In the pay-for-performance or network failure cases, inquirers may not go on to explore how the causal patterns they have uncovered might explain other examples of systems failure, or illuminate the undermining of other attempts to improve organizational performance.

If causal inquiry in organizations is peculiarly subject to such limitations and distortions—as I believe it is—then it may be enhanced by
social scientists who collaborate with practitioners to raise questions
like the ones listed above, develop frameworks for investigating patterns of wider scope, and model the processes of learning and incentive
creation through which managers and subordinates reciprocally create
their shared behavioral worlds.

Conclusion

I have explored a particular way of responding to the dilemma of
rigor or relevance that afflicts social science in general and the social science of organizational behavior in particular. Because normal social
science conceptions of causality and causal inference are inherently
unlikely to produce usable knowledge, I have proposed that we turn
upside down our familiar ideas about the relations between social science and social practice. Rather than asking how organizational practitioners might make better use of normal social science, or how normal
social scientists might make their research results more palatable to
practitioners, I have considered these practitioners as causal inquirers in
their own right. I propose that we ask what they already know how to
do, in order to see how a different kind of social science might enhance
the kinds of causal inquiry they conduct in their everyday practice.

The meanings of causality and causal inference are complementary in organizational inquiry as in normal social science, but the two
pairs of complementary meanings are significantly different from each
other. Organizational inquirers are concerned with pattern causality
that combines cause by reason with efficient cause. The causal inferences made by organizational practitioners are contained in episodes of
inquiry, in the Deweyean sense of that term. Their investigations aim
directly at interventions, and their interventions are experiments that
test, in the most decisive sense available to them, the adequacy of their
causal stories.

As a consequence, even though validity has the same meaning in
organizational practice as in normal social science, both the methods
and the logic of experimentation employed by organizational inquirers
are significantly different from those of normal social science. Causal
tracing and on-the-spot experiments are characteristic of organizational
inquiry but not of normal social science. And the affirmation of an intervention experiment—the discovery that an intervention derived from a
causal story produces the results intended for it while also producing
acceptable or desirable side effects—typically brings causal inquiry in

organizations to a close, which is not the case in normal social science.

In normal social science, the choice of questions, the selection of variables, and the design of experiments are all designed to produce externally valid causal generalizations of the covering law type. In contrast, causal inquiry in organizations typically centers on a particular situation in a single organization, and when it is successful, it yields not covering laws but prototypical models of causal patterns that may guide inquiry in other organizational situations—prototypes that depend, for their validity, on modification and testing in "the next situation." "Reflective transfer" seems to me a good label for this kind of generalization.

Some of the vulnerabilities of causal inquiry in organizations are very much the obverse of the vulnerabilities of normal social science, which extracts cause- and effect-variables from the local contexts of their occurrence. In its causal inferences, normal social science risks neglecting critically important contextual factors. Because of its reliance on the multiple settings essential to quasi-experimental method, it risks losing sight of important characteristics of a particular organization. And it risks distorting research results through the creation of the unilaterally controlled environments of its contrived experiments. In the case of organizational inquiry, on the other hand, practitioners are *in* the organizational situations they study. As they trace design and efficient causes and conduct on-the-spot experiments, they run the risk of unknowingly distorting both the phenomena they investigate and the meanings they derive from their observations. Because they are inquirers, rather than researchers in the normal science sense, they risk being captured by prevailing managerial objectives and ideologies in such a way as to neglect underlying causes, longer-term historical processes, and managers' contributions to the problematic features of the organization's behavioral world.

Finally, because inquiry always has a political meaning in the life of an organization, the inquirer risks becoming caught up in contests, games, and deceptions—the ordinary stuff of what Argyris and I have called "limited organizational learning systems."

These vulnerabilities to error help to define the sort of rigor appropriate to organizational inquiry, and also suggest in what directions we might try to develop a social science aimed at enhancing it. The central topics of such a science would include the nature of the theories-in-use by which practitioners, in their causal tracings and on-the-spot experiments, can increase the likelihood of producing valid information; the nature of the causal patterns through which organizations tend to inhibit causal inquiry and constrain the organizational learning derived from it; and the repertoire of prototypical models of pattern causality that inform, and might inform, organizational inquiry.

Argyris and I have worked at developing an approach to these questions, but my purpose in this paper has not been to present or defend that approach. It has been, rather, to argue for the importance of these questions and for the necessity of a practice-enhancing social science aimed at answering them.

Notes

1. R. Harre and P. F. Secord, *The Explanation of Social Behaviour* (Oxford: Basil Blackwell, 1972), v.

2. R. B. Zajonc, "Styles of Explanation in Social Psychology," *European Journal of Social Psychology* (September-October 1989), 360. This issue was devoted to controversies in the social explanation of psychological behavior. In the same issue, R. Harre, continuing his attack on the "Old Paradigm," questioned whether the idea of "cause" has any place in social science at all. See his "Metaphysics and Methodology: Some Prescriptions for Social Psychological Research," 452.

3. See D. A. Schon, *The Reflective Practitioner* (New York: Basic Books, 1983).

4. See also Chris Argyris and Donald A. Schon, "Conceptions of Causality in Social Theory and Research: Normal Science and Action Science Compared," *mimeo*, 1989. I am indebted to my work with Argyris for many of the ideas contained in the present paper, not only the ideas specifically related to the dilemma of rigor or relevance.

5. Harre and Secord offer a similar formulation: "In the Old Paradigm, a law has the form $f(x,y)$ where x and y are dependent and independent variables, and it is assumed that all properties of the system in which this 'law' is observed to hold can be treated as parameters, that is maintained constant without materially affecting the relationship between those allowed to vary. This assumption is thought to be justified in its turn by the general principle that the aim of science is to discover correlations between changes in the properties of systems. In the farthest background lies Hume's theory of causality, according to which such correlations *are* causal laws" (*Explanation of Social Behavior*, 20).

6. Quoted in L. R. James, S. A. Mulaik, and J. M. Brett, *Causal Analysis: Assumptions, Models, and Data* (Beverly Hills, CA: Sage, 1982). A very similar view of causality and causal inference in social science is to be found in the work of Donald Campbell: for example, D. T. Campbell and J. C. Stanley, *Experimental and Quasi-Experimental Designs for Research* (Skokie, IL: Rand McNally, 1963).

7. J. Dollard, L. Doob, N. E. Miller, O. H. Mowrer, and R. R. Sears, *Frustration and Aggression* (New Haven: Yale University Press, 1939), 1.

8. Spielberger, quoted in James, Mulaik, and Brett, *Causal Analysis*, 28.

9. John Stuart Mill, *A System of Logic* (London: Longmans, Green, 1949.

10. Campbell and Stanley, *Experimental and Quasi-Experimental Designs*.

11. See Chris Argyris, *The Inner Contradictions of Rigorous Research* (New York: Academic Press, 1980).

12. See Chris Argyris and Donald A. Schon, *Theory in Practice: Increasing Professional Effectiveness* (San Francisco: Jossey-Bass, 1974).

13. See John Van Maanen, *Tales of the Field* (Chicago: University of Chicago Press, 1988).

14. See Craig Zimring, "Normative Rationality and Evaluation by Large Building Delivery Organizations," paper presented at the Critical Approaches to Environmental Design Evaluation conference, Paris, 30 June-2 July 1990.

15. This case is described in detail in Argyris and Schon, "Conceptions of Causality"; research on the pay-for-performance case was conducted by Robert Putnam and Dolores Thomas (R. W. Putnam, "Organizational Action Map: Pay and Performance," in "Organizational Defense Routines," mimeo material, Harvard Graduate School of Education, 1988).

16. This description draws on an article by John Marlowe and Katharyn Culler, "How We're Adding Racial Balance to the Math Equation," in *The Executive Educator* 7.4 (April, 1987).

17. Whether "reasons," in this sense, are appropriately called "causes" is the subject of a long and still-continuing debate in the philosophy of action. See, for example, the work of Donald Davidson, *Essays in Actions and Events* (Oxford: Clarendon Press, 1980); and Donald Davidson, *Inquiries into Truth and Interpretation* (Oxford: Clarendon Press, 1984).

18. What Argyris and I have called "pattern causality" in organizational life turns out to have been anticipated in the context of collective social life by certain members in the Austrian School of Economics: Von Mises and Menger. See Donald LaVoie, "Between Historicism and Formalism: The Rise and Fall of the Austrian Schools' Calculation Argument," *Praxiologies and the Philosophy of Economics: The International Annual of Practical Philosophy and Methodologies*, 1992, ed., J. Lee Auspitz, Wojciech W. Gasparski, Marek K. Mlicki, & Klemens Szaniwski, vol. I (New Brunswick, NJ: Transaction Publishers).

19. John Dewey, *Logic: The Theory of Inquiry* (New York: Holt, Rinehart & Winston, 1938).

20. It is worth noting that a similar kind of exploratory activity and storytelling may also precede the more formal and systematic experiments of normal social scientists, although the latter rarely give us access to their preliminary explorations.

21. Charles E. Lindblom and David K. Cohen, *Usable Knowledge* (New Haven: Yale University Press, 1979).

22. The phrase is Thomas Kuhn's. See his "Second Thoughts on Paradigms," in *The Essential Tension* (Chicago: University of Chicago Press, 1977). The notion of seeing-as is taken from Ludwig Wittgenstein, *Philosophical Investigations* (New York: Macmillan, 1953).

23. Karl Popper, *Conjectures and Refutations* (New York: Harper and Row, 1968).

24. Geoffrey Vickers, Unpublished Memorandum, (Massachusetts Institute of Technology, 1978).

25. Recent developments in the philosophy of science—especially the work of Kuhn, Lakatos, and Feyerabend—develop the theory of the influence of the sociology of a community of inquirers on dispositions of individuals within that community to regard a scientific debate as "settled."

As for an *individual* social scientist's decision to bring a process of research to a close, see Lotte Bailyn's "Research as a Cognitive Process," *Quality and Quantity* 11 (1977): 97-117. Here, Bailyn argues that the stopping rule actually employed has something—though not everything—to do with the researcher's sense that her findings are compatible with her prior intuitions, values or inclinations.

26. Matters are complicated by the fact that relatively successful interventions need not always be based on a prior analysis of the causes of error. Without fully disentangling the welter of causes involved in road accidents, for example, one may institute stiffer, faster, and more reliably applied penalties for hazardous driving—and such an intervention may effectively reduce the accident rate. "What will fix x" is not necessarily based on an analysis of "what caused x." But this is not incompatible with the view that inquirers' causal stories tend to be selectively constructed with an eye to a future intervention.

27. See, for example, Donald A. Schon, "Designing: Worlds, Rules and Types," *Design Studies* (Spring 1990).

28. Zajonc, "Styles of Explanation in Social Psychology," 357.

29. It is, of course, Erving Goffman who is best known for having described such essays in presentation of self in everyday life.

30. George Devereaux, *From Anxiety to Method in the Behavioral Sciences* (The Hague: Mouton, 1967).

31. See Harre and Secord, *Explanation of Social Behavior*, 238.

32. Chris Argyris and Donald A. Schon, *Organizational Learning* (Reading, MA: Addison Wesley, 1978).

33. See, for example, Chris Argyris, Robert Putnam, and Diana McLain Smith, *Action Science* (San Francisco: Jossey-Bass, 1985). See also Argyris and Schon, "Conceptions of Causality in Social Research."

Bruner - ethnographer
as embodied discourse

6

The Redesign of Ethnography after the Critique of Its Rhetoric

George E. Marcus

The recent critical examination of ethnography as the key research practice of anthropology has attracted widespread attention, perhaps because of all American social science disciplines that were formed more or less committed to the idealized model of knowledge production in the natural sciences, anthropology is where the recent critique of social science rhetoric and its implications have been central rather than marginalized, as I believe they have been so far in political science, history, economics, and sociology. Traditionally placed in the social sciences and humanities as the source of the exotic otherness, of exceptional cases at the margins of dominant themes, ethnography in anthropology now has the possibility of redefining its position within Western intellectual discourses by freeing itself of its historic identification with the exotic and the primitive (objects of highly dubious empirical and ethical value in the late twentieth century anyway) and by exemplifying a discipline that not only heeds the continuing critique of its practices and discourses but also embraces such critique as the very source of its projects of knowledge. As will be seen, the experimental redesign of ethnographic representation does not merely react to the critical deconstruction under present historic circumstances but, rather, breeds on it.

Ethnography has been at the heart of anthropology for over seventy years, and has played an integral role in overthrowing the evolutionary paradigm on which much anthropological inquiry had been founded in the nineteenth century. Indeed, one might view ethnography itself as the historic mode of experimentation made doctrine by Franz Boas in the United States and Bronislaw Malinowski in England, and intended to move beyond the grand universalizing schemes of writers like Sir James Frazer and Lewis Henry Morgan. Yet, a scientific, ethnography-based anthropology, in scaling down the grand framework of a science of Man, nonetheless retained much of the latter's sense of problem as well as its central focus on the conditions of universal Man as specifically primitive man outside modernity, the presumed locus in which the essential questions about humanity could be addressed. So anthropology seems to have no other contemporary overarching purpose other than to create a detailed ethnographic archive of the exotic to the modern West, so that certain notions of human universals might eventually be addressed. Certainly, late-twentieth-century developments in other fields, such as the cognitive sciences, generally have left anthropology with the predicament of an archive—indeed, of intrinsic interest, but addressing a long outmoded grand project—but also with a distinctive approach to knowledge production, unique in the social sciences or humanities.

Ethnography has been forged largely outside the Western notion of history, and has been predicated on the thoroughly merged romantic/scientific quest of fieldwork—life in other communities of distinctive, if not exotic, difference, in which the sensitive task of cultural translation and interpretation has absorbed the intellectual energies and defined the ethos of the contemporary discipline. Some, indeed, have resisted the historicism embedded in the ethnographic paradigm; and, particularly after World War II, the focus on the primitive expanded to include peasants, urban migrants, and the formation of ethnic groups in the era of new nation building, decolonization, and the ideology of economic development. Nonetheless, even in change-oriented ethnography, which found an intellectual home in Marxist political economy, the basic conventions and rhetoric of the ethnographic production of knowledge held fast: Anthropologists continued to produce cases of cultures, circumscribed by the historic and circumstantial conditions of fieldwork, and displayed the mark of a nomothetic science that anthropology through its history has claimed to be.

It was only in the late 1960s and through the 1970s that effective critiques of the various elements of the ethnographic paradigm emerged. First, an increasingly sophisticated and historically informed discussion of anthropology as a situated intellectual formation in the history of Western colonialism has developed. Second, a critical discussion of fieldwork as an explicitly hermeneutic method has finally evolved from a longstanding silence among anthropologists about this key emblem of their disciplinary distinction into an outpouring, from the late 1960s up to the present, of romantic, confessional, but nonetheless epistemologically revealing accounts of the trials and tribulations of fieldwork. And third, anthropologists, in conjunction with intellectual historians and cultural critics, produced an ideological critique of the historically distinctive subject of their own discipline—the primitive, the exotic other, and, behind this representation, that of universal Man or humanity.

These important strands of critique all came together in a focused way during the 1980s in the critique of ethnographic rhetoric and discourse, perhaps most fully expressed in the 1986 volume that Jim Clifford and I edited, *Writing Culture: The Poetics and Politics of Ethnography*. At the heart of this critique was the manner in which ethnographic authority is constructed rhetorically in the textual production of what counts as anthropological knowledge. For example, the legitimacy and validity of ethnographies have rested on "having been there," that is, direct experience of another world in which knowledge of the other's language and everyday idioms makes the ethnographer a competent translator of a distinctive form of life that should be presented to and grasped by the ethnographer's readerships at home both vividly and holistically. The various blindnesses, evasions, and, indeed, fictions that had to be created to reap the very important insights that ethnography has produced, and their prominent exposure in the current environment of intellectual skepticism pervading the social sciences and humanities, have suggested most immediately the need for new vocabularies, new concepts, and new rhetorics—in short, new modes other than the available legacy and intellectual capital of nineteenth-century social theory, for the basic function of describing the social and the cultural.

The most interesting analytic problems in cultural and social anthropology today, being worked out in experimentation with the traditional conception and rhetoric of the ethnography, concern ways of opening up the local knowledge classically represented and described by ethnographers to contemporary processes of apparent global homogenization. The problem is no longer merely to place ethnography in the frame of historic metanarratives, since these are subject to critical scrutiny also, but to find new rhetorics of description for constituting the objects of inquiry that are not naive about the power of yet poorly understood transcultural processes that diversify and deterritorialize cultures just as they homogenize them. This is the kind of modernist—or, in its current version, postmodernist—doubletalk that ethnography, by redesigning its conventions, needs to demonstrate can be made into a project of research of rich possibility. Ethnography shares this problematic with other disciplines, but its advantage is that, as noted, it functions well and creatively without a sense that it needs a positive

Critique of
Ethnog. rhetoric +
discourse

e.g.

theoretical paradigm—that is, conventional social theory—to guide it, breeding off of the critique of its rhetoric instead.

By the late 1980s, the traditional interests of ethnography in culture as lived local experience and the acknowledged need to understand the latter in global perspective have come specifically to be about how collective and individual identities are negotiated in the various places that anthropologists have traditionally, and now not so traditionally, conducted fieldwork. As noted, such ethnography bears the burden of explaining how, in the conventional local contexts and sites familiar to ethnographic research, diversity emerges in a transcultural world. In the fact of global creolization processes, there is renewed interest among anthropologists in such topics as ethnicity, race, nationality, and colonialism. While such primordial phenomena as traditions, communities, kinship systems, rituals, and power structures continue to be documented, they can no longer in and of themselves serve as the grounding tropes which organize ethnographic description and explanation.

The most venturesome works are profoundly concerned with the shaping and transformation of identities (of one's subjects as well as, at the very same time, of the ethnographer and the ethnographic project itself). They are the most radically questioning of analytic and descriptive frameworks which rest on privileged exclusive identities emergent from an authoritative and holistic cultural structure, which can always be discovered and modeled. Instead, experimental ethnographies desire, find pleasure in, connecting phenomena worlds apart; in showing how cultural phenomena work systematically in decentered and fragmented ways; in overcoming the dualisms that have structured social theory and the resulting analytic cognitions that govern social science inquiry, such as traditional-modern, rural-urban, the individual-the social, *gemeinschaft-gesellschaft*, and the like; in discovering systematic relationships in the juxtaposition of what might conventionally have been thought to be incommensurate, as in finding the political content in poetic discourses and vice versa. In short, the practical writing and analytic task of much contemporary ethnography (and its greatest contribution to theory) is to redesign the spatio-temporal dimensions for representing processes of varying kinds in response to a perception that these dimensions must deal with the fragmentation, discontinuity, nonlinearity, and simultaneity that seem so characteristic of contemporary global and local realities.

Before actually suggesting a program of redesigning ethnography toward addressing these alternatives, I want to make a brief digression into the sociology (or ethnography) of anthropological careers, to indicate how experimentation is motivated as part of this context, and to sum up where the movement away from classic rhetoric of ethnography now stands for many (if not most) anthropologists of my own and succeeding generations who recognize that such disciplinary changes are both necessary and, indeed, already occurring.

I want to emphasize that experimentation is not prophesy on my part, based on the brilliant foreshadowings of a few examples, but is a documentable trend, not only in the current loosening up of the initiatory training model of ethnography in terms of what might be offered in dissertations but also in the predicament of second projects undertaken by already established scholars, who were credentialed in the late 1960s and early to mid-1970s. After all, ethnography is not only the central intellectual practice in anthropology, it is also the rite of passage that shapes careers. The initial training project to ethnographic research—one or two years of fieldwork, dissertation write-up, followed by publication of a monograph—constitutes the capital on which academic appointments are attained and then secured through tenure. While the training model is conservative and tends toward orthodoxy, what is orthodox (for better or worse), both as subject matter and conventions of writings, has changed markedly in the past decade, as much through student demand as through professorial will, I believe.

But for me personally and my own academic cohorts, the most interesting source of experimentation in the conduct of research occurs very commonly at the breakpoint with that initial career-making and conservative-tending research project in which the scholar (these days anyhow) attempts to do something very different from what she was trained to do. Since the initial project, often lasting more than a decade, by no means achieves deep ethnography mastery of another form of life—even work situated in a very focused space such as a village, town, or urban neighborhood, as most conventional fieldwork is—there has always been virtue attached to returning again and again to the original site of work and moving both geographically and conceptually beyond it in a painstaking manner. Yet few anthropologists now develop research careers in this manner. More commonly these days, I find breaks with first projects to be real departures and *de facto* experiments both in the conception of research and in its production. Yet, since careers do not depend on such projects, they tend to be more quietly developed, more intensely personal, more ambitious, and pursued less confidently. It is in the relatively silent production of second projects that the experimental trend that I posited exists on a widespread basis in contemporary anthropology.

The basic problem of these projects is precisely that of redesigning the conventions of ethnography for unconventional purposes, sites,

associations "It persons; a community or society characterized by this relationship

1) de facto: in reality; actually; from the fact

and subjects—particularly moving beyond the settled community as site of fieldwork toward dispersed phenomena that defy the way that classic ethnography is framed and persuades. For example, moving from a study of Italian villagers to the multinational European parliament, from the Amazon jungles to pain centers in Boston, from a study of a Japanese factory to the international fashion industry, from the study of ancestor worship in a Taiwanese village to medical versus American female discourses about the body, from Transylvanian villagers to Rumanian intellectuals, from the study of Sherpas in Nepal to one's own high school class: Each such career shift involves testing the limits of the ethnographic paradigm, and especially altering the form of the ethnography, while still trying to devise ways to remain within its ethos and tradition. For example, how does one reconstitute modes of ethnographic evidence and authority with nonlocalized subjects, emergent phenomena, not tied to well-articulated local history or tradition, in worlds that are not, on first analysis, that unfamiliar to the ethnographer?

With the critique of ethnographic discourse still the object of lively debate, I would argue that certain changes in ethnographic rhetoric and discourse, if not having been widely accepted, are at least widely countenanced. The two moves or strategies that the motivation to change ethnographic rhetoric is now widely understood to inject into ethnographies are reflexivity and what I will call the "resistance and accommodation" formula for resolving the need to open radically the local integrity of world historical forces. The danger is that these moves might be viewed as mere gestures, techniques, and adaptations of ethnographic discourse in response to the critique of its grounding rhetoric. Indeed, unless these moves, written into many contemporary ethnographies, are thought of as important elements in fuller strategies for the redesign of ethnographic discourse itself, they rapidly will lose their analytic or rhetorical power that they initially have.

Briefly, reflexivity involves working into ethnographic texts a self-conscious account and meditation upon the conditions of knowledge production as it is being produced. Crudely, this move is often viewed as replacing textually the observational objective "eye" of the ethnographer with his or her personal, sometimes pejoratively viewed narcissistic, "I." From the naive assumption of objectivity and unmediated realism, there is now tolerance for the explicit treatment of reflexivity in ethnographic analysis without any clear or systematic understanding of the intellectual functions such explicitness about reflexivity serves. Some might argue that it merely serves the ethical purpose of atoning for the bad faith of any blindness attributable to previously unmediated realism. But certainly there is more to reflexivity than this. Indeed, it is the integral basis of any hermeneutic practice. Extended most radically, it implies changes in the very notion of the kind of knowledge that ethnography can or should produce, knowledge that arises not from monologist authority or voice, however self-critical, but from dialogic relationships in the field that in turn might lead to experiments in intellectual collaboration which are *de facto* at the core of all ethnographic fieldwork. Initially, then, reflexivity means introducing discussion of these dialogic and collaborative relationships in the text. My own position, as I will elaborate, is that reflexivity, diversely deployed in different sorts of analytic and narrative tasks, is an essential dimension of any ethnographic analysis whose aim is to develop a critical knowledge of others' way of life and cultural representations.

Distinguishing the elements of resistance and accommodation in the formation of collective and personal identities at the site of any ethnographic project has become the almost sloganlike analytic formula to retain the coherence of locality, place, in the description of cultural processes, while recognizing the condition of "everything everywhere, everywhere different" created by the penetrations of world systems and consumer economies. The resistance and accommodation formula, however, can be explored with more or less radical departures from the conventional framing assumptions and purposes of traditional ethnography. In general, it might be understood as the remaking of the salvage rationale and the related narrative space that has served ethnography for so long. The ethnographer arrives on the scene of a world on the wane, and salvages it in texts before it is lost to inevitable modernization. The alternative in the resistance and accommodation narrative that is now being experimented with locates cultural survival and authenticity in much more subtle and complex ways, but constructs and valorizes survival and authenticity nonetheless.

In its more conservative use, this formula renegotiates the simultaneity of cultural homogenization and diversification in any locale through preserving the foundational framing power of such notions as community, subculture tradition, and structure. Such ethnographies often privilege some form of stable community, or culture structure, over any logic of enduring contradiction. The two poles of this experimental strategy most importantly serve to position traditional studies in a satisfactory ideological way in the face of the problematics of the profound globalization of the local. On one hand, admitting accommodation avoids the nostalgia for the whole, for the community, and more broadly avoids the allegory of the pastoral, the allegory which Jim Clifford has shown has narratively organized so much ethnography.

wane: dwindle; dim; ebb; to fall gradually from power, prosperity or influence

On the other hand, admitting resistance avoids the "iron-cage" pessimism of the totally administered world vision of modernity in the Frankfurt School critical theory of Theodor Adorno or in the theory of power and knowledge in the later work of Michel Foucault. However, what is really avoided or refused in the more conventional or conservative resistance and accommodation ethnographies is an exploration of the uncompromising sense of paradox in the intertwining of diversity and homogeneity that will not allow an easy parsing of these two terms.

These two contemporary innovative features of ethnographic writing, then, which are remaking the mode (unmediated realism) and rationale (salvage) of classic ethnography are, in the absence of an explicit theoretical paradigm for experimentation, what such experimentation is substantively taken to be about by many anthropologists. As noted, each of these strategies is in need of a project, a more systematic statement of its significance as an experiment with ethnographic narrative and description. What follows is my admittedly programmatic attempt to provide one comprehensive scheme for the redesign of ethnography that incorporates the above mores perceived largely as gestures of response to the critique of ethnographic rhetoric and discourse. What is missing from this attempt is, of course, discussion of current and emerging works that exemplify different aspects of this scheme, but also a consideration of the various other alternatives and sensibilities that might generate such a design. Far from a rejection of realism, or the possibility of narrative and description of the world, I see the following as a move toward a revitalized and defensible practice of realism that is informed by and arises from conversation with the most radical critics of realist narrative (those rhetoricians, skeptical philosophers, and charismatic cultural critics who question its validity, if not its possibility). What is off-stage here is that conversation and the origins of my scheme within it.

The following six stratagems[1] or moves arise appropriately from a systematic disqualification of the various structuring devices on which ethnographic realism has depended and which the critique of its rhetoric has highlighted. Three of them concern changing the parameters in the way that ethnographic subjects have been analytically and rhetorically constructed as subjects—redesigning the observed—and three involve altering the nature of the theoretical intervention that the ethnographer deploys in the texts she creates—redesigning the observer. Together I intend them to constitute a critical project for ethnography that takes the discipline well beyond its traditional archival function of classifying and describing the primitive and exotic otherness toward the postmodernist problematic of experimenting with

1) stratagem : an artifice or trick in war for deceiving + outwitting the enemy ; skill in ruses or trickery

ways of narrating (and thus understanding) the interpenetration of the social and cultural in their variety as simultaneously global and local forms of life.

Redesigning the Observed

problematizing spatial

1. Problematizing the spatial involves a break with the trope of community in realist ethnography. The concept of community in the classic sense of shared values, shared identity, and thus shared culture has been mapped literally onto locality to define one basic frame of reference orienting ethnography. The connotations of solidity and homogeneity attaching to the notion of community, whether concentrated in a locale or dispersed, has been replaced in the framework of modernity by the idea that the situated production of identity—of a person, of a group, or even a whole society—does not depend alone, or even always primarily, on the observable, concentrated activities within a particular locale. The identity of anyone or any group is produced simultaneously in many different locales of activity by many different agents for many different purposes. Where one lives, among one's neighbors, friends, relatives, or co-strangers, is only one social context, and perhaps not the most important one in which one's identity is shaped. It is this process of dispersed identity construction or mobile, related representations in many different places of differing character that must be grasped as social facts. Of course, such a requirement presents some new and very difficult problems of research method and textual representation in ethnography, but to capture the formation of identity (multiple identities, really) at a particular moment in the biography of a person or the history of a group of people through a configuration of very differing sites of locales of activity recognizes both the powerful integrating (rationalizing) drives of the state and economy in modernity, powered by constant technological innovation, and the resulting dispersals of the subject—person or group—in multiple overlapping fragments of identity that are also characteristic of modernity (see Marcus 1989).

The questions for study in this parallel processing, so to speak, of identity at many sites are, Which identities coalesce and under what circumstances? Which become defining or dominant and for how long? How does the play of unintended consequences affect the outcome in the coalescence of a salient identity in this space of the multiple construction and dispersed control of a person's or group's identities? And what is the nature of the politics by which identity at and across any site is controlled, perhaps most importantly at the site where identity in a literal sense is the embodiment of a particular human actor or group? Cultural difference or diversity arises here not from some local struggle for identity, but is a function of a complex process among all the sites in which the identity of someone or a group anywhere is defined in simultaneity. It is the burden of contemporary experimental ethnography to capture distinctive identity formations in all their migrations and dispersions. This multilocale, dispersed identity vision thus reconfigures and complexifies the spatial plane on which ethnography has conceptually operated in the past.

2. Problematizing the temporal involves a break with the trope of history in realist ethnography. The break is not with historical consciousness, or a pervasive sense of the past in any site or set of sites probed by ethnography, but rather with historical determination as the primary explanatory context for any ethnographic present. Realist ethnography has become dependent on—and revived by its incorporation within—existing Western historical metanarratives. There is a lively effort these days, in contradistinction to the classic period in the development of ethnography in Anglo-American anthropology, to tie the site of ethnographic close observation to a stream of history within which it can be explained by reference to origins, not in the generic sense of earlier anthropology, but in the framework of historical narrative. The contemporary experimental mood is not sanguine about the alliance between conventional social history and ethnography. The past that is present in any site is built up from memory, the fundamental medium of ethnohistory. Collective and individual memory in its multiple traces and expressions is indeed the crucible for the local self-recognition of an identity. While the significance of memory as the linking medium and process relating history and identity formation is well recognized by contemporary ethnographers, analytic and methodological thinking about it is as yet very undeveloped. The difficulty of descriptively grasping memory as a social or collective process under contemporary conditions is not unrelated to the inadequacy of the trope of the community to conceptualize the spatial plane of ethnography, as noted in the last section. The erosion of the public-private distinction in everyday life (on which community is constructed in Western narratives) as well as the displacement of the long-term memory function of orality and storytelling (again a condition of life in community as traditionally conceived) in the electronic information age makes the understanding and description of any straightforward "art of memory" especially problematic in modernity. Collective memory is more likely to be passed through individual memory and autobiography embedded in the diffuse communication between generations than in any spectacles

Macro vs. continuous flow of memory

or performances in public arenas, the power of which relies on ironic references to the present or what is emergent rather than on exhortations of varying subtlety to remember. Collective representations are thus most effectively filtered through personal representations. With this insight, redesigned ethnography transforms the conventional realist concern with history as it infuses, expresses, and even determines social identities in a locale into a study that is synonymous with addressing the construction of personal and collective identity itself. It is probably in the production of autobiography, as this genre has emerged with renewed presence particularly with a salient focus on ethnicity (see Fischer 1986), that the sort of historical experiences carried in memory and shaping contemporary social movements can best be appreciated.

Memory defines ethnog. present

The return of an ethnographic present—but a very different ethnographic present than the one that largely ignored by history in the classic functionalist anthropology of traditional, tribal society—is thus a challenge to the construction of the temporal setting for experimental ethnography. This is a present that is defined not by historical narrative either, but by memory, its own distinctive narratives and traces, an art of memory that is synonymous with the fragmented process of identity formation in any locale—one whose distinctly social forms are difficult to grasp or even see ethnographically—and that thus sets another problematic to be explored in the redesign of contemporary works.

Problem. Structure

3. Problematizing perspective/voice involves a break with the trope of structure in realist ethnography. Ethnography has opened to the understanding of perspective as "voice," just as the distinctly visual, controlling metaphor of structure has come into question. While indeed the trope of structure—that is, either social structure on the surface, derived from patterns of observed behaviors, or structure as underlying systematic meanings or codes that organize language and social discourses—may continue to be indispensable in rendering descriptions of the subject matter even of experimental ethnography, the analytic weight or heft of an account shifts to a concern with perspective as voice, as embedded discourse within the framing and conduct of a project of ethnographic inquiry.

In part, this shift came about as a result of questioning the adequacy of structural analysis of whatever kind to model the complexity of intracultural diversity. A Wittgensteinian family-of-resemblances problem confronted the ethnographer who would represent reality as organized by the operation of cultural models or codes (usually of a key or central model) and the more or less orderly transformations of their components. Controlling for context and the empirical recording of actual montage flows of association in data on discourse have challenged the adequacy of structural or semiotic models to account for associations that resist assimilation to a model of limited dimensions.

In part, the experimental alternative in voice, accepting the montage of polyphony as simultaneously the problem of representation and analysis, probably has had as much to do with the changing ethics of the ethnographic enterprise as with a dissatisfaction concerning the structural analysis of cultural phenomena. These changes are rooted in a marked sensitivity to the dialogic, oral roots of all anthropological knowledge, transformed and obscured by the complex processes of writing which dominate ethnographic projects from field to text, and of the differential power relationships that shape the ultimate media and modes of representing knowledge. Here, I merely want to comment on this shift in terms of the analytic difference in the way experimental ethnography creates its space-time field of discourse regardless of one's assessment of the possibilities for success in representing ethically as well as authoritatively voice and its diversity.

In the mode of cultural analysis that Raymond Williams developed (1977), a structure of feeling (the use of structure is quite idiosyncratic) would be the goal of ethnography, focused on what is emergent in a setting from the interaction of well-defined dominant and residual formations (these could be systems of social relations in the British sense of structure, but they also refer to possible and established modes of discourse) with that which is not quite articulable to subjects or to the analyst. Making it more sayable/visible is one of the critical functions of ethnography. In this vein, recognizing such properties of discourses as dominance, residualness, and emergence (or possibility), experimental ethnography would map the relationships of these properties in any site of inquiry not by immediate structural appropriations of discourse formations but by exposing, to the extent possible, the quality of voices by means of metalinguistic categories (such as narrative, trope, etc.). Voices are not seen as products of local structure, based on community and tradition alone, or as privileged sources of perspective but rather as products of the complex sets of associations and experiences which compose them. To enact this refocusing of ethnography from structure to voice/discourse involves different conceptions of the relationship of the observer to the observed, to which we now turn.

Redesigning the Observer

(It should not be lost on one that while a more complex appreciation of the dynamics of identity formation is one object of strategies for redesigning the conventions that construct the observed in ethnography, the parallel strategies for redesigning the presence of the observer in the ethnographic text are not less directed toward the dynamics of identity formation of the anthropologist in relation to his or her practice of ethnography.)

   4. The appropriation through dialogue of a text's conceptual apparatus. The realist ethnography has often been built around the intensive exegesis of a key indigenous symbol or concept pulled from its contexts of discourse to be reinserted in them according to the dictates of the ethnographer's authoritative analytic scheme. Much in recent cultural analysis has depended on this central organizing and analytic technique. On the quality and thoroughness of such exegesis often depends the professional assessment of the value of a particular ethnographic work.

   In one sense, the exegesis at the center of ethnography is a gesture toward recognizing and privileging indigenous concepts over those of anthropology. Most important, such targeted concepts come to act as synecdoche for identity—they stand for a system of meanings but also for the identity of a people in the anthropological literature and sometimes beyond it. Keying an account to particular concepts, myths, or symbols thus tends to impose an identity upon a people as a contribution (or course) of anthropology. *exegesis as imposition of identity*

   One alteration of the ethnography would be to remake this exercise into a fully dialogic one in which exegesis is foregrounded in the ethnography and the frame of analysis derives from at least the dual voices party to dialogue. In this basic process of cultural translation— one of the favored metaphors for characterizing the interpretive task in ethnography—the purpose is not so much to change indigenous concepts (that is the responsibility of the anthropologist's interlocutors) as to alter the anthropologist's own concepts. *transformation of the researcher*

   Indeed, it is the remaking of our concepts that is so much at stake generally in the contemporary cultural-studies movement in Western academia. In a recent interview, for example, Fredric Jameson (1987) responds to a comment about the difficulty of saying things about the whole in postmodernist discourse:

> One of the ways of describing this is as a modification in the very nature of the cultural sphere: a loss of autonomy of culture, a case of culture falling into the world. As you say, this makes it much more difficult to speak of cultural systems and to evaluate them in isolation. A whole new theoretical problem is posed. Thinking at once negatively and positively about it is a beginning, but what

¹)exegesis: an explanation or critical interpretation of a text we need is a new vocabulary. The languages that have been useful in talking about culture and politics in the past don't really seem adequate to this historical moment. (37)

From where might this vocabulary come, for the sake of Western social theory and cognition? Maybe from a reshaping of the translation of concepts at the core of realist ethnographies, through their appropriation for our own critical purposes. Perhaps moments of exegesis, of definition in context, would be replaced by the exposure of moments of dialogue and their use in the ethnographer's revision of familiar concepts that define the analytic limits of his or her own work, and of anthropological discourse more generally. Such a move would open the realm of discussion of ethnographies to organic intellectuals (to use Gramsci's term) and readerships among one's subjects wherever this is now feasible.

A different notion of exegesis, distinctively tied to a recognition of its dialogic character, becomes a thoroughly reflexive operation. While exploring the changing identity processes within an ethnographic setting, the identity of one's own concepts changes. The process of constructing an analysis thus can take on and parallel aspects of the process it describes. The key challenge here is whether an identity can ever be explained by a reference discourse when several discourses are in play, not the least of which is the ethnographer's in dialogue with specific other subjects. There are several resolutions in the way this activity might be represented textually, but the innovation is that the identity of the ethnographer's framework should not remain intact, authoritative, if the subject is being analytically pulled apart. This leads to a consideration of the bifocal character of any project of ethnographic research, a character that is heightened by the contemporary sense of the real— that the globe generally and intimately is becoming more integrated and that this, paradoxically, is not leading to an easily comprehensible totality but to an increasing diversity of connections among phenomena once thought disparate and worlds apart.

5. Bifocality. Looking in at least two ways, an embedded comparative dimension, has always been a more or less implicit aspect of every ethnographic project. In the evolving global modernity of the twentieth century in which anthropology has been pursued almost from its professional inception, the coevalness of the ethnographer with the Other as subject has, for the most part, been denied (Fabian 1983). There is, indeed, a history in ethnography of a developing critical juxtaposition, made explicitly between one's own world and that of the Other as subject, but the construct of separate, distant worlds in analytically making

such juxtapositions has been sustained. Only in the periodic internal
critique of anthropology's relationship to Western colonialism has the
thoroughly blurred historic relationship of the anthropologist's own
society and practices to the subject's under colonial domination been
argued.

Now that Western modernity is being reconceptualized as a global
and thoroughly transcultural phenomenon, the explicit treatment of
bifocality in ethnographic accounts is becoming more explicit and
openly transgressive of the us-them distanced worlds in which it was
previously constructed. In other words, the identity of the anthropologist and his world, by whatever complex chain of connection and association, is likely to be profoundly related to that of any particular world
he is studying. However, only the redesigning of the observed, outlined in the previous section, makes possible this revision of the bifocal
character of ethnography. For example, the multilocality of identity
processes across various levels of conventional divisions of social organization creates a mutuality of implication for identity processes occurring in any ethnographic site. The chain of preexisting historic or contemporary connection between the ethnographer and her subjects may
be a long or short one, thus making bifocality an issue of judgment and
a circumstance even of the personal autobiographical reasons for pursuit of a particular project, but its discovery and recognition remains a
defining feature of the current modernist sensibility in ethnography.
The mere demonstration of such connections and affinities, the juxtaposition of two identity predicaments precipitated by the ethnographer's project itself, stands as a critical statement against conventional
efforts to sustain distanced worlds and their separate determinations
despite the modernist insight about global integration through paths
that are transcultural as well as technological, political, and economic in
nature.

6. Critical juxtapositions and contemplation of alternative possibilities. The function of the experimental ethnography is primarily one
of cultural critique, not only of one's disciplinary apparatus through
an intellectual alliance with the subject, or of one's society that, in the
increasing condition of global integration, is always bifocally related
in transcultural process and historical perspective (or rather retrospective) to the site of ethnographic attention, but also of conditions within
the site of ethnographic focus—the local world which it treats. Given the
general commitment of modernist ethnographies to explore the full
range of possibilities for identities and their complex expressions
through voice in any setting, the enactment of this exploration is a key
form of cultural critique also. This move is, indeed, the distinct and

George E. Marcus

committed voice of the ethnographer in his text, and it operates from the critical attitude that things as they are need not have been, or need not be, the way they are, given the alternatives detectable within the situations—there are always more possibilities, other identities, and so forth, than those that have come to be enacted. Exploring all actual and possible outcomes through juxtapositions is itself a method of cultural critique which moves against the grain of the given situation and its definition in dominant identities which might otherwise be mistaken as authoritative models from which all variation is derived. The modernist treatment of reality allows, rather, for traces of the roads not taken or the possibilities not explored. Indeed, this kind of critical thought experiment incorporated within ethnography, in which juxtaposed actualities and possibilities are put analytically in dialogue with one another, might be thought to border on the utopian or the nostalgic if it were not dependent, first of all, on a documentation that these traces do have a life of their own, so to speak, and are integral to the processes that form identities, including the ones that appear defining or dominant. Such clarification of possibilities against the objective defining conditions, within the limits of the discourses "that matter" in any setting, is the one critical intervention and contribution that the ethnographer can make that is uniquely her own.

As a provocation, I leave readers, especially anthropologists, to see their own ethnography, or that of others, in the broad terms discussed above; or, if they cannot or choose not to, then I leave it to readers to revise and critique my own redesign in terms of other commitments and visions for what ethnography finally might become. Still, I am uneasy about letting the qualified statement of such a program stand, vulnerable to the complaint of "pie in the sky," without reference to exemplars that enact in their own ways the above redesign features. To end, I thus very briefly and as a mere gesture offer the following works which occur to me as exemplars of each of the features of experimental ethnography that I have outlined.

Bruno Latour's *Pasteurization of France* (1989), about the historic dissemination of Louis Pasteur's science in French society, attempts to construct a heterogeneous and discontinuous space in which to render an account of a process that is refracted in the simultaneous operations of multiple sites and actors without obvious cause-effect, linear relationships to one another. There's a stretching here to imagine the kind of complex space which enacts one design feature addressed by experimental ethnography.

Michael Taussig's *Shamanism, Colonialism, and the Wild Man* (1987), a vivid social history of the terror and genocide of the nineteenth-century Putumayo rubber boom, juxtaposed to the ethnographic present of disorder in backcountry Colombia, strives to subordinate conventional historical narrative to local media of memory, found in the healing performances of shamans. This work, one of the most self-conscious experiments available, enacts with variable power most of the redesign moves that I outlined.

Carolyn Kay Steedman's *Landscape for a Good Woman* (1987), a partly autobiographical account of an English working-class mother and her daughter, which tries to find an expression for this story in given theoretical frameworks and provocatively fails, is distinctive in the context of this paper in that it successfully sustains the quality of voice without intermediate structural determinations of the social space in which its discourses are evoked as voice. In fact, it directly challenges the available theoretical imageries of one notion of structure or another to subsume the voices Steedman orchestrates. More generally, revival of the life history or elicited autobiography as ethnographic text and document has been of keen interest in current experiments (one might think here of Vincent Crapanzano's *Tuhami: Portrait of a Moroccan* [1980]), especially where the double-voiced discourses that they generate often reshape in quite novel and unexpected ways the social and cultural spaces in which they are embedded. Such accounts radically subordinate the structural and structuralist modes of traditional ethnographic cognition.

Dennis Tedlock's recent work of poetry, *Days from a Dream Almanac* (1989), appropriates more seriously and thoroughly than any other anthropological work I know a framework dialogically derived from fieldwork and makes it his own, to remarkable effect. He renders a year in his own life as a Western man traveling in terms of the complex Maya Quiche organization of time. In so doing, he provides one kind of new vocabulary that Fredric Jameson called for as a response to postmodern conditions, one that convincingly revises the way one might understand time in contemporary Western experience.

Michael Herzfeld's *Anthropology through the Looking Glass* (1987) demonstrates the commonalties in the historic derivation of the culture concept in anthropology, which is Herzfeld's analytic capital or apparatus as observer, and the struggle to define the contemporary culture of Greece by Greeks themselves, which is his object of study and in which scholarly fields such as anthropology, folklore, and the classics played crucial roles. Herzfeld thus develops the bifocal dimension of ethnography by revealing in his project the complex historic relationship between the ethnographic gaze and what it focuses upon. Reflexivity is brought here from a mere gesture of the personal to a critical practice for ethnography that demonstrates the always already relationship existing between observer and observed in specific moments of inquiry.

Michael M. J. Fischer and Mehdi Abedi's *Debating Muslims* (1990), an account of contemporary Iranian Shi'ism, is developed in different genres of writing and from multiple perspectives, and exemplifies the collaborative ideal of ethnographic production; it critically lays out, better than any other work I know, the dominant, residual, and emergent formations of a particular intellectual and cultural space, one that in recent times has been most often characterized as fanatical and monolithic. Fischer and Abedi are especially good at capturing possibility and emergence in events after the 1979 Revolution and in the creation of a new and distinctive Iranian diaspora.

Conclusion

In this paper, then, I have surveyed a discipline that is currently powered by innovations in its empirical practice, responding to a critique of its past presumptions and aiming to represent the reality of distinctive forms of life worldwide. While experimentation with the forms of representation acknowledges the ongoing classic project of social theory and engages with it, it bypasses its authority in working out new narrative techniques as a means of materializing new subjects of inquiry and new questions. Such an experimental trend, as I have termed it, is clearly identifiable in other social sciences, and particularly in the newly emerging interdisciplinary spaces (for example, especially inspired by feminist thought), but nowhere does it have the disciplinary salience it has in anthropology, for reasons and in ways that I hope to have made clear.

Note

Portions of this paper appeared in my essay "After the Critique of Ethnography: Faith, Hope, and Charity, But the Greatest of These is Charity," in *Assessing Cultural Anthropology*, edited by Robert Borofsky (New York: McGraw-Hill, 1993), 55-67.

References

Clifford, James, and George E. Marcus. 1986. *Writing Culture: The Poetics and Politics of Ethnography*. Berkeley: University of California Press.

Crapanzano, Vincent. 1980. *Tuhami: Portrait of a Moroccan*. Chicago: University of Chicago Press.

Fabian, Johannes. 1983. *Time and the Other: How Anthropology Makes Its Object*. New York: Columbia University Press.

Fischer, Michael M. J. 1986. *Ethnicity and the Post-Modern Art of Memory*. In *Writing Culture*, edited by James Clifford and George Marcus, 194-233. Berkeley: University of California Press.

Fischer, Michael M. J., and Mehdi Abedi. 1990. *Debating Muslims: Cultural Dialogues in Postmodernity and Tradition*. Madison: University of Wisconsin Press.

Herzfeld, Michael. 1987. *Anthropology through the Looking Glass: Critical Ethnography in the Margins of Europe*. Cambridge: Cambridge University Press.

Jameson, Fredric. 1987. "Regarding Postmodernism—A Conversation With Fredric Jameson." *Social Text* No. 17:29-54.

Latour, Bruno. 1989. *The Pasteurization of France*. Cambridge: Harvard University Press.

Marcus, George E. 1989. "The Problem of the Unseen World of Wealth for the Rich: Toward an Ethnography of Complex Connections." *Ethos* 17(1): 114-23.

Steedman, Carolyn Kay. 1987. *Landscape for a Good Woman: A Story of Two Lives*. New Brunswick: Rutgers University Press.

Taussig, Michael. 1987. *Shamanism, Colonialism, and the Wild Man*. Chicago: University of Chicago Press.

Tedlock, Dennis. 1989. *Days from a Dream Almanac*. Urbana: University of Illinois Press.

Williams, Raymond. 1977. *Marxism and Literature*. London: Oxford University Press.

Can ~~an~~ E.H. be done using oral texts rather than written? using cultural performances?

knowledge is biosocial

biologically constituted
socially constituted
knowledge: the symbolic representation of what we know to be true about reality

7

Toward an Evolutionary Hermeneutics: The Case of Wisdom

how is the biosocial construction of knowledge related to wisdom adaptable

Mihaly Csikszentmihalyi

knowl. def.

Knowledge, or the symbolic representation of what we believe to be true about reality, is biologically and socially constituted. It is biologically constituted in that our senses precondition what we can experience and set limits to what aspects of reality we can actually observe. Knowledge is socially constituted in that the symbolic representations of facts and their relations are formulated in terms of historical traditions that are largely accidental and always at the service of some local interest or another. It is not that the laws of physics, for instance, are arbitrary fabrications; what they claim about the material world does, indeed, correspond to our experience of it. But the laws of physics deal only with those dimensions of the world that we are able to grasp in terms of our current sensory and intellectual equipment, and are concerned with expressing knowledge in terms that will allow humans, or a specific subsection of humanity, to control the reality thus grasped.

If knowledge is biosocially constituted, it follows that it will change, like other biological and social structures, in response to relevant changes in the environment. The process by which organisms acquire knowledge is selected, stored, and transmitted through ceaseless interactions with the environment.

"There are no such things as mind, reason, thought, . . . or truth. . . . It is [just] a question of a particular species of animal which can prosper only by means of a certain exactness, or better still, a regularity in recording its perceptions," wrote Friedrich Nietzsche about a hundred years ago, expressing a view that was to become the basis for a later evolutionary epistemology. The purpose of knowledge, according to this view, is to provide a living species with enough predictable information so as to allow it to make adaptive responses to the environment.

Nietzsche

knowledge's purpose is to help us survive

The utility of preservation—and not some abstract or theoretical need to eschew deception—stands as the motive force behind the development of the organs of knowledge; . . . they evolve in such a way that their observations may suffice for our preservation. . . . [A] species gets a grasp of a given amount of reality, in order to master it, in order to enlist that amount in its service. (Nietzsche 1960, 11-12).

it's not absolute

The truth our organs of knowledge provide is valuable not because of its formal qualities or because it approximates some absolute certainty but simply because, in the past, it has given our species an advantage in the struggle for survival. More recent psychological epistemologists are in essential agreement with this position, although they rarely endorse it with Nietzsche's radical abandon (Campbell 1960, 1974; Dennett 1991; Piaget 1971; Popper 1965).

history

If we wish to understand how knowledge works, then, we must reconstruct the history of our adaptive efforts to represent reality throughout time. The traces of current certainties are to be found in mankind's past gropings. Similarly, the blind spots that make us oblivious to some aspects of reality are rooted in our past. As Jean Piaget (1971) wrote,

horizons

> the very nature of life is constantly to overtake itself, and if we seek the explanation of rational organization within the living organization including its overtakings, we are attempting to interpret knowledge in terms of its own construction, which is no longer an absurd method since knowledge is essentially construction. (362)

Mihaly's purpose

★The purpose of this essay is to apply this apparently absurd method—that is, the interpretation of knowledge in terms of its own construction—to a specific question: What is wisdom? But whereas Piaget gave special prominence to the biological construction of knowledge, I shall pay particular attention to the social and cultural aspects of the process. Instead of looking for the key to wisdom in the adaptation of the nervous system to its environment, we shall look for it instead in the transformations of the symbolic representations that our culture has selected and transmitted through time.

An Outline of Evolutionary Hermeneutics

To illuminate what wisdom is about, I shall adopt a method that, for lack of a better term, we might call "evolutionary hermeneutics."

evolut. herm.

This approach assumes that concepts that relate to the evaluation of human behavior—such as virtue, courage, freedom, or wisdom—and that have been used for many centuries under very different social and historical conditions are likely to have adaptive value for humankind. The method is based on the further assumption that, to understand the significance of such concepts, it helps to compare their meanings across time, in order to identify invariant components as well as possible variations in response to differing conditions in the surrounding cultural environment.

To find out what we mean by "wisdom" at the end of the twentieth century is important, but it is not sufficient. No matter how advanced we think we are in terms of understanding the human psyche compared to former times, we still only have access to a limited cross-section of the growing tree of knowledge. To ignore the hard-won insights of the past about issues that are vital for survival is like blinding ourselves on purpose, out of false pride.

e.g. sexual behavior

A simple example may help illustrate this point. Up to a few generations ago, children in our culture were warned against promiscuous sexuality. Such behavior was labeled wrong, sinful, or immoral. In the last half-century, scientific knowledge discredited many of the assumptions and explanations on which these prohibitions were based. This led to the conclusion that sexual restraint was backed only by obsolete superstitions, and hence everyone should feel free to satisfy his or her sexual urges *ad libitum.* The medical and biological sciences, partly because they lacked hard "data," partly because they did not want to appear reactionary and spoil the fun, tacitly endorsed this position. What followed is history: a rampant increase in all forms of sexually transmitted diseases, and the AIDS epidemic.

STD's, AIDS

ev. herm. - corrective to view that present knowl. is superior

Evolutionary hermeneutics is a corrective against the naive assumption that present knowledge is in all respects superior to that of the past and that it is safe to ignore the cultural adaptations that were positively selected over time. It suggests, for instance, that the ancient and universal warnings against promiscuous sexuality might have been based on valid past experience. At the same time, it also suggests that the explanations for why such behavior is dangerous are likely to be given in terms of reasons that have lost their relevance. To say that promiscuity is "sinful" no longer means anything to a great number of people. Nevertheless, the meaning contained in the concept of "sin" may still be extremely relevant—indeed, a matter of life and death. Therefore, the task of an evolutionary hermeneutics is to uncover the meanings of concepts discovered in the past that have stood the test of time, to translate these meanings in the relatively timeless categories of

task of E.H.

¹) ad libitum - ad lib? in accordance w/ desire

evolutionary theory, and, finally, to translate them back into current concepts applicable to the present state of knowledge and to contemporary problems.

Evolutionary hermeneutics is a method that logically follows from evolutionary epistemology. Donald Campbell was one of the first psychologists to observe that changes in knowledge systems—including "hardware" as well as "software"—obey the evolutionary laws of variation, selection, and transmission (Campbell 1960, 1974, 1976; Csikszentmihalyi and Csikszentmihalyi 1988; Csikszentmihalyi and Massimini 1985; Csikszentmihalyi and Rathunde 1990; Csikszentmihalyi 1993; Simon 1969; Simonton 1988). According to Campbell, for instance, scientific experimentation is functionally equivalent to sensory organs which enable smell, touch, and vision. Science makes it possible to know what is happening around us, and allows us to test the environment vicariously. There is an unbroken line of gradual change from the physiological development of the senses to the development of memory to logic and then to the extrasomatic organs of knowledge such as language and myths, all the way to cultural knowledge systems culminating (temporarily) in science—a line of development shaped by selective pressure favoring the ability to obtain objective information about the environment at the least cost to the organism.

The notion of evolution on which this perspective is based is not limited to biochemical instructions mediated by genetic selection and transmission. I believe, instead, that it is useful to expand the evolutionary model to include within its compass instructions for behavior that are mediated by cultural learning. Tools and weapons, as well as ideas, to the extent that they influence adaptation, can be seen as *memes*[1] that are selected and transmitted across generations and that carry instructions which affect the survival of the human phenotype[2] (Dawkins 1976, 1982; Lumsden and Wilson 1981, 1983; Boyd and Richerson 1985; Csikszentmihalyi 1993; Csikszentmihalyi and Massimini 1985). The meme of "wisdom," for instance, contains a nucleus of meaning that has been transmitted relatively unchanged for at least eighty generations, providing directions for human thought and behavior.

Cultural selection, as opposed to genetic selection, does not necessarily favor the selective fitness of the individual who is the carrier of positive variations (Burhoe 1976; Csikszentmihalyi and Csikszentmihalyi 1988). Wise, creative, or intelligent persons are not likely to produce more numerous offspring—in fact, they may very well have fewer children than other people. Yet wise, creative, and intelligent behavior is likely to be noted, appreciated, and preserved by the com-

[handwritten margin notes:]
wisdom-as-meme
Cultural (vs. natural) selection

[handwritten footnotes:]
1) memes: an idea, behavior, style, or usage that spreads from person to person within a culture
2) phenotype: the observable properties of an organism that are produced by the interaction of the genotype & the environment

munity, and the people who display such behaviors will be remembered. They may or may not pass on more of their genes to posterity, but they will pass on their memes—i.e., the memory of their thoughts, actions, and works. In Burhoe's terms, genetic and cultural traits evolve together in a co-adaptive symbiosis; and commonly shared values provide the bonds that keep people working together who otherwise might compete to maximize their genetic progeny at each others' expense (Burhoe 1976).

The folk conception about "progress" in knowledge suffers from a misconception that is not inherent in the theoretical model. It assumes that if one method for getting knowledge comes after another, the latter is more credible and must displace the former. Because scientific knowledge is more recent than philosophy and religion, for instance, it is thought to be a more reliable symbolic system for representing reality, one that makes its predecessors obsolete. There are two problems with this assumption. In the first place, the majority of variations in the evolutionary record are not advantageous, and do not survive. Thus, just because an organ of knowledge is more recent, it does not mean it is better; in fact, the presumption is that it will be worse. Second, even if the new organ is more sensitive or more powerful in some respects, it does not mean that it must displace earlier ones. Just as sight and smell present different pictures of the world, so myth, religion, philosophy, and science provide complementary yet discrete windows on experience. Science may be a more evolved eye, but it does not compensate for being blind. It does not make sense to say that science, as a more evolved organ for providing information, is a substitute for the ability to see. For the same reason, science may not be a substitute for earlier epistemologies such as religion or wisdom.

Evolutionary hermeneutics is simply the name given to the attempt at reconciling what has been said in the past about certain important concepts with what is being said about them now, within the framework of current psychological knowledge informed by evolutionary theory. The aim is to integrate the experience of previous generations with our own, trying to understand the adaptive value of former responses, thereby providing a deeper and richer context for present understanding. In practice, the method consists in reviewing what has been said about a concept by previous writers as distant from us in time and cultural background as possible. The next step consists in identifying whether there are common meanings attributed to the concept and whether these change over time. Then the following questions are put to the data: What is the adaptive significance of this concept? For instance, what did the ancient Israelites mean when they wrote:

"Wisdom is the principal thing; therefore get wisdom" (Proverbs 4:7)?[1] What purposes did this idea serve? If the concept has changed over time, was this in response to relevant changes in the social and cultural environment? What is likely to be its present value?

It is, of course, impossible to apply this method with anything resembling its ideal intent. There is just too much potentially relevant information to assimilate, and our knowledge of past conditions is necessarily incomplete. Any application will have to be woefully approximate, especially in this first attempt. Yet the goal is worth pursuing even if the means, at this point, are inadequate. In the present case, I will explore only three aspects of the concept of wisdom and review only a narrow selection from mainly the Western classical literature, in the hope of demonstrating the usefulness of evolutionary hermeneutics and contributing to the substantive understanding of wisdom as a human trait.

What Is Wisdom?

There is widespread agreement among past thinkers that the concept of wisdom has three major dimensions of meaning. It refers, first of all, to a cognitive process, or a peculiar way of obtaining and processing information; second, to a virtue, or socially valued pattern of behavior; and finally, to a good or personally desirable state or condition. All three dimensions of the concept are relevant for its understanding, and therefore I will take up each of them in turn.

Wisdom as a Cognitive Process

The most obvious meaning of the term "wisdom" refers to a way of knowing. But how does it differ from other cognitive processes, such as intelligence or creativity? The various uses of the term in the past point to several distinguishing characteristics. In contrast to other forms of knowledge, it has been claimed that wisdom (a) deals not with the appearance of fleeting phenomena but with enduring universal truths; (b) is not specialized, but is an attempt to apprehend how the various aspects of reality are related to each other; (c) is not a value-free way of knowing, but implies a hierarchical ordering of truths and actions directed at those truths.

Considering the first of these three characteristics that usually define the cognitive dimensions of wisdom, we immediately run into a problem. There is not now, nor has there ever been, universal agreement about what it is that lies hidden behind the veil of appearance. What is to be counted as "universal truth" varies depending on the particular

See p. 130

cosmology of the times. For Plato, the visible world was made up of objects and of their images, to which corresponded a hidden but intelligible world of universal ideas (*Republic* 6.510, 533-34; *Philebus* 30; *Phaedo* 79). True knowledge consisted in discovering the outlines of this world. Wisdom was the state of the soul when she reflects on eternity and immortality instead of appearances (*Philebus* 30; *Phaedo* 79). Similarly, Aristotle viewed wisdom as the chief of sciences, because it was its role to prove the principles on which all other knowledge rested (*Ethics* 6.7).

Christian thinkers such as Augustine and Aquinas agreed in several important respects with the viewpoint of the classical philosophers. They also held that wisdom consisted in seeking the invariant and ultimate causes behind the variability of superficial phenomena. They differed, however, in believing that universal truth could be found only with the help of God. "He who considers absolutely the highest cause of the whole universe, namely God, is most of all called wise" (Aquinas, *Summa* 1.6).[2] Human reason could reach up to a point, but to behold the real order of things one needed additional faith in divine inspiration (Aquinas, *Summa* 2.12 passim; 32.1). Immanuel Kant also saw wisdom as the discovery of the relation of all cognitions to the ultimate and essential aims of human reason, which were contained in God (*Critique of Pure Reason* div. 2, 2, 3); but he derived the necessary existence of God from the existence of reason, rather than the other way around.

What all ancient thinkers seemed to realize is that without wisdom, ways of knowing are constrained by a tragic paradox: The clearer the view they provide, the more limited the slice of reality they reveal. *[classical paradox]* The integrated thought of "primitive" men and women—who did not distinguish between religion, art, science, habits, and instincts—slowly gave way to more and more specialized "domains" of knowledge. Nowadays, knowledge is divided into innumerable branches that appear to be unrelated to each other or to the world as we experience it. Specialization enables us to exert a powerful control on specific, limited aspects of reality. But it does not help us to know what to do with the control thus achieved.

In line with these classical conceptions, much of the impetus for the contemporary study of wisdom is a reaction to the overspecialization of modern culture. For instance, Holliday and Chandler (1986) claim that the present technological *Zeitgeist* has influenced psychology's exclusive concern with behavioral explanations, its concentration on the young, and its devaluation of "essences." They, as well as Meacham (1983), see research on wisdom as attempting to balance scientific/analytic "accumulation" models of truth with integrative

Zeitgeist: the general intellectual, moral, + cultural climate of an era hermeneutic inquiries that emphasize critical, historical, and practical dimensions (Habermas 1972).

Others concerned with higher stages of cognitive development in adulthood (Labouvie-Vief 1980; Kramer 1983; Riegel 1973) echo the same concerns, and try to expand beyond "formal operations" (abstract, logical, hypothetical, and problem-solving thought) as the preferred mode of information processing. Kramer (1983) notes the similarity between formal operations and "mechanistic" or "analytic" worldviews (Reese and Overton 1970), both of which are conducive to an atomistic conception of reality and supposedly less desirable than their mirror opposites, "organismic" and "synthetic" worldviews.

However, in contemporary discussions on wisdom, as in contemporary discussions on almost any human way of knowing, one would seldom come across such integrative notions as "universal truth" or "God." Thus, it is legitimate to ask whether or not an essential component of the ancient conception of wisdom has been fundamentally lost or altered. While it is certainly true that modern variations on the concept of wisdom appeared, it is unlikely that wisdom—conceived as a relatively holistic cognitive process—has completely disappeared from contemporary thought.

This, in fact, seems to be the case. Consistent with ancient distinctions between a holistic wisdom and other specialized ways of knowing are the results of current empirical studies of what the category "wise person" means in everyday language. Holliday and Chandler (1986) found a consistent multidimensional picture of the wise person as having: (a) general competence (a dimension which overlaps with logical intelligence, or technical ability), (b) an experience-based pragmatic knowledge, and (c) reflective or evaluative metaanalytic skills. They fit these three components into a Habermasian framework which recognizes three complementary "types" of knowledge, or knowledge-constitutive interests: technical interests concerned with instrumental action, practical interests concerned with social consensus and understanding, and emancipatory interests concerned with self-critical reflection and autonomy (Habermas 1972). Clayton and Birren (1980) found a similar multilevel picture of the wise individual as possessing the integration of intellectual, affective, and reflective skills for the processing of information. Finally, Sternberg's (1985) analysis of implicit theories of wisdom has uncovered dimensions that overlap with the above views. The wise individual is seen as having reasoning ability and superior intellectual functioning; but, in addition, good pragmatic judgment and skills of reflection that allow her to profit from past mistakes.

A similar portrait of the wise individual is implied by those who postulate a "postformal" operation stage of optimal adult development. Post-formal thought supposedly has the following characteristics: *(a)* One recognizes the relativity of various formal systems through life experience and is able to assume contradictory points of view; *(b)* one acknowledges the interrelatedness of all experience and the inevitability of change and transformation; *(c)* one adopts a more "metasystemic" or reflective and integrative approach to thinking (often dialectical); and *(d)* one makes choices with commitment to a certain course of action (Labouvie-Vief 1980, 1990; Kramer 1983; Riegel 1973; Perry 1970; Commons, Richards, and Kuhn 1982).

[margin handwriting: "Post formal" operation Stage of optimal adult development]

The picture emerging in contemporary thought concerning the cognitive functioning of "wise" adults, while it is incomplete and a long way from achieving a consensus, is consistent. This consistency is nicely expressed by Kramer's (1983) comment, "Post-formal operational thought is at the same time more practical and concrete, and more detached and abstract" (97). It is more concrete because the individual "transcends reason," through commitment based on self-examined life-experience (Perry 1970; Labouvie-Vief 1990); it is more abstract because of its metasystemic vantage point (i.e., operations on formal operations [Common, Richards, and Kuhn 1982]). It reminds one of Emerson's (1929) remark on wisdom: "Affection blends, intellect disjoins subject and object" (12:44); "A blending of these two—the intellectual perception of truth and the moral sentiments of right—is wisdom" (12:45).

It is easy to stress the differences between the ancient and contemporary ways of conceptualizing the meaning of wisdom. But I shall focus on the commonalities instead, in the belief that those aspects of a meme which remain the same despite great changes in the social and cultural milieu are the ones that will have the more enduring consequences for human survival.

[margin handwriting: Similarity b/t ancient & contemp wisdom]

While contemporary discussions of wisdom fail to evoke the traditional categories of universal truth or God to denote the pursuit of wisdom, there is an underlying emphasis in both accounts on the value of holistic cognitive processes that move beyond a fragmented and impassive relativity, toward a more "universal" or metasystemic awareness of interrelated systems. Attributes such as reflectivity or the capacity for self-examination are seen as providing the needed impetus to escape from relativistic intellectualization. What remains the same in these ways of conceiving of wisdom (and other similar ones in different cultures), despite many other divergent aspects, is the insight that the specific knowledge of the world we have at any given time is only a pale reflection of reality. Our eyes, our telescopes, the latest scientific

[margin handwriting: knowl. is partial]

theories provide only a narrow glimpse of the structure of the universe. These disjointed views, while clear, can be very deceptive. They make us believe that we know what lies outside, while they only give us selective, and hence misleading, information. This message is as relevant today as it was twenty-four centuries ago, in Plato's time.

In *War and Peace*, the Mason gives this explanation to Pierre: "The highest wisdom is not founded on reason alone, nor on those worldly sciences of physics, chemistry, and the like, into which intellectual knowledge is divided. The highest wisdom is one. The highest wisdom has but one science—the science of all, the science explaining all creation and man's place in it" (Tolstoy 1968, 429).

This view suggests what the "universal truth" of our time may turn out to be. Not immutable Platonic ideas nor the eternal, all-embracing will of God, but a systemic ecological consciousness in which the consequences of events and actions are understood to be causally related and to have long-term effects for the survival of human life and for the environment that sustains it.

The need for understanding the requirements of the total system of nature is foreshadowed by many thinkers of the past. Plato, in the *Statesman*, writes about the golden age in which men and animals could communicate; Montaigne discourses at length on the human folly of ignoring the natural context of which we are a part (*Essays* 2.12); Kant urges us to develop a morality based on an understanding of the "world as an ordered whole of interconnected goals, as a system of final causes." Wisdom consists in paying attention to the ends of nature, and inquiring after the stupendous art that lies hidden behind its forms (*Critique of Teleological Judgment* 86). Just as in the earliest time of recorded human thought, but with an even greater urgency, we are becoming increasingly aware of the fact that the separate branches of knowledge are not designed to reveal ultimate truths. For this we need wisdom, or the systematic pursuit of the connection between the branches—a "science of the whole."

Wisdom as Virtue [at both individual + social level]

The sense in which wisdom is a virtue follows from its characteristics as a cognitive process. If wisdom is a mode of knowledge for understanding the ultimate consequences of events in a holistic, systemic way, then it is also the best guide for what is the *summum bonum*, or supreme good. The knowledge of how causes and effects are connected shows the way to action, and becomes the basis of morality.

This will be true both at the individual and at the social levels. At the individual level, wisdom helps the person decide the best course of

[handwritten margin notes: "wisdom: a science of the whole"; "② follows from ①"; "1) summum bonum: the supreme good from which all others are derived"]

wisdom as indiv. virtue

action, by mediating between the local and often conflicting knowledge provided by instincts, habits, and reason (cf. Plato, *Republic* 4.442).
"All . . . things hang upon the soul," Socrates says in *Meno* (88), "and all
things of the soul herself hang upon wisdom." Time after time, Plato, as
well as many other thinkers of the past, points out that, without wisdom, other advantages—such as wealth, health, power, honor, and
even good fortune—are useless, because the person will not know how
to get benefit from them (e.g., *Meno* 87; *Protagoras* 349, 352, 358).
Therefore, "Wisdom is the only good, ignorance the only evil"
(*Euthydemus* 281). Inasmuch as he reflects on the "divine order," the
lawfulness behind the chaos of appearances, the mind of the philosopher himself will become orderly and divine, as far as the nature of
man allows it to be (*Republic* 6.500).

Kant saw an even closer connection between the cognitive and
the moral aspects of wisdom. To follow the logic of reason is a duty, and
a person is wise to the extent that he is not distracted by foreign influences in its pursuit (*Metaphysics of Ethics* II). The task of wisdom is to
seek the unconditioned totality of the effects of pure practical reason—
in other words, what is best for humankind (*Critique of Practical Reason*
1.1). Thus, the goals of radical cognition and of moral action blend into
one.

wisdom as social virtue

From this it follows that wisdom is also the foremost public virtue,
because it is the only approach that takes into account long-term consequences for the entire social system: "First among the virtues found in
the state, wisdom comes into view" (Plato, *Republic* 4.428). The wise
person is the one best equipped to judge (Aristotle, *Metaphysics* 1.2)
and to keep the commonwealth in order (Aquinas, *Summa* 1.8). The
ultimate requirement for ruling is knowledge of how to optimize the
well-being of the community as a whole (*Republic* 6.505). Hence Plato's
insistence that only when philosophers become kings, and kings
philosophers, will a good society come into being.

The assumption behind the view of wisdom as a virtue is that a
person confronted with the knowledge of what really goes on—i.e.,
ultimate truth—is unable to resist its logic, and will follow the right
path. "No man voluntarily pursues evil," writes Plato (*Protagoras* 358).
The divine order is so compelling that those who get a glimpse of it
will gladly submit to its pattern.

The findings of modern psychology, and the social sciences in
general, may be seen as casting grave doubts on the possibility that
"truth shall set ye free." We have learned from psychoanalysis how
childhood experiences distort our interpretations of adult reality. We
have learned from the behaviorists how much of our learning is condi-

tioned by fortuitous associations. Social psychologists have shown how strongly other people's opinions affect our judgment. Anthropologists have revealed the deep hold that the cultural patterning of symbols and values have on the mind. Marxists have argued that self-interest built into unequal social positions prevents men from ever being impartial. Given these merciless revelations about the limits of our ability to reason objectively, are there any grounds left for hoping that wisdom is possible and that it can lead to a better life?

Here again, as in the case of searching for universal truth, it seems apparent, at least at first glance, that modern thought has completely abandoned the quest and given up as hopeless Plato's suggestion that the contemplation of Truth will lead to a compelling ethic. However, the ethical dimension of wisdom has also survived in a new conceptual terminology. Habermas (1972) has traced the original development of ethics through "mimesis" in classical thought, through its contemporary rejection. He finally offers a formulation of how philosophy (love of wisdom) can remain "true to its classical tradition."

Habermas claims, "Philosophy remains true to its classical tradition by renouncing it" (317). According to Habermas, philosophy can remain true to its classical tradition (i.e., finding a connection between wisdom and virtue) only by first rejecting the ancient ontological formulation (especially its concealed "objectivism"). This allows, in turn, a new foundation for the connection of practical efficacy and human knowledge to be built.

Habermas's reformulation is not a radical proposal; ultimately, it amounts to the sound methodological advice that informs all epistemology: In order to free ourselves from narrow interests (in traditional terms, to achieve "disinterest"), we must continually uncover and then transcend implicit human interests.

The essential point of these observations is that, as with Nietzsche's rejection of universals, Habermas's rejection of the ancient link between wisdom and virtue (ethical order from divine order) is a preliminary step to the reintroduction of a formulation that serves a similar function. Thus, while the concept of wisdom has changed over time, essential attributes of the wisdom-virtue equation have, again, been renewed.

The evolutionary perspective suggests that the ancient equation of wisdom and virtue is still viable and, in fact, that it is more relevant now than it ever had been. It can be argued that the various limits on objective perception and reasoning the social sciences have revealed— repressions, defenses, bad faith, false consciousness, ethnocentrism, conditioned responses, suggestibility, and so on—are precisely the concrete "particulars" of experience that Plato argued the philosopher must

1) fortuitous: occurring by chance ; fortunate, lucky

overcome in order to see the underlying truth and thus get closer to wisdom. They are also the parochial "interests" that Habermas claims we must come to terms with. So the accumulating knowledge about our imperfections need not paralyze us into helplessness; on the contrary, it should help us make the right decisions with a clearer idea of where the obstacles are.

Wisdom is needed to help make these decisions. As the current empirical studies have shown (Holliday and Chandler 1986; Clayton and Birren 1980; Sternberg 1985), awareness of this important decision-making function of wisdom has not disappeared from the language. For instance, descriptors chosen for wise individuals include: "Is able to take the long view (as opposed to considering only short-term outcomes)" and "Has a huge store of information" (Sternberg 1985). This emphasis is particularly strong in the work of Baltes and Smith (1990) who define wisdom as knowledge and good judgment concerning the "fundamental pragmatics of life" (87).

With the daunting challenges that face modern society, one-dimensional technological thinking will not resolve many problems critical to our survival. There is no question that, now more than ever, we need a holistic, long-range understanding of actions and events—let's call it "wisdom"—so as to avoid the unforeseen consequences of narrowly specialized interests and ways of knowing. It took marvelous ingenuity to invent aerosol sprays based on chlorofluorocarbons—the knowledge that went into this artifact puts all the philosophers of ancient Greece to shame. But how wise will this invention turn out to be if it destroys part of the ozone layer surrounding the planet, allowing the harmful ultraviolet components of sun rays to kill much of the life inside the sea, or to kill us through skin cancer? Measured against such effects, clean windows and odorless underarms do not seem like such a bargain. If wisdom is a process by which people try to evaluate the ultimate consequences of events in terms of each other, wisdom is more necessary now than Plato could ever have anticipated it to be more than two millennia ago.

Unfortunately, wisdom is no more a priority now than it was at the time Socrates was invited to drink his hemlock. While specialized knowledge shows immediate effects, the benefits of wisdom are by definition slower to appear, and less obvious. Knowledge is expressed in declarative certitudes, whereas wisdom must compare, raise questions, and suggest restraints. Hence, wisdom rarely gets much respect and is seldom popular. Yet an evolutionary analysis indicates that unless we cultivate an interdisciplinary knowledge of our systemic needs, we will not be able to understand what is happening, or to see what is good or bad for us in the long run.

3 Wisdom as a Personal Good

There is a great unanimity among thinkers of the past about the fact that wisdom not only gets us closer to the truth, and not only provides a basis for making sound value judgments, but that it is also good for us here and now. Two main reasons are advanced for this claim. The first is that without it none of the other "goods" will be rewarding; we need wisdom to get pleasure from health, satisfaction from fame, and good use out of wealth (cf. Plato, *Meno* 87; Plato, *Euthydemus* 278-79). The second is that the contemplation of universal order wisdom affords is a supreme pleasure in its own right—that it is intrinsically rewarding.

[margin note: 2 reasons the ancients valued wisdom as good for us]

In the final chorus of *Antigone*, Sophocles writes: "Wisdom is the supreme part of happiness." Plato echoes the thought: "Wisdom and intelligence and memory . . . are better and more desirable than pleasure" (*Philebus* 11), and "All that the soul attempts or endures, when under the guidance of wisdom, ends in happiness" (*Meno* 88). So does Aristotle: A large part of the *Nichomachean Ethics* (e.g., Books 1 and 10) are devoted to the question of happiness. In it, he concludes that the contemplation of universal truth is the closest human beings can come to perfect happiness. "He who exercises his reason and cultivates it seems to be in the best state of mind and most dear to the gods. . . . And he who is that will presumably be also the happiest: so that in this way too the philosopher will more than any other be happy" (*Ethics* 10.8.1179a).

[margin note: wisdom is pleasurable]

The scholastics, for whom the search for universal truth inevitably led to God, also concluded that nothing compared with the happiness one could derive from the pursuit of wisdom (e.g., Aquinas, *Summa* 1.5, 1.64). "Contemplation is promised us as being the goal of all our actions, and the everlasting perfection of our joys" (Augustine, *De Trinitate* 1.8). And Spinoza: "It is therefore most profitable to us in this life, to make perfect the intellect or reason as far as possible, and in this one thing consists the highest happiness or blessedness of man; for blessedness is nothing but the peace of mind which springs from the intuitive knowledge of God." And Montaigne echoes the idea: "The most manifest sign of wisdom is continual cheerfulness" (*Essays* 1.25).

In spite of this overwhelming agreement of past thinkers that the pursuit of wisdom brings with it the most intense joy; this aspect of wisdom is clearly the least emphasized and least understood in modern thought. Is the ancient choir of praise an example of the self-delusion to which we are so prone, a whistling in the dark? Or is there a genuine foundation for the claim that the pursuit of wisdom is so enjoyable? One way to address this question is to appeal to what has been learned about the class of experiences and behavior referred to as "intrinsically motivating," or enjoyable for their own sake.

Contemporary research on intrinsically rewarding behavior has clearly demonstrated that people tend to lose interest in activities they once enjoyed after so-called extrinsic rewards, such as money or praise, are given to them for doing what they used to do spontaneously (Hennessey and Amabile 1988; Lepper and Greene 1978). That wisdom also gets clouded when it is directed by self-interest has been intuited by the most ancient writers: "The wisdom of a learned man cometh by opportunity of leisure; and he that hath little business shall become wise" (Ecclesiastics 38:24). "How can he get wisdom . . . whose talk is of bullocks" (Ecclesiastics 38:34). Similarly, Plato argues that philosophy must be intrinsically motivated, detached from politics and business (*Theaetetus* 172-75), and Aristotle stresses on several occasions that wisdom must be pursued in order to know, and not for any utilitarian end (e.g., *Metaphysics* 1.2.982b; *Ethics* 10.6-9).

Habermas (1972) also claims that in self-reflection "knowledge and interest are one"; the emancipatory cognitive interest in autonomy and responsibility pursues "knowledge for the sake of knowledge" or "the pursuit of reflection as such" (see pp. 313-14). The reflective dimension of wisdom belongs to a class of growth-oriented behaviors that do not provide a direct and immediate benefit for the individual in any technical or practical way. Such autotelic (*auto* = self, *telos* = goal) behaviors (Deci and Ryan 1985; Csikszentmihalyi 1975, 1990; Csikszentmihalyi and Csikszentmihalyi 1988) have consistently been shown to produce an optimal state of enjoyment in the consciousness of the actors and to be perceived as rewarding in themselves.

Habermas goes on to claim that this autonomy-oriented reflection (or wisdom) should "reflect back on the interest structure that joins subject and object a priori" (314), and is consistent with other recent perspectives on the connections between wisdom and intrinsically rewarding experience. For instance, Eastern philosophies and religions place the highest value on the experiential dimension of wisdom through pursuing satori or nirvana (Suzuki 1971). The attainment of such a state is believed to depend on a disciplined and mature awareness of the childlike ability to get engaged in experience (a childlike attitude without being childish) (Clayton and Birren 1980). Jung (1960) speaks of pursuing this childlike, playful modality consciously in later life, for the purpose of exploration and adult growth. Chinen (1984) refers to this potential for wisdom and intrinsically rewarding experience as coming from experiencing, rather than just attending to the content of experience.

Wisdom by all these accounts pursues a "higher" awareness of the motivations (interest structures) that lead us to process information in particular ways. Wisdom thus provides a better perspective on evolutionarily "lower" interests, so one's energy or attention does not become trapped in immediate need cycles, and can instead be directed toward long-term goals. Similar to the Greek conception of wisdom, this meta-awareness affords a twofold personal good: It is an intense joy in its own right, and it provides a higher perspective from which one can balance the various instrumental or practical "goods" that benefit human life.

Intrinsically rewarding transcendence, or self-overcoming, is arguably the most important aspect of wisdom in that the cherished past is spun from the axis of momentary joyful experience, and so is the anticipated future, as one desires to experience such intense joy again. Maslow (1968) understood this "transformational" power to be the value of peak experiences. Such lasting effects on everyday life seem to be characteristic of what subjects describe as a "flow" experience: ego-lessness, merged action and awareness, high concentration, clear feedback, control, and enjoyment of the activity for its own sake (Csikszentmihalyi 1975, 1990). The following quote comes from a rock climber describing his experience of flow: "Up there you have the greatest chance for finding your potential for any form of learning. . . . Up there you see man's true place in nature, you feel one with nature." Aldous Huxley (1972) made the same point about the value of transcendent experiences: "But if they are properly used, if they are co-operated with, if the memory of them is felt to be important and people work along the lines laid down during the vision, then they can be of immense value to us and of great importance in changing our lives" (56).

Transcendent experience places the person in a "betweenness" with her environment in the sense that previous limitations of perspective are at that moment surpassed, and one is raised to a new interactive posture with the world. Such experiences are felt to be universal, ethically compelling, and intrinsically motivating; thus—at their moment of occurrence—the three dimensions of wisdom discussed in this paper (cognitive process, virtue, and personal good) are expressed simultaneously.

To summarize, then, the connection of wisdom and supreme joy is still relevant today in important ways. The joy associated with the contemplation of divine order for its own sake is manifested in our days as an interest in growth, freedom from limitations, and in self-transcendent experience. Such an interest, like a variation in a phenotype, is a risky attempt to reach a new level of organization and order. The short-term consequences of such a move are not instrumental or practical. In this sense, the motivation and rewards for it are intrinsic, and the use of such terms as "survival" and "adaption" to describe the evolutionary process must be complemented by the notion of "expansion." Nietzsche (1974) has emphatically stressed this point: "The really fundamental instinct of life which aims at the expansion of power . . . frequently risks or even sacrifices self-preservation" (291-92). Thus the evolutionary importance of wisdom as a personal good (a supreme joy in its own right) lies in its connection to variation, experimentation, curiosity, and other similar expansive processes. The freedom to transcend oneself has an immediate appeal that does not have to be justified in any other way.

Conclusion

The application of an evolutionary hermeneutics to the concept of wisdom has shown a number of continuities in the meaning this term has had over a period of more than twenty-five centuries. The assumption underlying this analysis has been that such continuities represent relatively unchanging functional prerequisites of human adaptation and survival.

In other words, by recognizing a peculiar psychological process called "wisdom," by holding it in high esteem, and by learning to enjoy it, we have forged a powerful conceptual tool for managing information about the world and thus for helping us adapt to it. If we did not differentiate wisdom from other forms of knowledge, if we did not think highly of it, or if we accepted its value without question, presumably we would be less likely to fit in with our environment.

The reasons for this adaptive function are expressed by the characteristics generally attributed to wisdom. We have seen its three main dimensions: as a cognitive process, as a guide to action, and as an intrinsic reward.

As a cognitive process, wisdom refers to attempts at understanding the world in a disinterested way, seeking the ultimate consequences of events as well as ultimate causes, while preserving the integration of knowledge. Its survival implication is as an antidote to knowledge which pursues selfish, short-term, and limited goals that often turn out to have disastrous consequences for the very persons they were intended to benefit—not to mention other people or the nonhuman environment. More specifically, wisdom is the approach of choice to such contemporary problems as the escalation of nuclear power, the concentration of energy in any form, the pollution of air and water, the creation and cessation of life, and to issues of social inequality.

Wisdom is a virtue because, by reflecting and synthesizing in a disinterested way the broadest spectrum of knowledge, it provides the most compelling guide to action. Although we no longer believe in the existence of a perfect divine order beyond appearances on which to base a good life, we still must believe, if we are to survive, that it is possible to improve life by understanding how to order our actions in ways that will bring us in closer harmony with the laws that constrain the physical universe. As long as we act purely in terms of present needs and desires, it is doubtful the rest of the world will be able to afford keeping us around much longer. The egocentric, ethnocentric, anthropocentric impulses of mankind are bringing so much destruction into the planetary environment that the probability of the continuation of life keeps steadily diminishing. Only a truly disinterested, long-range, organic understanding of consequences can pull us back from the brink of disaster.

Finally, wisdom is a personal good, an intrinsically rewarding experience that provides some of the highest enjoyment and happiness available to human beings. When a person attempts to fathom the connection between events in a disinterested way, she has a chance to enter a flow experience, an ecstatic state common to those who concentrate consciousness on a challenging, ordered, goal-directed task. As the goal of wisdom is to understand the ultimate consequences and causes of things, it presents the greatest challenges of any mental activity and hence, presumably, also the most profound enjoyment. The evolutionary significance of this is twofold: On the one hand, it provides the mechanism for cultural evolution by motivating people to ever-expanding efforts at understanding; secondly, it provides an alternative for the extrinsic rewards based on pleasure and materialism, which tend to be zero-sum, expensive, and hence conducive to social and ecological conflict.

Of course, just because an analysis of past meanings reveals a message relevant to the present and to the future does not guarantee that evolutionary hermeneutics is a method that will reveal the truth. If there is one thing we have learned from the evolutionary perspective, it is that life always involves risks, that the safety of immutable knowledge is not available to mortals. We must keep making decisions that affect our survival in partial ignorance, trusting instincts and intuitions as well as knowledge. But as we go about weighing alternatives, we should not discard the hard-won wisdom of millions of years of continued learning just because it is couched in terms no longer familiar to us. It is to this essential task of preservation that an evolutionary hermeneutics hopes to contribute.

Notes

1. Biblical references are to the King James version.

2. All volume and page references for classical writers and philosophers, unless otherwise noted, are to the *Great Books of the Western World* series (Chicago: Encyclopaedia Britannica, 1987).

References

Baltes, P. B., and J. Smith. 1990. "Towards a Psychology of Wisdom and Its Ontogenesis." In *Wisdom: Its Nature, Origins, and Development*, ed. R. J. Sternberg, 87-120. New York: Cambridge University Press.

Boyd, R., and P. J. Richerson. 1985. *Culture and the Evolutionary Process*. Chicago: University of Chicago Press.

Burhoe, R. W. 1976. "The Source of Civilization in the Natural Selection of Co-Adapted Information in Genes and Cultures." *Zygon* 2(3): 263-303.

Campbell, D. T. 1960. "Blind Variation and Selective Retention in Creative Thought and Other Knowledge Processes." *Psychological Review* 67: 380-400.

———. 1974. "Evolutionary Epistemology." In *The Library Of Living Philosophers*, ed. P. A. Schlipp, 14: 413-68. LaSalle, IL: Open Court.

———. 1976. "On the Conflict between Biological and Social Evolution and between Psychology and the Moral Tradition." *Zygon* 2(3): 167-208.

Chinen, A. B. 1984. "Model Logic: A New Paradigm of Development and Late-Life Potential." *Human Development* 27: 42-56.

Clayton, V. P., and J. E. Birren. 1980. "The Development of Wisdom across the Life-Span: A Reexamination of an Ancient Topic." In *Life-Span Development and Behavior*, ed. P. B. Baltes and O. G. Brim Jr., 103-35. New York: Academic Press.

Commons, M. L., F. Richards, and D. Kuhn. 1982. "Metasystemic Reasoning: A Case for a Level of Systematic Reasoning beyond Piaget's State of Formal Operations." *Child Development* 53: 1058-69.

Csikszentmihalyi, M. 1975. *Beyond Boredom and Anxiety*. San Francisco: Jossey-Bass.

———. 1990. *Flow: The Psychology of Optimal Experience*. New York: HarperCollins.

————. 1993. *The Evolving Self: A Psychology for the Third Millennium*. New York: HarperCollins.

Csikszentmihalyi, M., and I. Csikszentmihalyi, eds. 1988. *Optimal Experience*. New York: Cambridge University Press.

Csikszentmihalyi, M., and F. Massimini. 1985. "On the Psychological Selection of Bio-Cultural Information." *New Ideas in Psychology* 3(2): 115-38.

Csikszentmihalyi, M., and K. Rathunde. 1990. "The Psychology of Wisdom: An Evolutionary Interpretation." In *Wisdom: Its Nature, Origins, and Development*, ed. R. J. Sternberg, 25-52. New York: Cambridge University Press.

Dawkins, R. 1976. *The Selfish Gene*. Oxford: Oxford University Press.

————. 1982. *The Extended Phenotype*. Oxford: Oxford University Press.

Deci, E. L., and R. M. Ryan. 1985. *Intrinsic Motivation and Self-Determination in Human Behavior*. New York: Plenum Press.

Dennett, D. C. 1991. *Consciousness Explained*. Boston: Little, Brown.

Emerson, R. W. 1929. *The Complete Works of Ralph Waldo Emerson*. New York: Wise.

Habermas, J. 1972. *Knowledge and Human Interest*. Boston: Beacon Press.

Hennessey, B. A., and T. M. Amabile. 1988. "The Conditions of Creativity." In *The Nature Of Creativity*, ed. R. J. Sternberg, 11-38. New York: Cambridge University Press.

Holliday, S. C., and M. J. Chandler. 1986. *Wisdom: Explorations in Adult Competence*. Basel, Switzerland: Karger.

Huxley, A. 1972. "Visionary Experience." In *The Highest State Of Consciousness*, ed. J. White, 34-57. New York: Anchor.

Jung, C. G. 1960. "The Stages of Life." In *The Collected Works of C. G. Jung*, ed. H. Read, M. Fordham, G. Adler, and W. McGuire, 8: 387-403. Vol. 8. Princeton, NJ: Princeton University Press.

Kramer, D. A. 1983. "Postformal Operations? A Need for Further Conceptualization." *Human Development* 16: 91-105.

Labouvie-Vief, G. 1980. "Beyond Formal Operations: Uses and Limits of Pure Logic in Life-Span Development." *Human Development* 12: 141-61.

————. 1990. "Wisdom as Integrated Thought: Historical and Developmental Perspectives." In *Wisdom: Its Nature, Origins, and Development*, ed. R. J. Sternberg, 52-86. New York: Cambridge University Press.

Lepper, M. R., and D. Greene, eds. 1978. *The Hidden Costs of Reward: New Perspectives on the Psychology of Human Motivation*. Hillsdale, NJ: Lawrence Erlbaum.

Lumsden, C. J., and E. O. Wilson. 1981. *Genes, Mind, Culture: The Coevolutionary Process*. Cambridge: Harvard University Press.

———. 1983. *Promethean Fire*. Cambridge: Harvard University Press.

Maslow, A. H. 1968. *Towards a Psychology of Being*. New York: Van Nostrand.

Meacham, J. A. 1983. "Wisdom and the Context of Knowledge: Knowing That One Doesn't Know." In *On the Development of Developmental Psychology*, ed. D. Kuhn and J. A. Meacham, 11-134. Basel, Switzerland: Karger.

Nietzsche, F. W. 1960. *The Will to Power in Science, Nature, And Art*. [1901.] New York: Frederick Publications.

———. 1974. *The Gay Science*. New York: Vintage.

Perry, W. I. 1970. *Forms of Intellectual and Ethical Development in College Years*. New York: Holt, Rinehart, and Winston.

Piaget, J. 1971. *Biology and Knowledge*. Chicago: University of Chicago Press.

Popper, K. 1965. *The Logic of Scientific Discovery*. New York: Harper & Row.

Reese, H. W., and W. F. Overton. 1970. "Models of Development and Theories of Development." In *Life-Span Developmental Psychology*, ed. L. R. Goulet and P. B. Baltes, 115-45. New York: Academic Press.

Riegel, K. F. 1973. "Dialectical Operations: The Final Period of Cognitive Development." *Human Development* 15: 1-12.

Simon, N. A. 1969. *The Sciences of the Artificial*. Cambridge: MIT Press.

Simonton, D. K. 1988. *Scientific Genius: A Psychology of Science*. New York: Cambridge University Press.

Sternberg, R. J. 1985. "Implicit Theories of Intelligence, Creativity, and Wisdom." *Journal of Personality and Social Psychology* 49(3): 607-27.

Suzuki, D. T. 1971. *What Is Zen?* New York: Harper & Row.

Tolstoy, L. 1968. *War and Peace*. [1869.] Trans. by Ann Dunnigan. New York: Academic Library.

III

Values, Reason, and Responsibility

8

Responsibility without Grounds

Jane Flax

And although I sensed that everything going on inside me remained blurred, inadequate in every sense of the word, I was once more forced to admire the way in which everything fits together with a sleepwalker's precision: the desire of most people for a comfortable life, their tendency to believe the speakers on raised platforms and the men in white coats; the addiction to harmony, and the fear of contradiction of the many seem to correspond to the arrogance and hunger for power, the dedication to profit, unscrupulous inquisitiveness, and self-infatuation of the few. So what was it that didn't add up in this equation?[1]

Dreams of Innocence

Questions of knowledge and practice must be situated historically. In the contemporary West these questions are especially puzzling, because the metanarrative in which each term and the relations between them acquired meaning has broken down. Part of the appeal of this metanarrative—which may be called the Enlightenment—was its promise to solve a problem that has plagued political theorists and philosophers since Plato: how to reconcile knowledge and power. Without power, there can be no practice; yet, in practice, power and desire or right do not always converge. The problem, then, is to discover knowledge which will enable us to exercise power appropriately.

Power can take many forms and be exercised for a variety of purposes, some of which implicate its user and destroy her innocence— that certainty of beneficence and freedom from doing harm or exercising unwarranted domination. Many philosophers and political theorists have found the potential loss of innocence unacceptable. They wish to ensure and preserve the innocence of knowledge, power, and themselves.[2] One solution, which is promised by the Enlightenment, is to mediate the relationship of knowledge and practice by truth. This truth must be simultaneously universal and benign so that governing according to its principles will result in the best for all and the domination of none. Only reason can discover such truth. Reason both represents and embodies truth and partakes of universality. It can grasp laws that are objectively true, that is, are knowable by and binding on every person. In turn, conflicts between knowledge and power can be overcome by grounding claims to and the exercise of authority in reason.[3] Since reason operates identically in each subject, rational discourse can resolve conflict by consulting the universal principles that govern everyone. All will benefit; no one will be hurt or disadvantaged; hence the innocence of power can be maintained.

Knowledge in this scheme has a curious double character. The Enlightenment hope is that utilizing truthful knowledge in the service of legitimate power will assure both freedom and progress. If knowledge is grounded in and warranted by a universal reason, not particular "interests," it can be *both* neutral and socially beneficial (powerful). The accumulation of more knowledge (the getting of more truth) results simultaneously in an increase in objectivity (neutrality) and in progress. To the extent that power/authority is grounded in this expanding knowledge, it, too, is progressive—for example, it becomes more rational and expands the freedom and self-actualization of its subjects who naturally conform their reason to its (and their) laws. Power can be innocently or purely emancipatory; "rational" power can be other than and not productive of new forms of domination. Such power can be neutral (it cannot hurt anyone), and transparent in its exercise and effects. Hence, it is not really power at all, especially when it works by/through such neutral mediums as the law.

Obviously this dream rests on a number of wishes. We must assume that the social as well as the physical universe is governed by a uniform, benign, and harmonious set of laws. Conforming our behavior to heterogeneous or malevolent laws would generate conflicts and differences that could not themselves be peacefully resolved. No neutral "decision procedure" would exist that could determine how conflict could be resolved without privileging one position over another. Without its protective grounding in a universal, neutral good for all, power would lose its innocence. Order would have to be (at least to some extent) imposed rather than dis-covered. Knowledge would be seen as useful for some (persons and effects) and oppressive to others. Actions generated by knowledge would have unpredictable and differential effects.

We must also assume that a homogeneous form of reason exists within all humans and that this reason itself is not determined or affected by other (heterogeneous) factors such as desire or historical experience. Humans must have "privileged access" to the operation of their own reason and be able to understand its intrinsic limits (if there are any). Otherwise, the reason that is our lawgiver would itself be contaminated by particularity and contingency. This reason could not be a reliable source of knowledge about ourselves, a dis-coverer of objective truth or an authority that a noumenal being ought to obey.

Liberal political theorists, Marxists, and social scientists all share some form of this Enlightenment dream. Much of the legitimacy of their claims to authority rests on a combination of these assumptions, especially the innocence of their knowledge claims, their privileged relation to a unitary truth, and their role as a pure reason's voice and representative. Liberal political theorists from John Locke to John Rawls attempt to distinguish legitimate authority from domination by listening for and recording reason's voice. They claim to articulate a set of rules or beliefs in Reason's own language. To hear Reason's language a rite of purification must be undergone (imagining a "state of nature" or drawing the "veil of ignorance" around oneself)[4] to strip away the merely contingent or historical. The rights or rules that are truly Reason's own and hence binding on all will then re-present themselves. Conformity to these (neutral) laws by the state and its subjects guarantees the rationality, justice, and freedom of both.

Marxists have their own variant of this dream. Their "objective" ground tends to be History rather than Reason, although, in their account, History itself is ultimately rational, purposive, unitary, law governed, and benign. In the Marxist view, events in history do not occur randomly; they are connected by and through an underlying, meaningful, and rational structure comprehensible by reason/science. The pregiven purpose of history is the progressive perfection of humans (especially through labor) and the ever more complete realization of their capacities and projects. Marxist theory and its articulator (the Party, the working class, the engaged intellectual) have a privileged relation to History.[5] They speak but do not construct its "laws," and legitimate their actions by invoking its name. Since History, like Reason, has an essentially teleological and homogeneous content, we can look forward to its "end." Then all sources of irresolvable conflicts or contradictions will disappear and authority will take the form of the administration of things rather than the domination of persons. Power will be innocent and human actions in conformity with our highest and most benign potentials.[6]

Social science also inherits, reflects, and is the beneficiary of Enlightenment dreams. Here the relationship between knowledge and power is mediated by science, or at least by a particular understanding of science. Just as Enlightenment philosophers privilege reason as the unique means of access to and voice of the Real, they privilege science as the ideal form of knowledge. Modern philosophy, after all, began with the task of explaining *how* scientific knowledge is possible, that is, how physics could develop such accurate and reliable knowledge of the physical world.[7] Philosophers such as Bacon or Kant do not attempt to throw into doubt the belief that science does generate such knowledge.

In science, reason takes the form of a "logic of discovery." This logic is universal and binding on all scientific practitioners. It is neutral in the sense that it affects neither the subject/investigator nor the object/data. Science's "successes" (dis-coveries) are due to the adherence to this logic by its practitioners. The "scientific method" enables all those who use it to dis-cover (not construct) the truths of its objects— bits of the Real which exist independent of the scientist and the scientific modes of investigation.[8]

Until recently, social scientists also did not question science's relationship to the Real. Their concern was whether such knowledge *could* be obtained about the *social* world and, if so, which methods were most likely to produce such results.[9] They accepted the Enlightenment belief that science is the ideal form of knowledge, the exemplar of the right use of reason, and the methodological paradigm for all truth claims.

A grounding in science preserves the innocence of the social scientist. Knowledge acquired by the proper methods must reflect the Real (which is also the rational, the benevolent, and the true). Hence, knowledge produced by social science can be simultaneously (and without contradiction) neutral, useful, and emancipatory. It can be on the side of good and have no unjustifiable costs. As the author of a recent textbook on social science claims, "By testing thoughts against reality, science helps liberate inquiry from bias, prejudice, and just plain muddleheadedness."[10] Having restated (without acknowledgment) his faith in the Enlightenment belief that superstition/knowledge is an antimony, the author continues, "Knowledge built on evidence, and captured in clear transmissible form, makes for power over the environment."[11] Despite the martial language, apparently social scientists' knowledge and power is innocent of bias, prejudice, or ill effects for anyone. Its innocence is warranted by the (universal) truth/laws in which it is grounded.

The plausibility, coherence, or even intelligibility of these claims requires a set of unstated background assumptions. These assumptions include a belief that truth and prejudice are clearly distinguishable and dichotomous categories. There must be a neutral language available to report our discoveries. The "logic of discovery" can operate independent of and without distorting either its subject (user) or object of investigation. The "scientific" process will eventually be self-correcting and governing (it will eliminate any biases or false knowledge). The social world is stable, homogeneous, and lawfully structured, and these laws are benign and free from contradictions. They work to the equal benefit of all.

If these conditions exist, there will be no fundamental disjunction between the discovery and administration of social laws. Social scientists can make claims for their expertise (and its funding) based simultaneously on its "scientific neutrality" and its utility for the creation of more rational/beneficial public policies.[12] The real of science has an unchanging and unchangeable existence independent of the knower: it is not merely created or transformed by humans in the process of doing science. Since the scientist speaks with and represents the voice of the Real, "primary" and "applied" social sciences are merely two facets of the same process—displacing ignorance and prejudice and replacing them with the neutral rule of reason. Action grounded in scientific/expert knowledge is, hence, an innocent form of power whose operation and effects are as transparent and universally accessible as the scientific enterprise. Expert rule generates neither privilege nor domination in its exercise; rather, it results in the good of all.[13]

Twentieth-Century Nightmares: The Centers Will Not Hold

The modern Western sense of self-certainty has been undermined by political and intellectual events. The meanings—or even existence—of concepts essential to all forms of Enlightenment metanarrative (reason, history, science, self, knowledge, power, gender, and the inherent superiority or Western culture) have been subjected to increasingly corrosive attacks. The challenge to Western political-economic hegemony by Japan and other countries, the rise of nationalist and anticolonialist movements in the Third World, women's movements everywhere, and antiracist struggles have disrupted the order of things.

Western intellectuals' sense of epistemological security has been further disrupted by internal dissent. Psychoanalysts, feminists, and postmodernists have undermined the "foundations" of Western thought by challenging their constituting and interdependent girders.[14] As the Enlightenment metanarrative continues to decay, the essential contestability (and the "all too human" contingency) of notions such as reason, truth, self, gender, science, culture, power, history, and knowledge are exposed. This exposure creates a crisis of innocence, since these notions then threaten to become mere artifacts that humans have created and for whose effects and consequences we alone are responsible. It is amazingly difficult for humans to live without secure grounds below and ontological or transcendental guarantees from above.

Unstable Selves

Psychoanalysts continue to develop and extend Freud's "third blow" to the "naive self-love of men."[15] Despite his own attachment to Enlightenment notions of science and the emancipatory effects of rational thought, Freud contributes to the undermining of confidence in the character and powers of reason. He suggests that the conscious/rational self is "not even master in its own house, but must content itself with scanty information of what is going on unconsciously in its mind."[16] Furthermore, he challenges Enlightenment ontological premises by placing desire, rather than reason, as the definitive and motivating core of our being.

Freud's increasingly complex structural theories undermine the concepts of mind upon which Enlightenment ideas of knowledge depend. His theories of mind also contradict and challenge many contemporary epistemologies. Unlike many philosophers, Freud conceptualizes the mind as fully embodied,[17] inherently conflict ridden, dynamic, heterogeneous, and constituted in and through processes that are intrinsically discordant. These processes cannot be synthesized or organized into a permanent, hierarchical organization of functions or control. Both the rationalist's faith in the powers of reason and the empiricist's belief in the reliability of sense perception and observation are grounded in and depend upon the mind's capacity to be at least partially undetermined by the effects of the body, passions, and social authority or convention. However, Freud renders such beliefs highly problematic. As he continues to analyze the mind, its structures and processes appear increasingly fragmented, fluid, and subject to complex and often unconscious alterations. The equation of mind and conscious thought or reason, or the psychical and the conscious, becomes untenable.

Neither the ego's "transcendental meditations" nor its empirical observations can be fully trusted or their reliability assumed. It is increasingly difficult to locate any aspect of the mind capable of engaging in or sustaining autonomous, "pure" thought. Reason cannot engage in a secure transcendental investigation of its own limits. Thought is always affected by forces whose effects and boundaries can never be transparent to us. Such forces include bodily experience, libidinal wishes, authority relations, and cultural conventions. Insight into the mind's operations must be considered incomplete and provisional in principle, because even aspects of the observing ego may be repressed. Bias cannot be "controlled for" if its source is in the dynamically unconscious repressed material to which the conscious mind lacks direct access. The agency of our knowing is "contaminated" by the influence of these unconscious forces, including desire and authority. The ego is not always a reliable witness or source of information, because in its relations with the id, the ego "too often yields to the temptation to become sycophantic, opportunist and lying, like a politician who sees the truth but wants to keep his place in popular favor."[18]

The ego may be modified by its own defensive processes as well as by its ongoing struggle with the superego and the id. The ego may seek accommodation with, or even glorify, tutelage as readily as express the will to freedom. Being able to give reasons for one choice of action or definition of self-interest cannot be treated as straightforward evidence of rationality or freedom from the unconscious. A "rational reconstruction" of the reasons for a choice or belief may be an elaborate rationalization of, or reparation for, an irrational wish or fear. Reason can become the ally or servant of unreason in other ways. Out of fear of a punitive superego, the ego may learn to comply with the authorities (familial, intellectual, political). It may even convince itself that, in so doing, it is pursuing truth or is expressing its own will. The self can be so dependent on and attached to its capacity for self-deception that its sense of reality is threatened if its rationalizations unravel.

These claims undermine the Enlightenment belief in the intrinsic relationships among reason, self-determination, and freedom or emancipation. The mind loses its privileged status as a private internal space. It can be neither a Lockean blank slate, as required by empiricism, nor any variety of monad, as envisioned, for example, by Descartes or Sartre. Radical individualism becomes untenable, as do all the epistemologies social scientists depend upon (or take for granted) that rely on the possibility of accurate self-observation and direct, reliable access to and control over the mind and its activities.

Unstable Stories

Postmodernists challenge Enlightenment ideas about truth, knowledge, power, history, self, and language still predominant in the West.[19]

Many social scientists have been dependent on philosophies situated within this metanarrative for their epistemological self-under-

standings and security; postmodernist deconstructions disrupt these
knowledges as well. Postmodernists believe that the deconstruction of
philosophical metanarrative is one of their responsibilities and (at least
qua philosophers) their most salient and subversive contribution to
contemporary Western culture. The process of deconstruction requires
one to enter into the terrain of philosophy and to engage in its arguments. However, the purpose of this process is not to reconstruct or
repair the traditional discourses of philosophy but to loosen their grip
so that conversation may move elsewhere.

According to postmodernists, Western philosophy has been under
the spell of the "metaphysics of presence" at least since Plato.[20] Most
Western philosophers took as their task the construction of a philosophic system in which something Real would and could be re-pre-
sented in thought. This Real is understood as an external or universal
subject or substance, existing "out there," independent of the knower.
The philosophers' task is to "mirror," register, mimic, or make present
the Real. Truth is understood as correspondence to it.

For postmodernists, an unacknowledged will to power lies concealed within and generates claims to truth. The quest for the real con-
ceals most Western philosophers' desire, which is to master the world
once and for all by enclosing it within an illusory but absolute system
they claim re-presents or corresponds to a unitary Being beyond history,
particularity, and change. To mask his idealizing desire, the philosopher
must assert that this Being is not the product, artifact, or effect of a particular set of historical or linguistic practices. It can only be the thought
of the Real itself.

The philosopher also obscures another aspect of his desire: to
claim a special relation and access to the True or Real. He believes that
the presence of the Real for us depends on him—the clarity of his consciousness, the purity of his intention. Only the philosopher has the
capacity for Reason, the love of wisdom (philo-sophia), the grasp of
method, or the capacity to construct a logic adequate to the Real. Just as
the Real is the ground of Truth, so, too, philosophy, as the privileged
representative of the Real and interrogator of truth claims, must play a
"foundational" role in all "positive knowledge." Thus, epistemology
is particularly important to philosophers. Epistemology serves as the
means to purge, clarify, or demarcate the philosopher's consciousness,
for himself, for the benefit of other philosophers, and ultimately for
humanity as a whole.

Postmodernists attack the "metaphysics of presence" and Western
philosophers' self-understanding in a number of ways. They question
the concepts of mind, truth, language, and the Real that underlie and

ground any such transcendental or foundational claims. They wish to remove discussions of knowledge from the terrain of truth, and instead seek to construct genealogies of the histories of our beliefs and to analyze their pragmatic consequences. Discourses are evaluated according to the specific, historically situated projects and interests they generate, permit, marginalize, and prohibit, not according to their truth content.

Postmodernists claim that there is and can be no transcendental mind; on the contrary, what we call mind or reason is an effect of discourse. There are no immediate or indubitable features of mental life. Sense data, ideas, intentions, or perceptions are already constituted. They only occur in and reflect a variety of linguistically and socially determined practices. The problem of the relation between the "mind" and "things in themselves" becomes infinitely more complex. One cannot even assume that the mind has some universal, transcendental, a priori categories or concepts that always shape experience in the same, even if unknowable, ways. Instead, the categories or concepts by and through which we structure experience are themselves historically and culturally variable. "Mind" is no more homogeneous, lawful, and internally consistent in or over time than is History.

Truth for postmodernists is an effect of discourse. Each discourse has its own distinctive set of rules or procedures that govern the production of what is to count as a meaningful or truthful statement. Each discourse is simultaneously enabling and limiting. Discourses enable us to make certain sorts of statements and to make truth claims, but we can only make statements that conform to their necessarily restricted set of rules. A discourse as a whole cannot be true or false, because truth is always contextual and rule dependent. Discourses are local, heterogeneous, and incommensurable. No discourse-independent or transcendental rules exist, especially ones that could govern all discourses or a choice between them. Truth claims are in principle "undecidable" outside of or between discourses.

Postmodernists do not claim there is no truth but rather that truth and our desire for it is discourse dependent. Postmodernism is not a form of relativism, because relativism only takes on meaning as the partner of its binary opposite—universalism. Relativism assumes the lack of an absolute standard is significant: for example, "everything is relative" because there is no one thing by which to measure all claims. If the hankering for an absolute universal standard were absent, "relativism" would lose its meaning and force, and we would turn our attention to the limits and possibilities of local productions of truth.

Postmodernists contest all concepts of language in which it is described as a transparent, passive, or neutral medium. Each of us is born into an ongoing set of language games that we must learn in order to be understood by and to understand others. Since human beings are speaking animals, our personhood is (at least partially) constructed by language. Language speaks us as much as we speak it. Furthermore, the *meaning* of our experience and our understanding of it cannot be independent of the fact that such experience and all thought about it are grasped and expressed in and through language. To the degree that thought depends upon and is articulated (to ourselves and others) in language, thought and the "mind" itself will be socially and historically (pre-) constituted. Postmodernists deny the possibility that a historical or transcendental standpoint exists from and by which the Real can directly and without construction or distortion be apprehended in and reported by thought. Instead, they investigate the sources of desire which generate a wish for such a standpoint, and analyze how such claims function within certain discourses.

In addition, they claim there is no stable, unchanging, and unitary Real against which our thoughts can be tested. Western philosophers create an illusory appearance of unity and stability by reducing the flux and heterogeneity of the human and physical worlds into binary and supposedly natural oppositions. Order is imposed and maintained by displacing chaos into the lesser of each binary pair—for example, culture/nature or male/female. The construction of such categories as and through oppositions expresses and reveals the philosopher's desire for control and domination. Once these oppositions are seen as fictive, asymmetric, and conditions of possibility for the philosopher's story, then a premise that underlies all variants of the metaphysics of presence can be revealed: To be other, to be different from the defining one, is to be inferior and to have no independent character or worth of one's own. For example, "woman" is defined as a deficient man in discourses from Aristotle through Freud. The superior member of the pair maintains his innocence. Unlike the inferior, "he" is secure in his independence and natural superiority; he is within but not of the dyad. Like Aristotle's master or husband, his is the active matter, determining and generative within, but never affected by his coupling. There is no disorder within him, and hence none within Being as such, but there may be disorderly objects requiring the exercise of his mastery. In the Enlightenment self-understanding, this view is an "optimistic," humane, and "progressive" one; eventually all difference/disorder will be brought within the benign sovereignty of the One.

Postmodernists regard all such wishes for unity with suspicion. Unity appears as an effect of domination, repression, and the temporary success of particular rhetorical strategies. According to postmodernists, all knowledge construction is fictive and nonrepresentational. As a product of the human mind, knowledge has no necessary relation to Truth or the Real. Philosophers create stories about these concepts and about their own activities. Their stories are no more true, foundational, or truth adjudicating than any others.

Postmodernists do have ideas about what they would like to replace epistemological and ontological practices based in general truth claims. They are committed to opening up possibilities and creating spaces in which multiple differences can flourish. Hence, they recommend that philosophers and other knowledge constructors seek to generate an infinite "dissemination" of meanings. They should adjure any attempt to construct a closed system in which the other or the "excess" are "pushed to the margins" and made to disappear in the interest of coherence and unity. Their task is to disrupt and subvert rather than (re-) construct totalities or grand theories. Postmodernists are obligated to situate themselves within their own discourses. The imperial, impersonal Cartesian ego is to be deconstructed and its desires set free to play within and as language. The "view from nowhere" is replaced by admittedly partial and fragmentary multiples of one.[21]

The Instabilities of Gender

Feminists define gender as a changeable set of social relations that pervade many aspects of human experience from the constitution of the "inner self" and family life to the "public worlds" of the state, the economy, and knowledge production. Gender cannot be understood as a consequence or effect of "natural sexual differences" or be reduced to any set of anatomical or biological attributes, although the relations of gender to embodiment is an interesting and controversial question. Gender is not a universal or unitary relation, but it is an indispensable category in the analysis of current Western cultures.

Within contemporary Western cultures, neither men nor women exist outside gender systems. One of their effects is the constitution of masculinity/feminity as exclusionary and unequal opposites. Masculine and feminine cannot be understood simply as positions in language which any subject can assume.[22] These categories are partially constituted in and through relations of power and domination. In relations of domination, no subject can simply or voluntarily switch sides. We receive certain privileges or suffer certain injuries depending on our structural positions, no matter what our subjective intent or purposes may be. Men can no more easily resign from masculinity and its effects than I can from being a white woman. Both men and women are marked by gender/race relations, although in different and unequal ways.

Feminists have successfully engaged in genealogical investigations of the generative powers of male dominance. We have begun to
track the effects of gender in the structuring of individual experience,
social relations, and knowledge itself. The necessary connections
between the marginalization of certain experiences and forms of knowledge and the persuasiveness and power of claims about the truth of
dominant beliefs have become more evident.

In particular, feminists have begun to delineate the gendered qualities of a central element in Enlightenment metanarrative: Reason. This
metanarrative both constructs and depends upon a certain notion of
Reason as disembodied and ahistoric. Reason and hence the ideal
knower appear to be ungendered. Since the Enlightenment philosophers define Reason as the essential human quality, presumably any
and every person possesses and can exercise it.

Yet is this so? If we ask a feminist question—which gendered
experiences could this concept of Reason represent?—the claim becomes
more problematic. The Enlightenment view of Reason depends upon
antinomies between reason and body, reason and passion, thought and
imagination, objectivity and subjectivity, truth and belief, and fact and
value. Under what conditions is it possible to imagine that reason and
embodiment are disjunctive and ultimately unequal as sources of
knowledge or as expressions of human beings? Why would we devalue
the passions and daily life as experiences or ways of knowing?

Feminists have begun to answer these questions by examining a
division of labor that is common in contemporary Western societies.
In these societies, some people engage only or primarily in abstract
thought while others take care of the necessities arising out of embodied
existence including childbearing and rearing.[23] Philosophers have
argued that engagement in such activities disqualifies one from the life
of reason. No true knowledge can arise out of these activities, and,
indeed, involvement in them impedes or clouds "true" thought. They
produce biases that must be "controlled for." Hence, only those who can
separate themselves from embodiment and reproduction can be rational
producers of true knowledge.

The relevance of gender to this view of Reason is more apparent
when the *sexual* division of labor prevalent within the modern West is
considered. Necessary labor is divided along gender as well as race
and class lines. Women have primary responsibility for the reproduction of daily life, including the care of small children. The premodern
distinctions between the household/private world and the public world
are incorporated and transformed in modern societies. The public now
includes the economy, the state, and knowledge/culture production.[24]

The household remains the locus of passion, feeling, the concrete and particular, the subjective, the mortal, the familial and kinship. These qualities are posited as opposite and inferior to reason, the abstract, the universal, objective, immortal (soul and/or knowledge) and the productive employment of labor or thought. Women can only partake of the higher order of things to the extent that we can divorce ourselves from embodied existence. Since "nature" is more fully present in us (we are potentially pregnant and reproductive beings for a long time), such separation is more difficult (and always more suspect) for women than for men.

The claim of universality and universal access to Reason has a gendered dimension—to the extent that women can be like men, to the extent we can transcend or control the unique (relative to men) aspects of female bodies, then we, too, can be producers of rational knowledge. Yet our capacity to do so is always suspect because of the particular conditions of our embodiment. Women remain the different to the (masculine) same.

In fact, the very *appearance* of neutrality or universality of Reason depends upon an independent and simultaneous set of moves: naming women as different in relation to the true measure of humanity: men, devaluing difference (the difference is always inferior to the same) and suppressing men's dependence on and complicity in this difference. Our understanding of Reason depends on what it is not, on its difference from and superiority to other faculties such as the passions. Associating women with the body and the particular are two of the necessary conditions for the possibility of conceptualizing a disembodied and universal faculty (e.g., the Cartesian ego or Kant's pure reason). The effects of male embodiment and social experiences on Reason and its products are denied out of existence. With the contaminating effects of difference located in women, suppressed or denied, Reason acquires its unitary and universal appearance. By situating men as well as women within gender relations, their purity/privilege is removed and both Reason and knowledge production are socialized. Rather than insisting that women's reason can be as "pure" as men's, it is more productive to question the purity of reason itself and the claim that no valuable or truthful knowledge can arise from the activities traditionally associated with women or the passions.[25]

We can also investigate the motives for insisting on such splits and this hierarchal ordering of human qualities. The insights derived from feminist object relations psychoanalysis are especially helpful in this investigation.[26] Since children develop in and through the context of relations with others, given the current sexual division of labor, both men and women will first begin to develop a self in interactions with a woman—a mother and/or other female relations. To some extent, male identity is built out of oppositional moves. He must become not-female, and in a culture where gender is an exclusionary and unequal pair of opposites, he must guard against the return of the repressed—his iden- tification with his mother and those "female" qualities within him. This provides a powerful unconscious motive for identifying with and over- valuing the abstract and the impersonal and for reinforcing gender seg- regation, including within intellectual work, to ensure that women will never again have power over men.

The End of Innocence and the Crisis of Representation

Feminists, psychoanalysts, and postmodernists challenge the posi- tions and self-understandings of intellectuals and raise fundamental questions about the possible relationships between knowledge, power, and practice. Their discourses disrupt master narratives of the West and the language games in which terms such as "freedom," "emanci- pation," or "domination" acquire meaning. Lacking "privileged" insight into the "laws" of history or reason's operations, firmly situated within discrete, contingent but constituting gender, race, and geographical locations, no longer serving as the neutral instrument of truth or the articulator of a homogeneous "humanity's" best hopes, what autho- rizes the intellectual? We become hesitant to speak for or prescribe our good(s) for others. Contemplating Auschwitz or a possible "nuclear winter," we can no longer sustain the illusion or the hope that "true" knowledge is sought only by the virtuous, is a priori generated by the good, and will, when put into practice, have only the beneficial results we intend. Normative discourse cannot be isolated from potential exer- cises of power, and it is increasingly difficult to conceptualize power entirely innocent of domination.[27]

Nonetheless, many intellectuals, including some feminist ones, are reluctant to abandon Enlightenment beliefs, including the assump- tions that justice/injustice are binary oppositions and that truth/jus- tice/the good are necessarily interdependent.[28] These theorists assume that domination and emancipation are binary opposites and that to dis- place one necessarily creates space for the other. They assume (rather than demonstrate) that there are necessary connections between truth, knowledge, emancipation, and justice. They believe the defects and incompleteness of our current knowledge is a necessary consequence of asymmetric power relations. People oppressed by such relations have a unique potential to create "better" (i.e., less distorted) knowledge. Such knowledge, they believe, will be benignly emancipatory—for example, it will not be generated by and generative of its own will to power. They assume rather than prove that truth and power are exclusionary. They are not content with constructing discourses which privilege some who have previously lacked power at the necessary expense of others but wish to claim dis-covery of ways to increase the total sum of human emancipation and truth.

Yet why should we assume that effective emancipatory political action and epistemologically secure knowledge are necessarily inter-dependent? At this time, such a belief is far more likely to encourage a dangerously blind innocence rather than prepare the ways for freedom or justice.[29] Operating on the terrain of "truth" does not exempt one from the effects of or complicity in relations of power. Just because false knowledge can be utilized to justify or support domination, it does not follow that truer knowledge will abolish it or that the possessor of "less false" knowledge will be free from complicity in the domination of others. Such necessity is an effect of certain discourses, not a law that governs political life.

In contemporary society, the will to truth and the will to power are inextricably linked. Part of the purpose of claiming truth is to compel agreement with our claim (if it is true, then you as a "rational person" must agree with me and change your beliefs and behavior accordingly). Appeals to truth appear least coercive and most innocent when the disputants are already within the same discursive frame and a consensus exists that all parties will respect the same rules. However, this appearance is an effect of the power exercised to achieve consensus, not the innocence of truth.

We must also take responsibility for our desire in such cases: what we really want is power in the world, not an innocent truth. We are often seeking a change in behavior or a win for our side. If so, there may be more effective ways to attain agreement or produce change than to argue about truth. Political action and change require and call upon many human capacities including empathy, anger, and disgust. There is no evidence that appeals to reason, knowledge, or truth are uniquely effective or ought to occupy privileged positions in strategies for change. It is simply not necessarily the case (especially in politics) that appeals to truth move people to action, much less to justice. Nor do epistemologies necessarily reassure people that taking risks are worthwhile or convince them that political claims are justified.[30]

Speaking in knowledge's voice or on its behalf, we can avoid taking responsibility for locating our contingent selves as the producers of knowledge and truth claims. A concern for truth can mask the desire to claim a position of innocence in which the possibility that one person's clarity rests on the exclusion of an other's experience is obscured. It can perpetuate the illusory hope that we can discover and follow a neutral set of rules which will not distort or erase someone else's truth. These exclusions are not primarily a consequence of poor methods or theories that could therefore be remedied by better ones. Rather, they reflect and are a consequence of the relations of domination prevalent throughout our culture. The solutions are primarily political—the distribution of power and authority and white people's racial privileges must be challenged. It is more comfortable (and comforting) to discuss epistemology (potentially neutral and common ground) than racism and other forms of domination.[31]

Responsibility without Grounds

Claims about domination concern *injustice*. Once we begin to make claims about any form of injustice, we irrevocably enter the realm of politics. Claims about injustice belong in the realm of persuasive speech, action, and (sometimes) violence. Such claims cannot be given extra force or justification by reference to Truth or even the "facts," because facts acquire meaning only within particular, contestable discursive schemes. Claims about injustice can operate independently of "truth" or, indeed, any corresponding counterclaim about a transcendental good or formal theory of justice.[32] In the worlds of politics, chance rather than rational principles rules. The actions of the inhabitants of such worlds are motivated by a complex and shifting set of forces, including moral commitments, desire, and relations to others. We need to make claims about and act upon injustices without transcendental guarantees or illusions of innocence. As Machiavelli argues, politics requires a morality and knowledge appropriate to its unique domain.

Transcendental notions of justice or knowledge are not only unnecessary but dangerous. They release us as discrete persons from full responsibility for our acts. We remain children, waiting, if our own powers fail, for the higher authorities to save us from the consequences of our actions. Such wishes depend on and express our complicity with what Nietzsche calls the "longest lie," the belief that "outside the haphazard and perilous experiments we perform there lies something (God, Science, Knowledge, Rationality, or Truth) which will, if only we perform the correct rituals, step in to save us."[33]

Feminists, psychoanalysts, and postmodernists have all begun to analyze our stubborn attachment to this lie. Feminists point to the pervasive effects of gender relations, to the splits between nurturance or caretaking and autonomy or history making.[34] Such splits impede the development of persons who can live comfortably within (or at least tolerate with an ironic sense of humor) political worlds. Psychoanalysts point to the connections between our conscience and our desires, to the impurity of our reason and its longings for an "objective" authority. Postmodernists point to the logocentrism at the heart of Western culture, to the equating of the rational and the human and the collapsing of the rational and the real. All three discourses tell stories about a being who refuses to grow up and fails to recognize that there is no one else here but our fragile and unstable selves and that nothing can guarantee happy or secure endings for our efforts.

To take responsibility is to situate ourselves firmly within contingent and imperfect contexts, to acknowledge differential privileges of race, gender, geographic location, and sexual identities, and to resist the delusory and dangerous recurrent hope of redemption to a world not of our own making. We need to learn to make claims on our own and others' behalves and to listen to those that differ from ours, knowing that ultimately there is nothing that justifies them beyond each person's own desire and need and the discourses which both generate and support such desire. Each person's well-being is ultimately dependent on the development of a sense of tolerance, empathy, friendly concern, and even benign indifference in the others. Lacking such feelings, as the Jews in Europe or people of color in the United States (among many others) have discovered, all the laws and cultural development civilization can offer will not save us. It is far from clear what contributions knowledge or truth can make to the development of such feelings.

As unstable and contingent subjects, we can engage in the process of dis-illusionment and of refusing the grandiose fantasies that have brought us to the brink of annihilation. For this is part of what is missing from Christa Wolf's equation: In different situations, people in the West are on both sides, the few and the many, and it is extremely difficult for us to accept and live such ambivalence. But these junctures are exactly where responsibility beyond innocence looms as a promise and a frightening necessity.

Notes

1. Christa Wolf, *Accident: A Day's News* (New York: Farrar, Straus, and Giroux, 1989), 17.

2. I have been deeply influenced in the development of this essay by Stuart Hampshire's recent book, *Innocence and Experience* (Cambridge: Harvard University Press, 1989). Some of the themes Hampshire explores in this book—

the contingency of politics and the need for distinctively political ethics—are also discussed in Agnes Heller and Ferenc Feher, *The Postmodern Political Condition* (New York: Columbia University Press, 1988).

3. Immanuel Kant, "What Is Enlightenment?," reprinted with his *Foundations of the Metaphysics of Morals* (Indianapolis: Bobbs-Merrill, 1959).

4. On the state of nature, see John Locke, *The Second Treatise of Government* in John Locke's *Two Treatises of Government,* ed. Peter Laslett (New York: Cambridge University Press, 1960). On the veil of ignorance, see John Rawls, *A Theory of Justice* (Cambridge: Harvard University Press, 1971), ch. 24. For a brilliant deconstruction of such rites or myths, see Carole Pateman, *The Sexual Contract* (Stanford: Stanford University Press, 1988).

5. For more extensive critiques of a variety of Marxist theories, see Isaac D. Balbus, *Marxism and Domination* (Princeton: Princeton University Press, 1982); and Hilary Manette Klein, "Marxism, Psychoanalysis, and Mother Nature," *Feminist Studies* 1.2 (Summer 1989): 255-78.

6. "The knell of capitalist private property sounds. The expropriator are expropriated. . . . [c]apitalist production begets, with the inexorability of a law of Nature, its own negation." Karl Marx, *Capital* (New York: International Publishers, 1967), 1:763.

7. Immanuel Kant, *Critique of Pure Reason* (Garden City, NY: Doubleday, 1966), esp. the introduction. See also René Descartes, *Discourse on Method and Other Writings* (Baltimore: Penguin, 1968); and Francis Bacon, *The New Organon* (Indianapolis: Bobbs-Merrill, 1960).

8. Thomas Kuhn, in *The Structure of Scientific Revolutions* (Chicago: University of Chicago Press, 1962), is one of the first writers to question this set of assumptions. His work suggests that the "success" of science can be attributed to certain practices adopted by historically specific scientific communities. By locating science and its practitioners in history, Kuhn (somewhat inadvertently, I believe) posed a radical challenge to philosophers. He, in effect, implies there is no timeless, universal "logic of discovery" that exists independent of its subjects and objects. This claim poses a profound threat to the disciplinary constitution of modern philosophy. By the early nineteenth century, philosophers were forced to abandon the claim that they could provide objective knowledge about the natural world. Nonetheless, they were able to resituate philosophy as a "foundational discipline" by asserting its epistemological privilege. Philosophy could tell us how objective knowledge is possible and when it exists. The philosopher's claim to truth and expertise reflects the objectivity and truth of its object. If there is no "logic of discovery" to discover and no truth claims to adjudicate, what are philosophers to do? For further reflections on these questions, see the essays in *After Philosophy,* ed. Kenneth Baynes, James Bohman, and Thomas McCarthy (Cambridge: MIT Press, 1987); and *The Institution of Philosophy,* ed. Avner Cohen and Marcelo Dascal (La Salle, IL: Open Court, 1989).

9. For an overview of contemporary approaches in social science, see *Metatheory in Social Science*, ed. Donald W. Fiske and Richard A. Shweder (Chicago: University of Chicago Press, 1986). Many social scientists and philosophers of social science continue to write as if they are completely unaware of the implications of recent philosophic developments for their foundational notions. See, for example, Alexander Rosenberg, *Philosophy of Social Science* (Boulder, CO: Westview Press, 1988); *The Use and Abuse of Social Science*, ed. Frank Heller (London: Sage, 1986); or Terence Ball, "Is There Progress in Political Science?", in *Idioms of Inquiry*, ed. Terence Ball (Albany, NY: State University of New York Press, 1987). Feminist theories or postmodernism are absent from or segregated in these texts.

10. Kenneth R. Hoover, *The Elements of Social Science Thinking*, 4th ed. (New York: St. Martin's, 1988), 6.

11. Ibid., 7.

12. A recent example of such claims is *The Behavioral and Social Sciences: Achievements and Opportunities*, ed. Dean R. Gerstein et al. (Washington, DC: National Academy Press, 1988).

13. David Ricci, *The Tragedy of Political Science* (New Haven: Yale University Press, 1984); and Raymond Seidelman with Edward J. Harpham, *Disenchanted Realists* (Albany, NY: State University of New York Press, 1985) discuss the recurrent power of this belief in American politics and political science.

14. See the essays in *Gender/Body/Knowledge*, ed. Alison M. Jagger and Susan R. Bordo (New Brunswick, NJ: Rutgers University Press, 1989); and *Feminist Challenges: Social and Political Theory*, ed. Carole Pateman and Elizabeth Gross (Boston: Northeastern Press, 1986).

15. Sigmund Freud, "Fixation to Traumas—The Unconscious," in his *Introductory Lectures on Psycho-Analysis* (New York: Norton, 1966), 353.

16. Ibid., 353.

17. Cf. his notion of the bodily ego in Sigmund Freud, "The Unconscious," in *Collected Papers*, ed. James Strachey (New York: Basic Books, 1959), vol. 4.

18. Sigmund Freud, *The Ego and the Id* (New York: Norton, 1960), 46.

19. The term "postmodernist" is controversial and ill-defined. I have discussed it extensively in my book, *Thinking Fragments: Psychoanalysis, Feminism, and Postmodernism in the Contemporary West* (Berkeley: University of California Press, 1990), especially ch. 6. My account here is derived from a condensation (and probably unfair collapsing) of some of the ideas of Michel Foucault, Jacques Derrida, Jean-Francois Lyotard, and Richard Rorty.

20. This phrase is from Jacques Derrida, "Violence and Metaphysics," in his *Writing and Difference* (Chicago: University of Chicago Press, 1978); see also

Richard Rorty on "Foundational Illusions," in his *Philosophy and the Mirror of Nature* (Princeton: Princeton University Press, 1979), especially p. 6.

21. On what a postmodernist philosopher might do, see the essays in Cohen and Dascal, *Institution of Philosophy*; Baynes, Bohman, and McCarthy, *After Philosophy*; Rorty, *Philosophy and the Mirror of Nature*, ch. 8; Richard Rorty, *Consequences of Pragmatism* (Minneapolis: University of Minnesota Press, 1982); Jacques Derrida, *Positions* (Chicago: University of Chicago Press, 1981); Michel Foucault, *Power/Knowledge* (New York: Pantheon, 1980); and Nancy Fraser, *Unruly Practices: Power, Discourse, and Gender in Contemporary Social Theory* (Minneapolis: University of Minnesota Press, 1989).

22. Cf. Jacques Derrida, *Spurs/Eperons* (Chicago: University of Chicago Press, 1978); and the sympathetic critiques of postmodernist positions by Naomi Schor, "Dreaming Dissymmetry: Barthes, Foucault, and Sexual Difference," in *Men in Feminism*, ed. Alice Jardine and Paul Smith (New York: Methuen, 1987); Alice A. Jardine, *Gynesis: Configurations of Woman and Modernity* (Ithaca, NY: Cornell University Press, 1985), esp. ch. 9; Susan Bordo, "Feminism, Postmodernism, and Gender-Skepticism," in *Feminism/Postmodernism*, ed. Linda Nicholson (New York: Routledge, 1990); and Judith Butler, *Gender Trouble: Feminism and the Subversion of Identity* (New York: Routledge, 1990). It is odd that many postmodernists are so emphatic in their claims that the subject is a thoroughly constituted but not a constituting being, yet they adopt a voluntary (indeed, almost free will) approach to gender identity.

23. These questions are discussed in the essays in Pateman and Gross, *Feminist Challenges*; and Jagger and Bordo, *Gender/Body/Knowledge*. See also Luce Irigaray, *Speculum of the Other Woman* (Ithaca, NY: Cornell University Press, 1985); Helene Cixous and Catherine Clement, *The Newly Born Woman* (Minneapolis: University of Minnesota Press, 1986); and the essays in *Feminist Perspectives in Philosophy*, ed. Morwenna Griffiths and Margaret Whitford (Bloomington, IN: Indiana University Press, 1988).

24. On this point, see Joan B. Landes, *Women and the Public Sphere* (Ithaca, NY: Cornell University Press, 1988); Susan Moller Okin, *Justice, Gender, and the Family* (New York: Basic Books, 1989); and Pateman, *Sexual Contract*.

25. See especially the essays in Jagger and Bordo, *Gender/Body/Knowledge*; and Pateman and Gross, *Feminist Challenges*.

26. Especially the work of Nancy Chodorow, *The Reproduction of Mothering* (Berkeley: University of California Press, 1978); and Dorothy Dinnerstein, *The Mermaid and the Minotaur* (New York: Harper and Row, 1976).

27. This is one of Michel Foucault's most important points. See his *Power/Knowledge*; and also Michel Foucault, *Politics, Philosophy, Culture*, ed. Lawrence D. Kritzman (New York: Routledge, 1990); and *The Foucault Effect: Studies in Governmentality*, ed. Graham Burchell et al. (Chicago: University of Chicago Press, 1991).

28. See the essays by Seyla Benhabib, Sandra Harding, Nancy Hartsock, and Christine de Stefano in Nicholson, *Feminism/Postmodernism*; Mary E. Hawkesworth, "Knowers, Knowing, Known: Feminist Theory and the Claims of Truth," in *Feminist Theory in Practice and Process*, ed. Micheline R. Malson et al. (Chicago: University of Chicago Press, 1989); Jurgen Habermas, *The Philosophical Discourse of Modernity* (Cambridge: MIT Press, 1987); and Jurgen Habermas, *The Theory of Communicative Action* (Boston: Beacon, 1989), vol. 2.

29. This view is shared by Hampshire, *Innocence and Experience*; and Heller and Feher, *Postmodern Political Condition*. See also Jean-Francois Lyotard, *The Postmodern Condition* (Minneapolis: University of Minnesota Press, 1984); and Kathy E. Ferguson, "Subject-Centeredness in Feminist Discourse," in *The Political Interests of Gender*, ed. Kathleen B. Jones and Anna G. Jonasdottir (London: Sage, 1988).

30. I develop this position more fully in "Beyond Equality: Gender, Justice, and Difference," in *Equality and Difference: Gender Dimensions in Political Thought and Morality*, ed. Gisela Bock and Susan James (New York: Routledge, 1992).

31. Barbara Christian, "Race for Theory," *Feminist Studies* 14.1 (Summer 1988): 67-79; Audre Lorde, *Sister Outsider* (Trumansburg, NY: Crossing Press, 1984); Deborah K. King, "Multiple Jeopardy, Multiple Consciousness: The Context for a Black Feminist Ideology," in Malson et al., *Feminist Theory in Practice and Process*; Elizabeth V. Spelman, *Inessential Woman: Problems of Exclusion in Feminist Thought* (Boston: Beacon, 1988); Teresa De Lauretis, "Eccentric Subjects: Feminist Theory and Historical Consciousness," *Feminist Studies* 16.1 (Spring 1990): 115-150; Patricia Hill Collins, *Black Feminist Thought: Knowledge, Consciousness, and the Politics of Empowerment* (New York: Routledge, 1990); Patricia J. Williams, *The Alchemy of Race and Rights* (Cambridge: Harvard University Press, 1991); *Third World Women and the Politics of Feminism*, ed. Chandra Talpade Mohanty et al. (Bloomington: Indiana University Press, 1991).

32. As shown in Hampshire, *Innocence and Experience*; and Heller and Feher, *Postmodern Political Condition*. See also Judith N. Sklar, "Injustice, Injury, and Inequality: An Introduction," in *Justice and Equality in the Here and Now*, ed. Frank S. Lucash (Ithaca, NY: Cornell University Press, 1986).

33. Richard Rorty, *Consequences of Pragmatism*, 208.

34. Dinnerstein, *The Mermaid and the Minotaur*; and Jane Flax, "Contemporary American Families: Decline or Transformation?," in *Families, Politics, and Public Policy*, ed. Irene Diamond (New York: Longman, 1983).

9

Narration, Knowledge, and the Possibility of Wisdom

Walter R. Fisher

Science shows what exists but not what to do about it.

—Heinz Pagels,
*The Dreams of Reason: The Computer
and the Rise of the Age of Complexity*

The strong claim of this essay is that narration is *the* most appropriate, useful paradigm for understanding and assessing whatever is taken as an instance of knowledge.[1] The weak claim is that this position is worthy of exploration and testing. The underlying premise of my argument is Alasdair MacIntyre's observation that "man is in his actions and practices, as well as in his fictions, essentially a storytelling animal."[2] I shall pursue the argument by (1) clarifying my meanings for narration and knowledge; (2) contrasting my position in relation to those of Jerome Bruner and Arthur Danto, writers who acknowledge the significance of narration in regard to knowledge but who relegate narrative knowing to a parallel status with empirical knowing or to a lesser level than philosophical knowing; and (3) demonstrating the soundness of viewing knowledge in the context of narration by application to James D. Watson and Francis H. Crick's proposal of the double-helix model of DNA. Central to this demonstration will be a delineation of what I call "narrative rationality," a logic that entails consideration of both "reasons" and values—values being seen as potential reasons in and of themselves and as the principal force in what are usually taken as reasons.

Narration and Knowledge

By "narration" I do not refer specifically to such individuated forms of language as anecdote, depiction, or characterization; nor do I specifically intend to denote such literary or dramatic genres as saga, legend, myth, novel, or play. These modes of discourse are not excluded from consideration, but they do not capture my meaning. Narration, as it is used here, designates a conceptual frame, one that I think is intrinsic to the nature of human beings. Narration, then, would account not only for the kinds of discourse just mentioned but also all other discourse forms, including scientific, historical, philosophical, political, religious, and so on—*insofar as they lay claim to our reason*. In addition, life itself—that is, its interpretation and enactment—is to be understood in narrative terms. As David Carr notes in *Time, Narrative, and History*: "Action, life, and historical existence are themselves structured narratively, independently of their presentation in literary form, and . . . this structure is practical before it is aesthetic or cognitive."[3]

Another way of thinking about narration, as I am using it, is as a master metaphor. As such, it subsumes other candidates for master metaphor—Homo Faber, Homo Politicus, Homo Sapiens, and so on—making of them figures with Homo Narrans the ground. (Implicit here is the assumption that human beings are valuing and reasoning beings.) When any of the other metaphors is considered the master metaphor, narration is figure: simple storytelling, an art, a mode of expression, or a genre. When Homo Narrans is the master metaphor, the other metaphors can be seen as various ways of informing how humans recount or account for human choice and action. Recounting takes such forms as history, biography, and autobiography. Accounting for takes such forms as theoretical explanation or argument. Recounting and accounting for can also be expressed in poetic forms: drama, poetry, novel, and so on. In this capacity, aesthetic forms serve a cognitive function: to make manifest ideas concerning the nature of self, society, and the world. Regardless of the form they are given, recounting and accounting for constitute the stories we tell ourselves and each other to establish a meaningful life-world. Thus, all forms of discourse can be considered stories, that is, interpretations of some aspect of the world occurring in time and shaped by history, culture, and character. (The structure of specific stories, of particular instances of discourse, is shaped by the conventions that constitute the genre to which they belong.) This view entails the notion that there is no form of reasoned discourse that presents uncontested truths, and that the appropriate logic for assessment of such communication should be a "narrative logic" compatible with the very nature of human beings and the discourse they generate.

To say that all forms of communication should be construed as stories is not to say that one must reject traditional distinctions such as exposition, argument, and narration (as modes of discourse) or such categories as scientific, religious, philosophical, or political discourse. It is to say that insofar as these modes and genres lay claim to knowledge, to our beliefs and actions, they are properly interpreted and assessed by narrative logic—no matter the diverse ways in which they make their claims. To put the point concretely, although the essays in this book may be grounded in empirical investigations, verifiable observations, or strict logical constructions, they are still open to doubt, criticism, and direct contradiction. Whatever else they may be considered— exposition, argument, literature, philosophy, science, or social science discourse—they are rhetorical: that is, persuasive compositions advancing contested or contestable conclusions about some aspect of the world of knowing.

The essays are rhetorical not only in the sense that they are composed and presented to influence beliefs and actions, in that the author wants and intends that his or her theses/themes be accepted as the true and right way of conceiving of a matter, but also in the fact that they are the product of rhetorical art. Created with various discursive and nondiscursive symbols, each essay reflects the literary and rhetorical sensibility and sensitivity of the author. Each composition proceeds from an act of intellection marked by insight; reveals inventiveness of mind and imagination; demonstrates the capacity to achieve order, unity, coherence, and force in language; and indicates the author's perception and understanding of the audience and the time and place of presentation. Furthermore, the compositions commend themselves to the reader by virtue of how well they measure up to rival stories, the stories the reader knows that are relevant to the story that they are reading. The story that is read can become the story by which new ones will be interpreted and assessed. (Such is the case with Watson and Crick's proposal of the double-helix model of DNA.) The stories that we hold to be "true" are those that best satisfy the two basic criteria of the narrative logic I shall present later: coherence and fidelity. Whatever may be considered knowledge, at least as it is expressed through language, cannot be considered so unless it meets these criteria.

But what, then, is knowledge? Answers to this question vary over time—from Plato's noumenal view to the strict phenomenal position of the logical positivists—but a review of this history is unnecessary here. There is only one conception that need concern us. It is the notion that true knowledge (in contrast with praxial knowledge) is objective—the result of observation, description, explanation, prediction, and control. This conception informs the mind-set of researchers and consultants for virtually all levels of decision making in every social, political, educational, legislative, and business institution in society.[4] The "tacit knowledge" of this mind-set is that all problems are fundamentally "logical puzzles" that are to be solved by empirical investigation tied to such systems as "cost-benefit analysis."[5] Method, techniques, and technology are its means; efficiency, productivity, power, and effectiveness are its values.[6] Knowledge from this perspective combines what Gilbert Ryle called "knowledge of that" and "knowledge of how."[7] "What exists" is covered by these sorts of knowledge but not the *knowledge of whether*, whether or not some things are desirable to do beyond what is instrumentally feasible and profitable. The dominant notion of knowledge, which is the legacy of positivism, ill serves questions of justice, happiness, and humanity. It is for this reason, and others, that a number of writers have risen to revise radically or to reject traditional notions of knowledge and reason: Richard Rorty, Paul Feyerabend, Michael Foucault, Jacques Derrida, and Jean-Francois Lyotard most prominent among them.[8]

Knowledge of whether, as I am calling it, has its origins in Aristotle's concept of practical wisdom, and it is in line with Mihaly Csikszentmihalyi's construction (in this volume). It includes knowledge of that and knowledge of how, and adds to them a praxial consciousness. The construct may be clarified by these examples: Medical doctors *know that* by using certain technological devices they can keep one alive even when the brain is "dead." They *know how* to do this. The question of *whether* they should do this is beyond their science. Nuclear scientists obviously *know that* by combining certain materials they can build weapons of incredible destructive power. The also *know how* to deploy them for maximum effect. The question of *whether* nuclear weapons should be employed involves another sort of knowledge. Doctors and scientists, *as technicians*, may dismiss, ignore, or relegate this sort of knowledge to others—it's not their business—but they cannot do so without denying their humanity. (Needless to say, many doctors and scientists are keenly aware of this fact.) They may also deny this sort of knowledge by insisting that it is a matter of values, as though their enterprises do not entail values, as though nonaction does not imply values as clearly as action. What is at stake in the dominant objectivist conception of knowledge is a notion that gives one power but not discretion. Shortly before he died, physicist Heinz Pagels made this relevant observation:

Some intellectual prophets have declared the end of the age of knowledge and the beginning of the age of information. Information tends to drive out knowledge. Information is just signs and numbers, while knowledge has semantic value. What we want is knowledge, but what we often get is information. It is a sign of the times that many people cannot tell the difference between information and knowledge, not to mention wisdom, which even knowledge tends to drive out.[9]

The sort of knowledge (and information) that has tended to drive out wisdom, I have been maintaining, is objectivist knowledge. The sort of knowledge that is in need of reconstruction, I believe, is praxial knowledge, but the matter at hand is narration and knowledge, and the next task is to summarize the orientation that leads to objectivist knowledge and discuss the ways narration relates to it.

object knowl. drives out wisdom

The objectivist orientation is referred to by Jerome Bruner as the "logico-scientific" mode of cognition (in contrast with what he calls the "narrative mode"). Central features of the "logico-scientific" mode include its

logico-scientific mode

attempt to fulfill the ideal of a formal, mathematical system of description and explanation. It employs categorization or conceptualization and the operations by which categories are established, instantiated, idealized, and related to the others to form a system. Its armamentarium of connectives includes on the formal side such ideas as conjunction and disjunction, hyperonymy and hyponymy, strict implication, and the devices by which general propositions are extracted from statements in their particular contexts. . . . Its language is regulated by the requirements of consistency and noncontradiction. Its domain is defined not only by observables to which its basic statements relate, but also by the set of possible worlds that can be logically generated and tested against the observables—that is, it is driven by principled hypotheses.[10]

Taking this representation as accurate and fair, I propose now to answer the question, How does narration as a paradigm relate to the objectivist position?

Narration (as paradigm) respects reason as mythos/logos, as including metaphor as well as argument, as inextricably bound to values, and as historical and contextual. Thus, it is pertinent to objectivist thinking and discourse in four major aspects. First, as Holton documents in *Thematic Origins of Science*, objectivist thinking has its roots in concepts, methods, and hypotheses inherited from Parmenides, Heraclitus, Pythagoras, Thales, and others.[11] Much of the historical and

1) armamentarium : collection of resources available or utilized for an undertaking or field of activity

2) hyperonymy :

3) hyponymy :

N.~obj. thinking | ⓐ grounded in myths ⓑ relies on non-obj.
thinking ~ lang. ⓒ value laden
ⓓ historical + contextual
174   *Walter R. Fisher*

myths tacit assumptions of this thinking is, in other words, grounded in myths. A telling example of this fact is the story told by Stephen Jay Gould in *Time's Arrow, Time's Cycle: Myth and Metaphor in the Discovery of Geological Time*.[12] Second, objectivist thinking and discourse cannot be conceived or composed without reliance on nonobjectivist ideas and nonobjectivist language. The classic example here is the principle of *non-obj. lang — thinking — imagination* verifiability; to wit: "A statement intended to be a fact is meaningful only if it is either formally valid, or some kind of observation is relevant to its truth or falsehood"—which is neither a formally valid deduction nor an observable fact. Moreover, objectivist thinking and discourse cannot advance without recourse to imagination. As J. Bronowski saw, such a move cannot be "mechanized":

> It is a free play of the mind, an invention outside the logical pro-cesses. This is the central act of imagination in science, and it is in all respects like any similar act in literature; it can in fact be taken as a definition of imagination. In this respect science and literature are alike: in both of them, the mind decides to enrich the system as it stands by an addition which is made by an unmechanized act of free choice.[13]

Third, objectivist thinking and discourse are value laden. Paramount values in scientific inquiry, Bronowski maintained, are truth, independence, tolerance, dissent, freedom of thought and speech, justice, honor, human dignity, and self-respect.[14] In *Science and Values: The Aims of Science and Their Role in Scientific Debate*, Laudan examines the cognitive values internal to science and its controversies. These disputes revolve around facts, methods, and aims. He does not specify "what the central values, aims, and methods of science are," but he insists that "until we are clear about the dynamics of cognitive value change, . . . it would be premature to try to work our way through the mechanics of moral axiological debate."[15] It is noteworthy that both Laudan and Bronowski hold that "rules" and procedures of justification will not resolve scientific dispute, that science is ever changing. Fourth, objectivist thinking and discourse are historical and contextual: They arise at a particular time and place, and involve particular thinkers and writers in transactions with others to produce knowledge, whether thought to be a product of strict empirical research or argumentative exchange. That such is the case is brilliantly illustrated in Martin J. S. Rudwick's *Great Devonian Controversy: The Shaping of Scientific Knowledge among Gentlemanly Specialists*. He concludes, among other things, that the Devonian controversy was "pervasively rhetorical" and that the clearest evidence for this lies "in the metaphors and images participants used to describe what they were doing."[16] The same could be said of controversies surrounding Newtonian versus Cartesian mechanics, Einstein versus Bohr on quantum mechanics, and special creation versus evolutionary biology. In sum, no matter how objectively one thinks or writes, one does so in a storied context as a character acting in relation to other characters in some moment in time and space.

A Narrative Paradigm Critique of
Bruner and Danto on Narration and Knowledge

In two recent books, *Actual Minds, Possible Worlds*, and *Acts of Meaning*, Jerome Bruner has advanced the argument that "there are two modes of cognitive functioning, two modes of thought, each providing distinctive ways of ordering experience, of constructing reality."[17] As noted earlier, one of these modes is the "logico-scientific," which stresses "verifiable reference" and "empirical truth." Its characteristic language is argument, and its goal is to establish "actual worlds." The second mode of cognitive functioning is narrative: "good stories, gripping drama, believable (though not necessarily 'true') historical accounts." Imagination plays a role in both modes of thought, according to Bruner, but in the "logico-scientific" mode, it conceives of theories or hypotheses, "possible formal connections before one is able to prove them in any possible way."[18] Imagination in the narrative mode creates "possible worlds." In *Acts of Meaning*, Bruner insists that the "paradigmatic" and narrative modes do not "fuse."[19]

At the outset of my response to this argument, I would like to acknowledge the significant contribution that Bruner has made to the understanding and acceptance of narration as a cognitive mode of thinking and communication.[20] I also consider his advancement, in *Acts of Meaning*, of "folk" or cultural psychology a major move in the right direction for cognitivists. I agree with him when he writes that "our capacity to render experience in terms of narrative is not just child's play, but an instrument for making meaning that dominates much life in culture––from soliloquies at bedtime to the weighing of testimony in our legal system."[21] I further endorse his observation that "experience in and memory of the social world are powerfully structured not only by deeply internalized and narratized conceptions of folk psychology but also by historically rooted institutions that a culture elaborates to support and enforce them."[22] Where I disagree with him is in his tacit recognition that narratives are rhetorical: They constitute our consciousness and influence our beliefs, attitudes, values, and action; and his failure to recognize that argument, the "logico-scientific" mode of thinking, is also rhetorical, serving the same communicative functions. The difference between constituting consciousness and constituting the mind is not one that can withstand empirical or argumentative scrutiny. No matter how strictly a case is argued—scientifically, philosophically, theologically, or legally—it may always be most accurately viewed as a story, an interpretation of some aspect of the world that is historically and culturally grounded and is told by a character to other characters, revealing in the transaction what honor and hubris humans are heir to.

Narrative and argumentative discourse may serve other than rhetorical functions—at least in theory. They may be informative, consummatory, or phatic, or simply lead to contemplation. But when they lay claim to our reason, to how we should understand ourselves, others, and the world, they invite interpretation and assessment by a logic that pertains to both modes, and, as I have been contending, that logic is a narrative logic. This means that each mode, in its own way, presents good reasons for accepting whatever "truth" it would foster. By "good reasons" I mean those elements that provide warrants for accepting or adhering to the advice fostered by any form of communication that can be considered rhetorical. By "warrant" I mean that which authorizes, sanctions, or justifies belief, attitude, value, or action—including metaphor, characterization, depiction, exposition, charts, graphs, statistics, arguments, and whatever other symbolic modes of inducement that go into human communication. The term "good reasons," I should stress, does not imply that every element in discourse that warrants a belief, attitude, value, or action is as good as any other. It only signifies that whatever is taken as a basis for adopting a rhetorical message is inextricably bound to a value—to a conception of the good, desirable, or obligatory (or their opposites—disvalues). Needless to say, good reasons are not necessarily effective, persuasive reasons. And, it should be noted, good reasons are components of cognitive processes—deliberation and decision—as well as discourse.

My difference from Bruner on narration is perhaps made most clearly by raising this question: How is his argument about the "logico-scientific" and narrative modes of cognition to be interpreted and assessed—by "logico-scientific" or narrative thinking? On the one hand, he clearly intends to represent an actual world. His argument rests, however, not so much on direct "logico-scientific" thinking as on astute observation. The basic distinction between "logico-scientific" and narrative modes depends less on empirical data than on intuitive intellection—which is the principal gift of any creative, path-breaking thinker. Strict cognitivists are likely to read his argument as presenting a possi-

hubris: exaggerated pride or self-confidence

ble world rather than an actual one. On the other hand, viewing Bruner's representation as a narrative portrayal fails his characterization of narrative. His books are not imaginative stories featuring actors in conflict with each other or with challenges from an environment whether human (a totalitarian state, for example) or natural (a flood, earthquake, or pestilence). So how are his conclusions, especially the distinction between argument and narrative, to be interpreted and assessed? The answer to this question, I think, is to evaluate Bruner's books in terms of narrative rationality and to weigh the good reasons he offers in regard to their coherence and fidelity.

It is appropriate at this point to specify what is entailed by these two considerations of narrative rationality. Since this is a time when it is fashionable to celebrate discontinuity, fragmentation, and conceptual incommensurability, it may seem odd to stress coherence as a key aspect of rationality. But, then, it is even more strange that this or any other project to reconstruct reason exists—given the contemporary preoccupation with desire, ideology, uncertainty, power, and indeterminacy. One can only observe that declarations of incoherence or inconsistency are made coherently and consistently. Moreover, they are made seriously as interpretations of the way the world is, as truths that should be believed and acted upon. Besides, there is reason in them. To determine how much, one must assess the degree of coherence (as detailed here) and fidelity in each declaration.

Coherence has three aspects. First, there is a concern for *argumentative or structural coherence*. Second, there is a concern for *material coherence*, which is determined by comparing and contrasting Bruner's story with stories told in other relevant discourses. By juxtaposing stories that purport to tell the "truth" about a given matter, one is able to discern factual errors, omission of relevant arguments, and any other sort of distortion. It is important to recognize that any discourse is as good as it stands with or against other stories. There is, in other words, no story that is not embedded in other stories. Third, there is a concern for *characterological coherence*. Here there is regard for the intelligence, integrity, and goodwill (ethos) of the author, the values he or she embodies and would advance in the world (character).[23] The degree to which one adheres to the message of any story is always related to the degree to which the narrator is taken to be a character whose word warrants attendance, if not adherence. In each of these features of coherence, values are manifest; consistency, completeness, and character.

Testing for fidelity is not merely an assessment of formal or informal soundness in thinking. Since values inform "reasons," it is necessary, indispensable, to weigh values in discourse to determine their

3 aspects of coherence: concern for → argumentative or structural coher.
→ material coher.
→ characterological coher.

worthiness as a basis of belief and action. Testing for fidelity, for the truth qualities of a story, then, entails two major considerations: weighing the elements of a message usually regarded as its reasons and weighing the values it explicitly or implicitly conveys. In the first instance, one does what one has always been taught to do: one determines whether the statements in a message that purport to be fact are indeed facts, that is, confirmed by empirical tests, consensus, or reliable, competent witnesses; one determines whether relevant facts or arguments have been omitted or misrepresented (which can be determined through consideration of the text's material coherence); one determines whether the individuated forms of reasoning in it are sound, that is, assesses the sign, cause, definition, analogy, example, and authority arguments—using standards from formal or informal logics; and one determines whether the key issues have been addressed, the questions on which decision and action should turn.

    In the second instance, one tries to answer the following questions related to values: What are the explicit and implicit values in the story? Are the values appropriate to the nature of the decision or beliefs that the story concerns? What would be the effects of adhering to the values in regard to one's concept of self, to one's behavior, to one's relationship with others and society? Are the values confirmed or validated in one's experience, in the lives and statements of others whom one admires and respects? And even if a *prima facie* case has been made or a burden of proof has been established, are the values fostered by the story those that would constitute a humane basis for human conduct? This final question most clearly concerns the knowledge of whether, and is clearly the paramount issue that confronts those responsible for decisions that impinge on the nature, quality, and continued existence of human life, especially in the fields of medicine and weapons technology and employment.

    My intention in developing these questions about values, I should note, was to offer a scheme to generate a sense of what is good as well as what is strictly logical in the stories that people might adopt. It is a scheme that does not dictate what one should believe, but it does necessarily involve one in considering one's relations with others and the pragmatic consequences of one's choices in regard to self and society. In short, assessing the explicit and implicit values in a story or in a process of deliberation/decision transforms knowledge of how and of that into knowledge of whether to do this or that.

    Given the principles of narrative rationality, then, Bruner's argument can be seen as structurally coherent and truthful in regard to narrative as a mode of discourse which contributes significantly to human

prima facie: at first view; upon the first appearance

knowledge. However, it lacks material coherence and fidelity insofar as it maintains that argument and narrative, as modes of thinking and discourse, cannot be fused; they are, in fact, fused in *Actual Minds, Possible Worlds* and in *Acts of Meaning*. And, most important for my own argument, they are fused in the construction of narration as a paradigm. Bruner's books establish good reasons for believing that those who propose actual worlds do so from a narrative frame and their discourse is most aptly assessed by a narrative logic. Later, in the examination of Watson's and Crick's proposal of the double-helix model of DNA, I shall attempt to provide further reasoning and evidence to support this claim.

Where Bruner considers narrative from the perspective of cognitive psychology, Arthur Danto examines it as a philosopher. Both take the position that narration is one of the fundamental ways in which we construe and represent the world, that it may express knowledge, and that our very lives are lived narratively. Danto's assertion that "narration yields certain categories of thought that might be said to compose the metaphysics of everyday life"[24] could serve well as a thesis for both of Bruner's books. The closeness of their thinking is also revealed in Danto's distinguishing among philosophy, science, and literature. Philosophy, he maintains, "wants to be more than universal; it wants necessity as well: truth for all the worlds that are possible." Science, on the other hand, is "concerned with truths of just the particular, uniquely actual world." And literature, seen through the lens of philosophical semantics, is given the capacity to be "true of possible worlds."[25]

Even as Bruner and Danto agree on the significance of narration in relation to knowledge, they disagree as to what this relationship is. For Bruner, narration and knowledge are related by the very nature of cognition: Narrative accounts for cultural knowledge. For Danto, narration and knowledge are related by narrative discourse's capacity to provide explanations; he asserts: "A narration is a *form* of explanation." In particular, he has in mind narration as it appears in historical writing or as a component within such writing. There is, he writes, "as much justification for the claim that we reconstruct a 'scientific explanation' as narrative as there is for the reverse claim, and that an account in narrative form will not lose any of the explanatory force of the original, assuming it had any explanatory force to begin with."[26] Finally, however, Bruner and Danto agree that narration is productive of knowledge on a limited basis—as one mode of cognition and its discourse or as a genre that on occasion provides a compelling account of "reality" or reveals "to us what we are in virtue of our reading."[27]

My point of departure from Danto's position, as it was with Bruner's, is to question his distinctions, in particular his categorizing of discourse. I do not deny the utility of Danto's analytic markers among history, science, literature, and philosophy. As generic categories, they have their uses: pedagogical, critical, and perhaps political—as in the politics of scholarship. But, the idea that there is something sacrosanct about them, that they represent "necessary truths," is an error, a lack of respect for the fact that each of these forms of communication lays claim to our reason and does so strategically with the intent to convince or persuade. It is also an error to assume that the subject matters of these forms of communication are a direct reflection of "reality"—a "mirror of nature," to use Richard Rorty's apt expression.[28] Danto's own discourse, philosophy, illustrates the point. I do not want to go as far as Ernesto Grassi and maintain that rhetorical thinking and discourse are prior to philosophy,[29] but I do argue, along with philosophers Chaim Perelman[30] and Henry W. Johnstone Jr.,[31] that philosophical discourse is rhetorical. As already noted, Danto sees philosophy as pursuing necessary, universal truths. "Philosophy," he asserts, "is the study of those semantical forces which bond language to reality and enable the former to express truths." The province of philosophy is the "space between language and the world."[32] Thus, philosophy explores what Perelman calls "confused notions," such as truth, reality, reason, rationality, wisdom, and justice.[33] The fact of their "confusion" is evidenced by the inconclusive efforts to establish their meanings with certainty since philosophy began. If realism, ideal or objective, realistically represented the world, the "confused notions" would have been clarified to everyone's satisfaction long ago. Given the aspiration to necessary truths, the notions that are argued about, and the audience to which it is addressed, philosophy would seem clearly to be nonrhetorical. Yet, as noted in regard to the notions that philosophy pursues, necessary truths are never established absolutely, universally; they are approximate, historically constituted, and forever contested. The propositions advanced by philosophers are meant to be persuasively compelling and will be found to be so by particular, not universal, audiences. So, as with Bruner's position, Danto's arguments on narration and knowledge commend themselves by virtue of good reasons, not strict logical demonstrations, and are convincing to the extent that they are coherent and have fidelity with the subject matter.

Narrative Logic and the Double-Helix Proposal

Having presented my position on narration and knowledge and contrasted it with those of Bruner and Danto, the remaining task is to

[handwritten margin notes:] Fisher's critique of Danto

[handwritten margin notes:] Danto's arguments are narrative not logic

[handwritten note at bottom:])sacrosanct: most sacred or holy : treated as if holy ; immune from criticism or violation

apply the narrative construct to an analysis of Watson and Crick's proposal of the double-helix model of DNA. I shall consider their article,
"A Structure for Deoxyribose Nucleic Acid," as a rhetorical text; that is,
as a symbolically composed discourse meant to induce adherence, as
historically situated, as addressed to a particular audience, and as reasonable rather than rigorously empirical or logical.[34] Since the rhetorical
nature of the document has been well demonstrated by previous writers
(as will be noted later), I shall focus on the criteria, the logic, by which
one would decide whether or not to adhere to the message. The reader
who has followed the argument so far will not be surprised that I shall
maintain that those criteria are coherence and fidelity. Perhaps needless
to say, the way in which these criteria are interpreted is not exactly the
same for scientific discourse as for other forms of communication: aesthetic, political, religious, historical, cultural, and so on. But, then, they
are not entirely unique either, as I shall demonstrate.

Since there is such a strong disposition against considering science in any sense as rhetorical, I will begin this analysis with several
observations by John Ziman, former professor of theoretical physics at
the University of Bristol. Early in his book, *Public Knowledge: The Social
Dimension of Science*, he writes: "The word *rhetoric* here may seem out of
place; it carries hints of bolstering bad argument by appeals to the emotions rather than to the intellect. But this surely is the only word we
may use, once we have dethroned positivism, and challenged the abso-
lutism of 'scientific' proof. It implies an appropriate degree of skepticism and doubt concerning any alleged scientific discovery, without
suggesting that we should treat the whole matter as a fraud." He asks,
as I am doing in my analysis, "Why, in fact, do we *believe* a good scientific argument, whether or not we can give a complete logical justification for that belief?"[35] His answer to this question in the end is that
"Objectivity and logical rationality, the supreme characteristics of the
Scientific Attitude, are meaningless for the isolated individual; they
imply a strong social context, and the sharing experience of an opinion."
He goes on to claim "that all genuine scientific procedures of thought
and argument are essentially the same as those of everyday life, and . . .
their apparent formality and supposed rigor is a result of specialization."[36] Ziman's observations are confirmed, I believe, by Watson's
account of the thinking and interactions he and his colleagues had in the
processes of "inventing" the double-helix model and the composition
that announced it.

Watson's story in *The Double Helix* is obviously a narrative, a tale
of conflict, competing characters, resolution, and a "happy" ending.
What is of most interest in this story, for our purposes, is the revelation

of the thinking that produced the double-helix model. **Motivated by an intense search for the most reasonable representation of what could not be seen directly,** guided by relevant theories, x-ray crystallography data, and empirical research, **the thought processes were nurtured by luck, hunches, "doodling," speculation, "playing" with ideas, trial and error, insight, and imagination.** In contemplating the structure of the DNA molecule, Watson and Crick were in the position of the scientist, described by Albert Einstein, who studied the face of a clock (nature) and tried to conceive of the mechanisms behind the face which accounted for the movement of the clock's hands. Reminiscing about the experience, Watson notes that "much of our success was due to the long uneventful periods when we walked among the colleges or unobtrusively read the new books that came into Heffer's Bookstore."[37] Rigorous reasoning obviously was involved in the invention of the double-helix model, but so was reflection not guided by strict inferential rules but by alternative possibilities and choosing the most apt, persuasive ones. As the mental processes that produced the model were shaped by choices with an audience in mind, the thinking became rhetorical. Watson attests to this fact unknowingly in the preface to *The Double Helix*: "Science seldom proceeds in the straightforward manner imagined by outsiders. Instead, its steps forward (and sometimes backward) are often human events in which personalities and cultural traditions play major parts."[38]

Before getting to the analysis of the logic behind the acceptance of Watson and Crick's discovery, it is pertinent—perhaps even instructive in itself—to review the research establishing the rhetorical nature of this proposal. For S. Michael Halloran, the document is rhetorical by virtue of the figures of speech that permeate the literature (and thinking) in genetic biology, especially metaphors such as "codes," "message," and "transmission," which suggest that DNA operates as a communication system.[39] In *Shaping Written Knowledge*, Charles Bazerman identifies several other features that make the article rhetorical: how the presentation is adapted to its audience; how its persuasive force depends on its adherence to the principle of "correspondence between data and claim";[40] how the article conveys a persona for the authors—humble but authoritative; how the authors reveal their differences from some previous writers and their alliance with others; and how evidence for the model is briefly sketched, more suggested than developed. Notably, the authors do not "urge, but rather leave the audience to judge and act according to the dictates of science."[41] A clear implication of Bazerman's study is that the rhetoric of science has a formulaic quality that is indispensable to its appeal and possible acceptance. Put another way, unless a scientific paper conforms to certain conventions, *proper form* [handwritten: proper form] it will not be recognized as legitimately scientific. Proper form, then, constitutes one "good reason" to believe a message.

Lawrence J. Prelli, in *A Rhetoric of Science*, locates the rhetorical nature of Watson and Crick's article in the inventional processes by which it was composed. He argues that the article was strategically written in accord with topics that are constitutive of scientific discourse: conjectural, definitional, and qualitative.[42] Because the significance and value of their discovery was evident, the authors, Prelli maintains, did not deal with another conventional topic: "fruitfulness." He concludes that the article was persuasive "because by habit, reason, strategy, or all three, the authors argued that their model for DNA promised *empirical adequacy*, and possessed qualities of *consistency*, elegance, explanatory power, and *immediate fruitfulness*."[43] I hasten to note that each of these factors is a value and can be considered a good reason, a warrant, for believing and accepting Watson and Crick's proposal.

In *The Rhetoric of Science*, Alan G. Gross goes beyond the other writers on the rhetorical nature of Watson and Crick's article. He takes the position that "the sense that a molecule of this structure exists at all, the sense of its reality, is an effect only of words, numbers, and pictures judiciously used with persuasive intent."[44] After examining Watson and Crick's article and Watson's account of the discovery of the model in *The Double Helix*, Gross concludes that the persuasive power of the two writings may be attributed to the same measure: "the fit between the new view presented and a preferred view of the constitution of reality."[45] Both discourses, in other words, produce knowledge and are susceptible of confirmation. The article differs from the book, according to Gross, only in the strictness by which this confirmation may be made. In both instances, the knowledge produced by the writings "goes well beyond the establishment of fact."[46]

In sum, Watson and Crick's proposal of the double-helix model is rhetorical by virtue of its conception, composition, intent, relation to reality, and its reception. The question remains: What are, or appear to be, the criteria of its acceptance, the logic that determines belief in its message?

From my own stance, the narrative paradigm, Watson and Crick's article epitomizes what I call the rational world paradigm. Its presuppositions are that (1) humans are essentially rational beings; (2) the appropriate mode of human decision making and communication is argument—discourse that features clear-cut inferential or implicative structures; (3) the conduct of argument is ruled by the dictates of situations—legal, scientific, legislative, public, and so on; (4) rationality is [handwritten: Rational World Paradigm] determined by subject-matter knowledge, argumentative ability, and skill in employing the rules of advocacy in given fields; and (5) the world is a set of logical puzzles that can be solved through appropriate analysis and application of reason conceived as an argumentative construct. The principal differences between the narrative paradigm (outlined earlier) and the rational-world paradigm, at least for present purposes, concerns the conception of reason. The narrative paradigm accepts the fact that reason is expressed through clear-cut inferential or implicative structures and retains, in its attendant logic (narrative rationality), the formal and informal tests of arguments. But it broadens the conception of reason to encompass any symbolic form that provides a warrant for belief and action, and it offers tests of values, which may be, as I have said, good reasons in and of themselves. Thus, narrative rationality directs attention to features of discourse seen and unseen by traditional logics. In addition to the enlarged view of reason and the tests of values, narrative rationality includes explicit consideration of the coherence of the discourse: argumentative-structural, material, and characterological. To put the matter succinctly in regard to Watson and Crick's article, there is more reason in it than can be accounted for by looking only at its statements of fact and argument.

The truth of this observation should become evident as I proceed. I shall focus on how Watson and Crick's article satisfies the tests of coherence and fidelity. I shall begin with fidelity, because it is *the* measure of discourse reflecting the rational world paradigm. Watson and Crick's basic claim is that they have discovered a valid structure for the DNA molecule. Actually, there are two claims here: One, that they discovered the model; and, two, that it is a valid model. My concern is the second claim, and the initial question is: What facts do the authors offer to support the validity of the double-helix model? The most direct answer to this question is contained in the penultimate paragraph:

> The previously published X-ray data on deoxyribose nucleic acid are insufficient for a rigorous test of our structure. So far as we can tell, it is roughly compatible with the experimental data, but it must be regarded as unproven until it has been checked against more exact results.

Their model, they go on to say, "rests mainly though not entirely on published experimental data and stereochemical arguments."[47] If this is the case, if the model was not secured by facts, it was not so much valid as it was *veracious*, not so much true as truthful. Being truthful rather than true, of course, is not a detriment in the advancement of scientific

Veracious: truthful, honest; marked by truth, accurate

theory (or any other kind of theory); it is as much as the workings of nature (and human experience) will allow. The fidelity of Watson and Crick's model with known data and relevant "laws" of chemistry had to be the most compelling reason for belief in their proposal. Truthfulness is a value. It provides a good reason to entertain any theory.

The question with which this analysis began—What facts do the authors offer to support the validity of the double-helix model?—must now be revised: What arguments do the authors offer to support the *truthfulness* of the double-helix model? Their first argument was that the structure proposed by Linus Pauling and R. B. Corey was "unsatisfactory." The underlying reason for their rejection was that the Pauling-Corey model was not truthful; it violated chemical "laws" and prior research. Their second argument was that the structure put forward by Fraser was too "ill-defined" to warrant comment. Clearly, precision is a value and lack of it is sufficient reason, a good reason, for rejecting ideas that are "ill-defined." After describing their model—verbally and in diagram—Watson and Crick present an intertwined argument to establish its conformity with "laws" of chemistry and current research data. Here again, there is an implication of a good reason: Sound theory is in accord with prior knowledge. Each of these three lines of argument, it should be noted, is not a strict logical demonstration, either deductive or inductive. Each is, however, a proper deductive argument if one grants the premise on which it is grounded: good theory is truthful (that of Pauling-Corey is not truthful; it should be rejected); good theory is precise (Fraser's theory is not precise; it should be rejected); good theory is confirmed by the best available theory and evidence (ours is; therefore, it should be accepted). The "reasons" for believing, accepting Watson and Crick's proposal, then, are good reasons, reasons informed by values: truthfulness, precision, conformity with the best that is known, and the promise of useful results in its application in further theory and research.

So far, the analysis of Watson and Crick's claim that they have produced a truthful model of DNA has focused on facts and arguments, the usual concerns of the logic associated with the rational-world paradigm. The analysis, however, differs from the traditional approach in that it has brought to the surface the role of values in giving force to these facts and arguments. The stage is now set to consider whether or not these values provide good reasons to support Watson and Crick's basic contention. This consideration is not part of the assessment process dictated by traditional logics, but it is integral to the system of evaluation in the construct of narrative rationality. It is, moreover, I believe, impossible to adhere to Watson and Crick's position without endorsing the values their discourse affirms. Particularly pertinent are questions of the appropriateness (given the subject matter) of the explicit and implicit values in the message; the consequences of endorsing these values for the constitution of agents involved in the enterprise (of science) and the vitality of the enterprise itself; and if the values are those that are esteemed by significant actors in the enterprise. Without reservation, truthfulness, precision, conformity to the best that is known, and usefulness are values appropriate to the matter at hand; they are conducive to the make-up of good scientists and the conduct of science; and they are heralded by leaders throughout the discipline. They are, in fact, the bedrock values that inform knowing and communicating in all of the sciences—physical, social, and human. They are the stuff not only of good reasons but the best of reasons—in scholarship.

It is worthy of note, however, that truthfulness, precision, conformity with past knowledge, and usefulness are not sufficient values to constitute a praxial consciousness. Even as they are definitive of the scholarly/scientific mind/enterprise, they do not go beyond what exists, or what is thought to exist. Even when tied to the traditional values of pragmatism—efficiency, workability, success—they do not fully inform the mind to the knowledge of whether. The values that are necessary to this state of awareness are those that look not only to the past and present but also to the future. Those values include, as suggested earlier, justice, happiness, and wisdom. The bedrock value of a praxial consciousness, I believe, is love; that is, an abiding concern for the welfare and well-being of others.

An example of the difference between a mind oriented to the here and now, to the technical means and values by which problems are to be solved in laboratories or in society, and a mind that incorporates this sort of knowledge with a compassion for the consequences of using this knowledge should help to clarify my point. An engineer is commissioned to build a bridge; she is thereby confronted with a technical problem which she is well equipped to solve. The engineer knows the how and the that of the matter. The result is a structurally sound bridge. The engineer imbued with a feeling for those who will use the bridge, not only their safety but also their sense of the ecological and aesthetic qualities of the bridge, would design it differently from the one whose only concern was technical proficiency. The bridge would be built with caring competence; put another way, it would be built with a concern for the welfare *and* the well-being of its users. The difference between the technically minded engineer and the technically proficient, praxially conscious engineer comes down to a difference in their perceptions of audience: The former has in mind a technical audience; the latter has in mind the same audience, but she sees it as part of a larger one—potentially all of humanity.

The final component in this analysis concerns the coherence of Watson and Crick's presentation, another consideration left out in traditional logical assessment. There is good reason to accept the presentation because it is *argumentatively-structurally* sound. There is good reason to accept it because it is also *materially coherent,* that is, it is consonant with other relevant stories that relate to the matter, even as it supersedes them, becoming *the* story by which those that follow it will be read and evaluated. And there is good reason to accept it because it is *characterologically* credible. The voices of Watson and Crick achieve authenticity through the good reasons they provide in content and form. "A Structure for Deoxyribose Nucleic Acid" is, in short, not only a touchstone within its field, it is also a classic representation of scientific discourse. It is so because it is coherent and has fidelity to the matter at hand.

The point of this analysis has been to show that the construct of narrative rationality provides a more complete, adequate account of reason in discourse than traditional logics. If successful, it has demonstrated that the logical appeal of Watson and Crick's claim to have come up with a truthful model of DNA involved much more than the facts and arguments they presented. The principal revelation has been that *values* were the compelling force in their message, determining, even, the persuasive power of the facts and arguments. One more observation is suggested, if not warranted entirely, by this analysis: Certainty about "factual" or theoretical matters plays the same role in the physical sciences as it does in the social and human sciences. Each of these enterprises is sustained by ongoing rhetorical transactions. When a particular discovery in any one of them is confirmed by a relevant community of scholars, that particular line of inquiry and the specific rhetorical transactions that produced it wither and die—giving birth to new lines of inquiry and other specific rhetorical transactions, some of which may eventually disconfirm the certainties of the past and revive the original controversy in the language of the present. In any case, certainty is hardly the culmination of intellectual curiosity; it is the commencement or recommencement of a continuing desire to know.

Conclusion

In 1978, I concluded an essay with the following words: "Since the time of Francis Bacon, knowledge has been conceived largely as power over people and things. In my judgment, we have lost a sense of wisdom. To regain it, I think, we need to reaffirm the place of value as a component of knowledge."[48] This chapter is written in this spirit. The narrative paradigm and its attendant logic, narrative rationality, are designed to reveal the role of values in reason and action in order to restore a consciousness of *whether* in our conceptions of knowledge, which inevitably imply a praxis.[49] Without a sense of *whether*, knowledge of how and knowledge of that will continue to dominate, stifling the humane concerns of happiness, justice, and wisdom. We know that the structure of DNA is a double helix. We know how it can be altered. This knowledge is essential, but the question of whether DNA should be manipulated persists—and the answer is beyond the province of what merely exists.

Notes

1. This chapter incorporates portions of my book, *Human Communication as Narration: Toward a Philosophy of Reason, Value, and Action* (Columbia, SC: University of South Carolina Press, 1987). See Margaret Masterman's "The Nature of a Paradigm" in *Criticism and the Growth of Knowledge*, ed. I. Lakotos and A. Musgrave (London: Cambridge University Press, 1970), 65, which is an analysis of the uses of "paradigm" in Thomas S. Kuhn's *Structure of Scientific Revolutions* (Chicago: The University of Chicago Press, 1962). Metaparadigms are to be distinguished from "sociological" and "artefact" paradigms.

2. Alasdair MacIntyre, *After Virtue: A Study in Moral Theory* (Notre Dame, IN: Notre Dame University Press, 1981), 201. See also Fredric R. Jameson, "The Symbolic Inference; or, Kenneth Burke and Ideological Analysis" in *Representing Kenneth Burke*, ed. Hayden White and Margaret Brose (Baltimore: John Hopkins University Press, 1982), 72ff.; and Fredric P. Jameson, *The Political Unconscious: Narrative as a Socially Symbolic Act* (Ithaca, NY: Cornell University Press, 1981).

3. David Carr, *Time, Narrative, and History* (Bloomington, IN: Indiana University Press, 1986), 185

4. Frank Fischer, *Technocracy and the Politics of Expertise* (Newbury Park, CA: Sage, 1990), 13-55.

5. Michael Polanyi, *Personal Knowledge: Towards a Post-Critical Philosophy* (Chicago: University of Chicago Press, 1962), 132-202. See also Michael Polanyi, *The Tacit Dimension* (Garden City, NY: Anchor Books, 1967), 1-25.

6. William Barrett, *The Illusion of Technique: A Search for Meaning in a Technological Civilization* (Garden City, NY: Anchor Books, 1979).

7. Gilbert Ryle, *The Concept of Mind* (London: Hutchinson's University Library, 1949), 25-61.

8. See, for instance, Richard Rorty, *Philosophy and the Mirror of Nature* (Princeton, NJ: Princeton University Press, 1979); Paul Feyerabend, *Farewell to Reason* (London: Verso, 1988); Michel Foucault, *Madness and Civilization: A History of Insanity in the Age of Reason*, trans. Richard Howard (New York: Vintage Books, 1988); Jacques Derrida, *Dissemination*, trans. Barbara Johnson (Chicago: University of Chicago Press, 1981), 61-171; Jean-Francois Lyotard, *The Postmodern Condition: A Report on Knowledge*, trans. Geoff Bennington and Brian Massumi (Minneapolis: University of Minnesota Press, 1988).

9. Heinz Pagels, *The Dreams of Reason: The Computer and the Rise of the Age of Complexity* (New York: Simon & Schuster, 1988), 149.

10. Jerome Bruner, *Actual Minds, Possible Worlds* (Cambridge: Harvard University Press, 1986), 12-13. For another perspective on objectivist thinking, see George Lakoff, *Women, Fire, and Other Dangerous Things: What Categories Reveal about the Mind* (Chicago: University of Chicago Press, 1987), xii-xiii.

11. G. Holton, *Thematic Origins of Modern Science* (Cambridge: Harvard University Press, 1973).

12. Stephen Jay Gould, *Time's Arrow Time's Cycle: Myth and Metaphor in the Discovery of Geological Time* (Cambridge: Harvard University Press, 1987). See also Earl R. MacCormac, *Metaphor and Myth in Science and Religion* (Durham, NC: Duke University Press, 1976).

13. J. Bronowski, *The Identity of Man*, rev. ed. (Garden City, NY: Natural History Press, 1971), 126-27. See also Peter Medawar, *The Limits of Science* (Oxford: Oxford University Press, 1984), 45-54.

14. J. Bronowki, *Science and Human Values*, rev. ed. (New York: Harper & Row, 1972), 68.

15. Larry Laudan, *Science and Values: The Aims of Science and Their Role in Scientific Debate* (Berkeley: University of California Press, 1984), 139.

16. Martin J. S. Rudwick, *The Great Devonian Controversy: The Shaping of Knowledge among Gentlemanly Specialists* (Chicago: University of Chicago Press, 1985), 435. For how scientific knowledge was shaped through rhetorical transactions in regard to the discovery of the DNA model, see James D. Watson, *The Double Helix* (New York: New American Library, 1968).

17. Bruner, *Actual Minds*, 11. For another view of the relationship between narration and knowing, see Donald E. Polkinghorne, *Narrative Knowing and the Human Sciences* (Albany, NY: State University of New York Press, 1988).

18. Bruner, *Actual Minds*, 13.

19. Jerome Bruner, *Acts of Meaning* (Cambridge: Harvard University Press, 1990), 94.

20. Bruner is not the first to make the claim that literature produces knowledge. For instance, Benedetto Croce wrote at the turn of the century that "knowledge has two forms: it is either intuitive knowledge or logical knowledge; knowledge obtained through the imagination or knowledge obtained through the intellect; knowledge of the individual or knowledge of the universal; of individual things or of the relations between them; it is, in fact, productive either of images or of concepts." See Benedetto Croce, "Intuition and Expression," in *Critical Theory since Plato*, ed. Hazard Adams (New York: Harcourt Brace Jovanovich, 1971), 727. See also Allan Tate, "Literature as Knowledge," in *Essays of Four Decades* (Chicago: Swallow Press, 1968), 104-5.

21. Bruner, *Acts of Meaning*, 97. Empirical evidence to support the claim that trials are conducted through storytelling is contained in W. Lance Bennett and Marsha S. Feldman's *Reconstructing Reality in the Courtroom: Justice and Judgment in American Culture* (New Brunswick, NJ: Rutgers University Press, 1981).

22. Bruner, *Acts Of Meaning*, 57.

23. The relationship between ethos and character is delineated in my book, *Human Communication as Narration*, 148.

24. Arthur C. Danto, *Narration and Knowledge* (New York: Columbia University Press, 1985), xiv.

25. Arthur C. Danto, "Philosophy as/and/of Literature," in *Post-Analytic Philosophy*, ed. John Rajchman and Cornel West (New York: Columbia University Press, 1985), 77.

26. Danto, *Narration and Knowledge*, 237.

27. Danto, "Philosophy as/and/of Literature," 83.

28. Rorty, *Philosophy and the Mirror of Nature*.

29. Ernesto Grassi, *Rhetoric as Philosophy: The Humanistic Tradition* (University Park, PA: Pennsylvania State University Press, 1980), 18-34.

30. Chaim Perelman, "Rhetoric and Philosophy," *Philosophy and Rhetoric* 1 (1968): 15-24.

31. Henry W. Johnstone Jr., "From Philosophy to Rhetoric and Back," in *Rhetoric, Philosophy, and Literature: An Exploration*, ed. Don M. Burks (West Lafayette, IN: Purdue University Press, 1978), 49-66.

32. Danto, *Narration and Knowledge*, 310.

Possibility of Wisdom 191

33. Chaim Perelman and L. Olbrechts-Tyteca, *The New Rhetoric: A Treatise on Argumentation*, trans. John Wilkinson and Purcell Weaver (Notre Dame, IN: Notre Dame University Press, 1969), 130-35.

34. See Lawrence J. Prelli, *A Rhetoric of Science: Inventing Scientific Discourse* (Columbia, SC: University of South Carolina Press, 1989), 83-115.

35. John Ziman, *Public Knowledge: The Social Dimension of Science* (London: Cambridge University Press, 1968), 32.

36. Ibid., 144.

37. Watson, *Double Helix*, 128.

38. Ibid., ix.

39. S. Michael Halloran, "Toward a Rhetoric of Scientific Revolution," in *Proceedings: 31st Conference on College Composition and Communication: Technical Communication Session*, ed. John A. Muller (Urbana, IL: ATTW, 1980), 229-36; and S. Michael Halloran and Annette Norris Buford, "Figures of Speech in the Rhetoric of Science," in *Classical Rhetoric and Modern Discourse*, ed. Robert J. Connor, Lisa S. Ede, and Andrea A. Lundsford (Carbondale, IL: Southern Illinois University Press, 1984), 179-92. See also Walter B. Weimer, "Science as Rhetorical Transaction: Toward a Nonjustificational Conception of Rhetoric," *Philosophy and Rhetoric* 10 (1977): 1-29; Richard Harvey Brown, "Narrative in Scientific Knowledge and Civic Discourse," in *Current Perspectives in Social Theory*, ed. John Wilson (Greenwich, CT: JAI Press, 1991), 11: 313-29; Philip Levin, "Categorization and the Narrative Structure of Science," unpublished manuscript. For essays on the rhetoric of various of the human sciences, including mathematics, see *The Rhetoric of the Human Sciences: Language and Argument in Scholarship and Public Affairs*, ed. John S. Nelson, Allan Megill, and Donald N. McClosky (Madison, WI: University of Wisconsin Press, 1987).

40. Charles Bazerman, *Shaping Written Knowledge: The Genre and Activity of the Experimental Article in Science* (Madison, WI: University of Wisconsin Press, 1988), 29.

41. Ibid., 46.

42. Prelli, *A Rhetoric of Science*, 238.

43. Ibid., 249.

44. Alan G. Gross, *The Rhetoric of Science* (Cambridge: Harvard University Press, 1990), 54.

45. Ibid., 55.

46. Ibid., 65.

47. James D. Watson and Francis H. Crick, "A Structure for Deoxyribose Nucleic Acid," *Nature* 171 (1953), 737. The relationships between love and knowledge are explored extensively by Martha C. Nussbaum in *Love's Knowledge: Essays on Philosophy and Literature* (New York: Oxford University Press, 1990). See John Dewey, "The Quest for Certainty: A Study of the Relation of Knowledge and Action," in *The Later Works, 1925-1953, Vol. 4: 1929,* ed. Jo Ann Boydston (Carbondale, IL: Southern Illinois University Press, 1988).

48. Walter R. Fisher, "Toward a Logic of Good Reasons," *The Quarterly Journal of Speech* 64 (1978), 384.

49. On the relationship between conceptions of knowledge and praxis, see Stephen Toulmin, *Cosmopolis: The Hidden Agenda of Modernity* (New York: Free Press, 1990), 68ff.

IV

Knowledge and Schema Theory

10

Bridging Cognition and Knowledge

Helen Couclelis

It is no wonder that the question of knowledge holds such perennial fascination for human thought: Why else has the species named
itself *homo sapiens*? In western societies, the question of knowledge, and
of the growth of knowledge in particular, has been closely associated
with the idea of science and scientific progress, and its study has been
the realm of epistemology and the philosophy (recently also the sociology) of science. Most will agree that knowledge and science are not
quite the same thing, but there again, the etymologies are revealing.

Whether or not one includes in the definition of knowledge its
common sense and practical forms, the growth of knowledge in the
societal realm is widely understood as the expansion of the store of
facts available to humankind. The growth of knowledge in the individual, by contrast, is normally identified with the subjective experience of
learning. As such, it is considered the province of the educator, the psychologist, the cognitive scientist, and recently also the neurobiologist, all
of them concerned not with knowledge per se but with knowing as a
process inside a person's brain or mind. In fact, mainstream logic and
the modern philosophy of mind draw a sharp distinction between
knowledge and knowing, between facts and the cognitive phenomena
through which human minds discover, organize, process, and store
these facts, between the "truths in themselves" and the subjective
thought processes that may lead to such truths. In Karl Popper's (1972)
very influential philosophy of science, that dualism between cognition
and its externalized products is tellingly reflected in his definition of
two separate "worlds": World 2, the world of subjective experiences
and thought processes; and World 3, the world of statements, ideas,
arguments, problems, and theories in themselves. World 2 and World 3
interpret and codify World 1, the external world of physical objects.
Formal logic is the only discipline that makes an explicit connection

between (correct) reasoning and (valid) statements, but its normative approach to both cognition and knowledge makes it an unsuitable model for any empirical science of either or both of these realms.

By and large, then, some rare exceptions notwithstanding (see Polanyi 1958; Arbib and Hesse 1986), societal knowledge and personal knowledge are treated as two separate domains: the first having to do with what the world may really be like, the second exploring the powers and limitations of individuals as they strive to know that world. There is little doubt that the sharp distinction between the objective and subjective aspects of knowledge proved very fruitful in the history of ideas, and may be credited to a large extent with the success of modern science. But good ideas, in particular, have a tendency to outlive their purpose and to linger past the point where they start generating more conundrums than they help resolve. It is beyond the scope of this essay to argue that this is, indeed, the case with the separation of knowledge from knowing. My goal is simply to point out that the taken-for-granted dichotomy is neither logically inescapable nor practically inevitable for lack of a serious alternative. The alternative in this case lies in a conceptual framework that helps bridge cognition and knowledge, negating the premise that they reside in separate "worlds."

This essay is therefore intended as a contribution to that small and still unorthodox body of literature purporting to go beyond the dualism of cognition and fact, knowing and knowledge. At the core of my critique is an insidious assumption, encapsulated in the phrase "the container metaphor," which underlies much of the conventional understanding of both individual memory and the growth of societal knowledge. According to that view, new items of knowledge are produced (in a society) or learned (by the individual) and added to the store of pre-existing public or personal knowledge. Whether new volumes in a library or new facts or skills stored in the mind, these chunks of new knowledge are added to the contents already held by some kind of container. Clearly, the notion hardly ever appears in such crude terms, and nowadays there is widespread recognition of the fact that new knowledge not only complements but also modifies and displaces old knowledge. But the furor that greeted Thomas Kuhn's (1962) *Structure of Scientific Revolutions*, which dared challenge the view that the growth of scientific knowledge is linear, additive, and cumulative, is indicative of the great resistance of western thought to any suggestions to the contrary. The conviction that knowledge grows by accretion is not just a deeply rooted commonsense belief; it is also firmly grounded in traditional formal logic, which comes very close to equating knowledge with objective, timeless truth. It is only in recent years, in the newly defined area of nonmonotonic reasoning, that formal logic has begun to come to grips with the notion that inferences that are valid at some point in time may later be reversed as a result of new evidence. Still, what is at issue here is the validity of particular items of knowledge (the inference, say, that a particular bird can fly, given the further evidence that the bird in question is an ostrich) rather than the possibility of global "paradigm shifts" of the kind Kuhn adumbrated (see Genesereth and Nilsson 1987).

In the pervasive and largely unexamined adoption of the container metaphor I see the main obstacle to the bridging of cognition and knowledge. Containers imply contents, and contents can only be "things," discrete entities with an autonomous existence: They may be examined independently of context, moved around, replaced, combined with others, added to, pulled apart, analyzed, created and destroyed, named and classified, without losing their individual essence. To this dominant paradigm I wish to oppose the notion of a "schema." Although widely used in cognitive science and artificial intelligence, the notion of schema is difficult to pin down in a few words. In fact, it is easier to describe it by contrasting it with what it is not: It is a coherent pattern rather than a thing, a state rather than a content, a property rather than an entity; it is retained rather than stored in memory; it is re-created rather than re-called; it changes through restructuring rather than accretion; it is a holistic rather than an atomistic concept. Jean Piaget (1954) and his followers in developmental psychology have made different versions of the schema idea central to their theoretical approach to cognition, while others have helped develop it into a construct tangible enough to be implemented in computer models of learning and action (see Sowa 1984). Extensions of the notion from the cognitive to the social and cultural realms have only recently appeared and are still few and far between (Banerjee 1986; Casson 1983). *The Construction of Reality*, by Michael Arbib and Mary Hesse (1986), is, to my knowledge, still the only major work to develop a systematic schema-based framework that encompasses both individual and societal knowledge.

Viewing cognition and knowledge through a schema perspective not only may help resolve the traditional dualism but could also shed light on a number of other problems of knowledge, such as the question of the relationship between natural and social science. This is the main point of this essay. But before dismissing the container metaphor in favor of an alternative with far less respectable credentials, the reasons for its pervasiveness must be addressed. Nor is the schema paradigm itself without problems. I will discuss it first in connection with personal knowledge, bringing in some additional insights from areas as diverse as cognitive linguistics, geography, computer science, and neurobiology. And finally, I will adumbrate an alternative view of scientific knowledge that is compatible with the schema perspective. It is also more useful, I will claim, in helping understand the difference between physical and social science.

There is something about container metaphors that is strangely seductive. In the realm of knowledge, this is particularly true of our views of the individual mind. While we may readily think of items of societal knowledge as being "contents" in some Popperian World 3, it is the well-delimited spatial finiteness of the brain that makes the metaphor really compelling. Bank, storage place, warehouse, store, receptacle, black box, bucket, storehouse: Language is replete with ready images to help us speak of the container view of memory and the mind. Finding simple metaphors for the schema paradigm, on the other hand, is not as easy. Retaining states, preserving dispositions, actualizing potentials, reconstructing configurations, allowing capacities to emerge, are all phrases that aptly convey the alternative, schema viewpoint. Still, they have nowhere near the evocative power of the imagery aroused by the container idea. Somehow it is hard for us to think of the mind and memory in different terms.

Cognitive science and the philosophy of mind are not alone in granting a special place to the container metaphor. In other areas of thought, container views persist in the face of challenges that have been accumulating for several generations. The notion of space presents a case I am particularly familiar with, coming as I do from the discipline of geography. The space of traditional Newtonian mechanics is a container space, inert and indifferent to the existence and trajectories of the bodies inside it. Things are in space, just as oranges are in a box or fish are in water. This is the notion of "absolute" space. Yet the mathematicians Gauss and Riemann almost a century ago, and later Einstein, showed that matter and process don't just lie "in" space, but help constitute it: Space is thus "relative," its structure and properties being intimately linked with the enfolding of particular phenomena. In more recent years, the absolute space/relative space theme was picked up by human geographers and other social scientists, who, for once, seem to have reached a consensus on something: Space in the human realm is not a container of human activity; space is both a determinant and a product of socioeconomic and cultural processes and relations (see Gregory and Urry 1985). This hard-won insight seems, however, to have been lost on Geographic Information Systems (GIS). This is the new computer-based technology for the analysis and manipulation of spatially referenced data which some think is about to revolutionize the way empirical social science research is done. Despite its considerable technical sophistication, GIS is taking us back to a container view of space that seems to come straight out of the pages of Newton, and every phenomenon of interest is formally defined as an "object" within that neutral, absolute space (see Couclelis 1991).

More examples readily come to mind. Set theory, as we well know, is the basis of all mathematics. But how do we understand sets if not as containers of elements? Should one have doubts about this, think of the new term coined to designate a set of non-unique elements: it is called a "bag." This interpretation of sets in terms of container and contents is not the only logically possible one, as Nelson Goodman (1951) tried to show with his "calculus of individuals." And finally, what view is implied in phrases such as "things in the world" or even "the furniture of the world," routinely found in philosophical writings?

What comes out of these examples is the pervasiveness and persistence of the container metaphor, an issue much more general than the question of its adequacy, or inadequacy, in any particular instance. It seems that our intuitive understanding of some of the most fundamental entities—the mind and memory, space, the most basic concept in mathematics, the world itself—is in terms of the duality between content and container. In our theorizing, we are comfortable with notions such as organization, structure, process, operation, law, as long as they apply to operands or contents against the neutral backcloth of an unchanging container. But try to blur the line between the two—mention Gestalt, holism, emergence, context dependence, or, for that matter, schema—and watch for the embarrassed glances around the room.

Could so many be wrong about so many things? Paradoxically, an explanation of the power of container metaphors comes from a theory of cognition on the same side of the fence as the schema paradigm under discussion. From the perspective of cognitive linguistics, George Lakoff and Mark Johnson (1980) have argued forcibly that the container metaphor is an expression of one of a number of fundamental "image schemas" shared by all members of the human race, rooted in our direct physical experience with the material world, and in the very make-up of our bodies. This and a handful of other basic image schemas (such as up-down, source-path-destination, more-is-up, and so on), derive from our interaction with the material-cultural world we grow in, are at the basis of how we categorize the things around us, extend well into the most abstract forms of thought, and pervade language with the explicit or insidious metaphors that these authors have studied. If this line of thought is more or less correct, it is no wonder that container views of the mind, of memory, and of so many other things are difficult to avoid. But psychological power is not epistemological truth, and the search is on for other models of cognition and knowledge.

An increasingly popular interpretation of the schema paradigm of mind and memory is based on the work of the "connectionist" school of thought in cognitive and computer science. Systems programmed along connectionist principles can recognize patterns, learn from examples, make inferences about missing data, and generalize from the known to the unknown, exhibiting capacities thus far attributed exclusively to human minds. Here, too, memories of patterns and correct responses to particular stimuli are states of activation in a neural network rather than items of information tucked away somewhere; here, too, systems "remember" by re-generating states of awareness they have retained rather than by retrieving facts from a memory warehouse; here, too, learning is the development of a capacity to distinguish and respond correctly to new stimuli rather than the addition of new facts to a pre-existing store of knowledge (see McClelland and Rumelhart 1986). Popular expositions of that work, such as in Heinz Pagels's (1988) book *The Dreams of Reason*, have captured the public imagination. But in psychology and cognitive science, the connectionist view remains very much at odds with the mainstream, information-processing paradigm, which views knowledge as made up of items of information stored in memory, and thus represents the scientific formulation of the container perspective on cognition.

Still, some believe that even the connectionist view is not yet good enough. A most interesting line of critique comes from evolutionary biology (see Reeke and Edelman 1988; Rosenfield 1988). It questions, among other things, the assumption underlying connectionist as well as information-processing views of memory, that minds respond to information preexisting out-there. There is no conceivable neurobiological mechanism, so the argument goes, that could prepare an organism to recognize and distinguish among the potentially infinite variety of unique situations it might encounter. Nor is there any *a priori* way to group these situations into more amenable numbers of categories, because such groupings can again be made in an infinite number of different ways. The principles of evolution and selection suggest that organisms must construct for themselves, both at the phylogenetic and the ontogenetic level, the classifications and categories most appropriate for their own survival. Thus, it is the experience of an organism—both as an individual and as a member of a species which evolution has endowed with the disposition to recognize what is most relevant to its survival—that determines how the mindless clutter of the outside world is to be carved up into meaningful categories of entities and situations. There is ample neurological evidence to support this view. In humans, neural connections in the brain continue forming for several months after birth, in pace with the child's development of the ability to explore and recognize the most relevant things and properties of the world around it. While the neural networks capable of retaining these most basic distinctions appear to be formed early on, the strengths of the neural connections can be shown to change throughout a lifetime of experience. This argument from biology rejoins the insight of Eleanor Rosch (1975) in psychology, later also persuasively argued, from a linguistics standpoint, by George Lakoff (1987) in his much discussed book *Women, Fire, and Dangerous Things*. Categorization, perhaps the most fundamental operation of thought, is the result of (rather than the prerequisite for) the embodied person's growing up functional and conscious in the world of experience.

The argument also brings to mind a view much maligned in mainstream information-processing cognitive science—the view behind James Gibson's (1979) "affordances," Don Norman's (1988) *Psychology of Everyday Things*, Humberto Maturana's notion of "structural coupling" (see Winograd and Flores 1987), and Jon Barwise and John Perry's (1983) definition of "situations." In a nutshell, the idea is the following: Information, out of which knowledge is built, is neither "inside" the organism nor in the things out-there, waiting to be picked up; rather, it is in the active relationship between organism and world, as the former strives to survive in an ever changing environment, to adapt, and to thrive.

These insights—from areas as diverse as cognitive science, computer science, neurobiology, philosophy, and linguistics—lend strong support to the schema paradigm of personal knowledge. At the same time, they cast doubts on the view of scientific knowledge as a body of facts about the world that somehow reflects, however provisionally and imperfectly, how reality is constituted. The bipolar metaphor of Thing vs. Representation implicit in that view presupposes a pairing of corresponding *elements*, of known facts on the one hand and pieces of reality on the other, which is ill compatible with the notion of information as active *relationship* between world and mind.

Shadows on the walls of a cave, reflections, projections, partial views, sketches, maps: partial, flawed, biased, impoverished, oversimplified, imperfect, clumsy, distorted representations of "Real Things Out There." This kind of imagery is a vital part of our Greek intellectual inheritance and has been at the basis of all "spectator" epistemologies—to use Richard Rorty's (1979) phrase—that have constituted mainstream thinking on the problem of knowledge for the past three thousand years. What all such epistemologies have in common is the assumption that knowledge involves *representations* of things existing out-there. The concessions to the limits and imperfections of human understanding are caveats that are well taken but not very significant. The point is that we need to postulate a mechanical one-to-one correspondence between the contents of knowledge and the contents of the world, even though we may not know, or not trust, the rules of that transformation.

The question then becomes the following: How does one get away from a representational view of scientific knowledge without falling into the trap of denying the existence of a reality independent of the human mind? The schema paradigm appears to offer a plausible working answer to the question of knowledge in the individual. How could it be extended to cover natural and social science as well?

To begin tackling this question, we need to go back to the basic insight from the evolutionary schema view I mentioned earlier. Organisms develop the capacity to re-cognize, re-present, and re-create states of awareness and forms of behavior appropriate for their particular kind of relationship with the world. Thus, the existence of an external world is not in question. But the organisms carve out that world into categories, relations, events, and situations "as they see fit," obeying the principles of selection and evolutionary advantage.

This leads to an epistemology that is realist as to the existence of "something" out there in the world, but is idealist as to the question of how that something may, in fact, be structured, organized, put together, or working. I hasten to add that this idea is not new. Decades ago, several of the most distinguished scientists of our time came to similar conclusions. Hertz, Einstein, Poincaré, Eddington, Heisenberg, Planck, Schrödinger (to name only a few) have all thought and written about the problem of representation in physical theory, and the tentative answers they were able to give are very far removed from traditional "spectator" interpretations of knowledge (see, for example, Sir Arthur Eddington's *Philosophy of Physical Science* [1958]).

The question of what theories and models really represent is even more urgent in the context of the social sciences. This is because of the intrinsic inability of the latter to resort to instrumentalist, operationalist, and ultimately circular definitions of their object of study in the way the physical scientists seem to have done. For what seems to emerge from most conceptual analyses in modern theoretical physics is a view of the *intelligible* universe as a largely man-made, contingent construct, a world that owes its reality as much to some formless heap of "something" that is indeed out-there as to the properties of the theoretical languages and the conventions of measurement and observation that we humans use. But, while the physical scientist can say, "Physical knowledge . . . has the form of a description of a world. *We define* the physical universe to be the world so described" (Eddington 1958, 3), the social scientist cannot just substitute "social" for "physical" and leave it at that. That circular conception of the physical universe, and the ensuing logical closure of the corresponding system of knowledge, grants the theoretical constructs within that system an almost complete autonomy vis-à-vis factors that are by definition external. Such detachment is clearly extremely problematic in social science where theoretical constructs must, as in all science, be defined and related so as to fit the phenomena under study but also, *at the same time, be acceptable to the very entities these theoretical constructs are about*. To make this point a little more concrete, let us consider some of the basic categories dealt with in social science: society, culture, mind, human life, economy, class, power, social relations, cognition, consciousness, institutions, the state. These "unobservables" of social science differ from their natural science counterparts in at least one crucial respect—in that, because they are defined implicitly in social and linguistic practices and accompanying frames of thinking, they are the creations of all people at all times, and they do not allow themselves to be defined by any one observer-scientist at any one time. It may perhaps be said that the only significant distinction between the physical and the human world is that the human world is self-defining, whereas the physical world (the intelligible, structured universe we call the physical world) is, to a large extent, the result of the observer's definition (Couclelis 1983).

A last issue I will raise, before others raise it for me, is whether there is room for Truth in such a picture of scientific knowledge. I would like to refer once again to Arbib and Hesse's (1986) *Construction of Reality*, as they already said there pretty much everything I tried to express in these pages. The different insights I painstakingly gathered from a wide literature look like conclusions falling out of their own ambitious theory of schemas. Likewise, their conception of truth is the pragmatist one to which I am led by my own arguments: Truth is defined not in *essence* but in *use*.

What this implies is that, in the case of scientific theories, truth is the same as old-fashioned predictive success. In the case of schemas "representing reality" in some less rigorous manner, it means the generation of attitudes, expectations, and actions that adequately anticipate eventual outcomes. This pragmatic criterion of truth resolves the binary opposition between idealism and realism. There must exist a

204   *Helen Couclelis*

real world out there to provide the proof of the pudding at the moment when expectation meets outcome; and yet our conceptions and theories about that world need not themselves be reflections of how reality is *really* constituted. The world is only knowable through its manifestations: All else may be nothing but metaphor and myth.

In this view, then, the search for truth is the search for the development of *appropriate schemas*. These are the schemas which "make sense" because they cohere with our accumulated experience of the world, which are meaningful because they elicit dispositions and actions leading to pragmatically successful outcomes, and which are intellectually fruitful because they help connect together disparate pieces of the broader network of meanings, thus leading to ever more appropriate, though ever shifting, truths (Couclelis 1988).

Adopting such an informal, unrigorous view of truth will make it easier for us to accept that the structure of the world, though not its existence, may be the product of our evolutionary imagination. It may also lead us to look into some of the alternative, ascientific, arational, subjective accounts of the world as valid complements to the clear, cool, detached, powerful, though necessarily bounded view provided by science. It is strange that social scientists in particular should be so afraid to acknowledge the constitutive role of human thought in the shaping of that human world they strive to study. Ironically, it is a cosmologist, Brandon Carter, a "real" scientist working in the area of physics most remote from the world of human affairs, who expressed the most anthropocentric view of the world I have come across: "*Cogito, ergo mundus talis est*" (I think, therefore the world is as it is).

References

Arbib, M., and M. Hesse. 1986. *The Construction of Reality*. Cambridge: Cambridge University Press.

Banerjee, S. 1986. "Reproduction of Social Structures: An Artificial Intelligence Model." *Journal of Conflict Resolution* 30(2): 221-52.

Barwise, J., and J. Perry. 1983. *Situations and Attitudes*. Cambridge: MIT Press.

Casson, R. W. 1983. "Schemata in Cognitive Anthropology." *Annual Review of Anthropology* 12: 429-62.

Couclelis, H. 1983. "Some Second Thoughts about Theory in the Social Sciences." *Geographical Analysis* 15(1): 28-33.

———. 1988. "The Truth Seekers: Geographers in Search of the Human World." In *A Ground for Common Search*, ed. R. G. Golledge, H. Couclelis, and P. Gould. Santa Barbara: Santa Barbara Geographical Press.

———. 1991. "Requirements for Planning-Relevant GIS: A Spatial Perspective." *Papers in Regional Science* 70(1): 9-19.

Eddington, A. 1958. *The Philosophy of Physical Science*. Ann Arbor: University of Michigan Press.

Genesereth, M. R., and N. J. Nilsson. 1987. *Logical Foundations of Artificial Intelligence*. Palo Alto, CA: Morgan Kaufmann.

Gibson, J. J. 1979. *The Ecological Approach to Visual Perception*. Boston: Houghton Mifflin.

Goodman, N. 1951. *The Structure of Appearance*. Cambridge: Harvard University Press.

Gregory, D., and J. Urry. 1985. *Social Relations and Spatial Structure*. London: Macmillan.

Lakoff, G. 1987. *Women, Fire, and Dangerous Things: What Categories Reveal about the Mind*. Chicago: Chicago University Press.

Lakoff, G., and M. Johnson. 1980. *Metaphors We Live By*. Chicago: Chicago University Press.

McClelland, J. L., and D. E. Rumelhart. 1986. *Parallel Distributed Processing: Explorations into the Micro-Structure of Cognition*. 2 vols. Cambridge: MIT Press.

Norman, D. A. 1988. *The Psychology of Everyday Things*. New York: Basic Books.

Piaget, J. 1954. *The Construction of Reality in the Child*. New York: Basic Books.

Polanyi, M. 1958. *Personal Knowledge*. London: Routledge & Kegan Paul.

Popper, K. 1972. *Objective Knowledge: An Evolutionary Approach*. Oxford: Clarendon Press.

Reeke, G. N., and G. M. Edelman. 1988. "Real Brains and Artificial Intelligence." *Daedalus* 117(1): 143-74.

Rorty, R. 1979. *Philosophy and the Mirror of Nature*. Princeton: Princeton University Press.

Rosenfield, I. 1988. *The Invention of Memory: A New View of the Brain*. New York: Basic Books.

Rosch, E. 1975. "Cognitive Representations of Semantic Categories." *Journal of Experimental Psychology: General* 104: 192-233.

Sowa, J. F. 1984. *Conceptual Structures: Information Processing in Mind and Machine*. Reading, MA: Addison-Wesley.

Winograd, T., and F. Flores. 1977. *Understanding Computers and Cognition*. Reading, MA: Addison-Wesley.

11

The Schema Theory of Minds:
Implications for the Social Sciences[1]

Michael A. Arbib

1. Schema Theory as Cognitive Science

Elsewhere, I have developed the *schema* as the unit for an analysis of cognition rooted in brain research and computer science (Arbib 1992),[2] with emphasis on a theory of "schemas in the head," seeking to understand how perception, action, and language may be mediated in terms of interacting schemas (Arbib 1989). Where conventional computers store data passively, to be retrieved and processed by some central processing unit, schema theory explains behavior in terms of the interaction of many concurrent activities for recognition of different objects, and the planning and control of different activities. Given a schema that represents generic knowledge about some object, we may need several active *instances* of the schema to subserve our perception of a variety of such objects. The use, representation, and recall of knowledge is mediated through the activity of a network of interacting schema instances which, between them, provide processes for going from a particular situation and a particular structure of goals and tasks to a suitable course of action (which may be covert—such activity may involve self-modification and self-organization).

There is an everyday reality of persons and things. If you cut yourself, you bleed. If you drop a kettle, boiling water may scald you. How can we come to know this reality? Schema theory answers that our minds comprise a richly interconnected network of schemas. As we act, we perceive; as we perceive, so we act. Perception is not passive, like a photograph. Rather, it is active, as our current schemas determine what we take from the environment. Looking for someone as we walk down the street, we may recognize another friend; seeking a taxi, we may pass the same friend, not recognizing her. An assemblage of some of the perceptual schemas represents our current situation; planning then yields an assemblage (coordinated control program) of motor schemas which guide our actions.

1.1 Schemas and the Brain

In much of my work, I study how these schemas may be distributed across the brain or implemented in neural networks. When we study the brain, we probe its physiology, anatomy, and neurochemistry, with some questions in mind. Believing that a part of the brain is involved in vision, we might flash visual stimuli at an animal, use microelectrodes to measure activity of neurons in that part of the brain, and try to find correlations between stimulus and response. However, the brain is not one great, uniform neural network. The cerebellum is different from the hippocampus. The visual cortex is different from the motor cortex. That anatomical specialization can be linked to functional specialization. My claim is that both natural and artificial intelligence are to be understood in terms of networks of subsystems *cooperating* and *competing* to solve some overall problem. (This may also read as an analogy with social processes.) We need a vocabulary in which to express these interactions, and so, over the years, I have developed a two-level methodology of modeling, complementing neural networks with schemas which describe basic subcomponents of some overall computation. I will give one example from my study of *Rana computatrix* (Latin for "the frog that computes"), an evolving model of visuomotor coordination in frog and toad. Hypotheses about how schemas are played out over one or more regions of the brain are constrained by lesion data showing how the behavior of animals changes when one or more brain regions are missing. For example, toads snap at small moving objects and jump away from large moving objects. Thus, our first model of the toad brain at the level of schemas might look something like figure 1a. One perceptual schema recognizes small moving objects, while another recognizes large moving objects. The first schema activates a motor schema for approaching the prey; the latter activates a motor schema for avoiding the enemy.

Lesion experiments can put such a model to the test. It was thought that perhaps a brain region called the pretectum was the locus for recognizing large moving objects, with small moving objects recognized by the tectum. The model of figure 1a would then predict that an animal with lesioned pretectum would be unresponsive to large objects but would respond normally to small objects. However, Peter Ewert lesioned pretectum and discovered that the pretectum-lesioned toad will approach any moving object at all, and does not exhibit avoidance behavior. This leads to the new schema model of figure 1b. The perceptual schema in the pretectum does recognize large moving objects, but the tectum contains a schema not for recognizing small moving objects but for recognizing any moving object. We then add that activity of the pretectal schema not only triggers the avoid motor schema but also inhibits approach. This new schema model does fit the lesion data, since removal of the pretectum removes inhibition, and so the animal will now approach any moving object.

Is it the real toad that has schemas in it or just the artificial toad-models? My claim is that schemas are as real as any theoretical entity, such as gravity and electrons. But just as physical theory has evolved over the years so that our notion of what is real changes accordingly, so, too, will our theory of schemas as meaningful units of functional analysis change over the years. What makes this more than a game of "artificial realities" is that our scientific concepts evolve under the pressure of the *pragmatic criterion* in which models expressed in theory-language are brought as far as possible into a harmonious whole with observations expressed in observation-language (Hesse 1980). Both these languages may evolve in the process. The brain is as real at the level of interacting schemas and brain regions as it is in terms of the fine details of interacting neural networks.

1.2 Schemas and Learning

A schema—as a unit of interaction with, or representation of, the world—is partial and approximate. It provides us not only with abilities for recognition and guides to action, but also with expectations about what will happen. These may be wrong. We sometimes learn from our mistakes. Our schemas, and their connections within the schema network, change. Jean Piaget gives us some insight into these processes of schema change. He traced the cognitive development of the child, starting from basic sensorimotor schemas, through stages of increasing abstraction that lead to language and logic, to schemas for abstract thought. Piaget talks both of *assimilation*, the ability to make sense of a situation in terms of the current stocks of schemas, and of *accommodation*, the way in which this stock may change over time as expectations based on assimilation to current schemas are not met.

Moreover, there is no single set of schemas imposed upon all persons in a uniform fashion. Even young children have distinct personalities. Each of us has very different life experiences on the basis of which his schemas change over time. Each of us has his knowledge embedded within a different schema network. Thus, each of us has constructed a

FIGURE 1

(a) The "naive" schema program for the toad's snapping and avoidance
behavior, and *(b)* the schema program revised in light of data
on the effect of lesioning the pretectum.

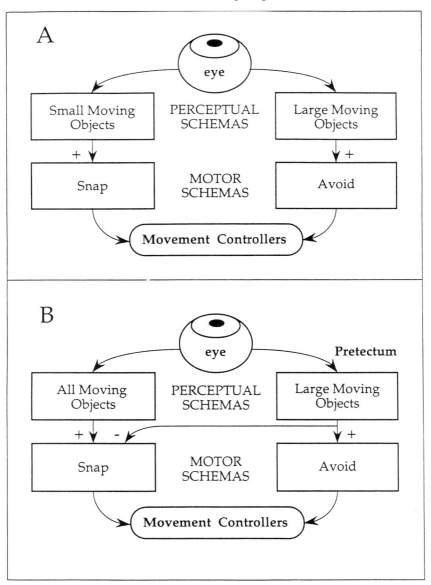

different worldview which each of us takes for reality. This observation will be very important when we try to reconcile the schemas of individual and society.

Having spoken of Piaget, let me offer as another sample of schema theory what might be called a computational neo-Piagetian approach to the acquisition of language in the two-year-old child. Chomsky's view of language acquisition is that the child's innate schemas incorporate a Universal Grammar, including such general categories as noun and verb, and certain constraints on the relationships between these categories. By contrast, Jane Hill (cf. Arbib and Hill 1988) looked at how a two-year-old child acquires language to show how the dynamics of the child's schemas could represent its ability to use language. The child assimilates what it hears to produce its response, and yet in the process accommodates, schemas changing so that the child's language matures. Hill provided a computer model embodying a causal explanation consistent with the general pattern of Piaget's findings but which gives more insight into underlying mechanisms.

This model of language acquisition in a two-year-old child starts not from innate syntactic constraints but from the observation that the child wants to communicate and likes to repeat sentences. However—and this accords well with our schema-theoretic basis—when the child "repeats" a sentence, she does not repeat the sentence word for word. Nor does the child omit words at random. To focus her study, Hill looked at a two-year-old responding to adult sentences either with a simple paraphrase or with a simple response. The child was studied once a week for nine weeks to provide a specific database to balance general findings in the literature. The child changed every week, and so the model had to be one of microchanges, in the sense that every sentence could possibly change the child's internal structures.

We know that certain portions of the brain have to be intact for a person to have language and that language is degraded in specific ways by removing certain portions of the brain. What is at issue is to determine what it is that the initial structure of the brain gives to the child. Hill's model indicates that innate patterns of schema change can yield an increasing richness of language without building upon language universals. The model has basic schemas for words, basic schemas for concepts, and basic templates which provided a grammar marked by a richness of simple patterns the child had already broken out of experience, rather than the grand general rules that we would find in the grammarian's description of adult language. And what was built in were not grammatical rules but, rather, processes whereby the child could form word classes and try to match incoming words to existing templates, using those templates to generate the response.

For a brief example of the way in which studies of this kind can give us insights, consider that, for a while, the child only produces two-word utterances. One simple way of accounting for this might be to have some notion of limited complexity which increases as the child matures. With such a model, one might next expect to see three-word utterances, but, in fact, what comes next, though only for a week, is a predominance of four-word utterances which seem to be concatenations of two-word utterances such as "second ball, green ball." By the next week, instead of saying "second ball, green ball," the child was saying "second green ball." Hill's model explains this by invoking a process that collapses four-word utterances down to three-word utterances by deleting the first occurrence of a repeated word. This hypothesis would explain the earlier findings of Matthei (1979). (In fact, the example "second ball, green ball" was not something that Jane Hill's subject had said, but was chosen from Matthei's study.) To probe the child's understanding, Matthei would place in front of the child a row of red and green balls and ask the child to pick out the second green ball. The young child looks to see if the second ball is green, and is frustrated if it isn't! It may even rearrange the balls so that the second ball is green. It will pick up the second ball if it is also a green ball. This seems to accord with Hill's hypothesis that, for the young child, the semantics of "second green ball" is really given by the flat concatenation of "second ball" and "green ball" rather than the hierarchical qualification of "green ball" by "second."

2. Schema Theory as Social Science

To bridge from such examples of "schemas in the head" to our concern with social science, note that the language experienced by the young child is a socially constructed reality. The key integrative concept in linking minds to society (akin to Durkheim's notion of a "collective representation") is that of a social schema (Arbib and Hesse 1986). In the theory of "schemas in the head," we may distinguish the *external* view of a schema (some characteristic family of overt behaviors exhibited by the individual) from an *internal* view (information-processing or brain mechanisms). However, consider the schema (itself a vast network of smaller schemas representing knowledge of words, idioms, grammar, *mots justes*, pun generators, etc.) for the English language. From an individualistic viewpoint, we may ask what patterns of behavior are evidence of a command of English and then probe inward for the underlying cognitive skills or brain mechanisms. But from a social point of view, a child can learn English by interacting with many speakers of the language—despite an immense diversity in individual accent, vocabulary, and syntax. We explain this by saying that the patterns of English-speaking behavior of many individuals have a coherence (we may temper this by invoking Wittgenstein's notion of a "family resemblance") which constitutes a reality, a *social schema*, which may shape the development of the child and the behavior of the individual in the society as strongly as do the externalities of the physical world.

How does the child extract patterns from the utterances of a community of mutually intelligible speakers to form the schemas which interiorize his own version of the language? Hill's model gives us something of an answer by showing how the child may form internal schemas which come to form a network which, in turn, enables it to function effectively in an English-speaking community. In short, we may think of language both as a social reality external to the individual and as an "idiolect" internalized in the schemas of each individual, so that the language community is constituted by the schemas of many individuals. A similar dichotomy may be seen in approaches to the study of society and ideology. A top-down, or *structuralist*, view conceives the relations of the members of society as determined by the roles (or the class) they occupy and the forces impinging on such roles at the level of social structures. In contrast, a bottom-up, or *interpretive*, view stresses the schemas that an individual has constructed in internalizing social roles, focusing on the intersubjective dimension acquired through growing up with others in a particular society.

Schema theory offers an interpretive view of the individual in society. However, individual schemas may cohere into an external social schema which provides a psychically tangible reality external to each individual in that society. As individuals accommodate to communal patterns, they provide part of the coherent context for others, but the uniqueness of both genetic endowment and individual experience ensures that no two members of a society have precisely the same individual schemas in their heads, and so the commonality of social behaviors still leaves space for discord. The individual can shape schemas that not only enable the playing of various roles but also provide a critique that may emerge in overt dissent. The attainment of coherent internalizations of social schemas may entail that people share understandings of social relationships and that their behavior may be conditioned by their appreciation of what social roles are open to them, but that does *not* entail identical patterns of behavior in different individuals.

We have now discussed the four levels of neurons, schemas, persons, and societies—the neural, cognitive, individual, and social levels. But perhaps we should, following the structure of the last section, make a more careful labeling of the levels as neurons, cognitive schemas, persons, and social schemas. Even this is a little sloppy: There is much about a person that depends upon interaction of brain and body that is not cognitive (just consider hormones and emotions), and society is a function of geography and economic infrastructure as much as of the cognitive reality that it presents to its members. But what I want to emphasize here is that I have made two distinct claims: (1) There is an existing schema theory for cognition; and (2) we begin to see how to extend this to provide a schema theory for social science.

People have a very special ability, namely, to come to know about all four levels—what might grandly be called "interlevel" coupling. They can acquire, adapt, or create networks of schemas which represent neurons and networks of schemas which represent societies—and communicate about them through the medium of language. I thus view social science as the process of socially structured schema formation whose subject is itself societies, their components, and the interactions of persons within and against the social matrix. By this last qualification, I mean two things: first, that eating is not part of social science if studied from a physiological perspective, but is such if we study, say, the effect of social custom on patterns of dining or seek to develop policy to combat starvation; second, that social science must be as interested in what leads to revolt as in the social patterns that create conformity to a social order (and we each live within many social orders).

3. Social Action and the
Decompartmentalization of the Social Sciences

"Action" plays a key role in cognitive organization—both in the "internal action" within a brain and in the interaction of the members of a society. It may be expressed in physical motion or symbolic choice behavior. Given one's perception of one's goal and one's current situation (no matter how distorted one's view of it), one has the ability to plan a course of action that will help achieve that goal. And given the plan, one may evaluate its cost and its chance of success—though the flames of passion may conquer the cool rational weighing of evidence— to commit oneself to a course of action. This whole process—of setting goals, forming plans, and weighing alternatives—leads to *social action* if the goal is to change society. In such a process, what is to distinguish social science from politics or from individual revolt? For background, consider the type of action—it is called "technology"—that flows from the physical sciences. The physical scientist seeks to isolate key variables and determine lawful relations between them to satisfy the pragmatic criterion of prediction and control—not only predicting how certain variables co-vary in the laboratory but also building technological systems. Such systems, while too complicated for full scientific analysis, may still be designed to achieve physical performances that might hitherto have appeared impossible: Think of jet flight, electronic computers, or genetic engineering, for just three examples. The phenomenal expansion in the power of computers—and we are truly just at the beginning—means that, increasingly, these analyses can be run on the computer. Scientific computation is enabling the physical sciences to break the confines of systems with restricted numbers of variables to handle hundreds of thousands of variables. This may provide the tools that social science needs to increasingly meet pragmatic criteria of its own.

I will sketch a schema-theoretic account of how an individual engages in "unscientific" social action so that I may then discuss what the scientific input to such action might look like. We grow up in a society, accommodating our schemas to assimilate social norms and standards of language and logic in a richly interconnected network that has no prespecified boundaries. Thus, the grounds for a critique of society may not (at least initially) even be perceptible in terms of the internal schemas which have accommodated the regnant social schemas of the community. Yet the very dynamics of individual schema change may lead to discord between an individual's schemas and the social schemas around her, and the result may, indeed, be a rejection of those social schemas. But the apparent utility of such changed schemas to an individual (whether or not they can be consciously articulated) is no guarantee of their wider acceptance. A social critique elaborated by a small group of individuals often becomes repressed or remains restricted to discussions within that small group. Only in exceptional cases will a critique spread to the point of effecting an enduring restructuring of society.

There is, of course, a vast literature on reformist and revolutionary movements in society. Here let me simply note the relevance of the vocabulary of qualitative analysis of dynamical systems. In most states of a system, a small change—corresponding to the action of any one individual in a social system—will only result in a small effect. But there is a relatively small set of situations in which a small change can be magnified to cause the overall system to effect a phase transition from one overall mode of behavior to a qualitatively differently one. Such a change may be referred to as a "bifurcation" from one regime to another. In the same way, only in certain situations may an individual critique become widely accepted, irrespective of its intrinsic merits— even though it is individual beliefs that in their cooperativity constitute the regnant social schemas.

I am now ready to return to the question of how policy making can be made more scientific, in the strict sense of science which (according to the *Oxford English Dictionary*) is concerned "with observed facts systematically classified and more or less colligated by being brought under general laws and which includes trustworthy methods for the discovery of new truth within its own domain." This work has two components.

1. There is the task of data gathering, of developing and applying reliable methods for the discovery of new truth, and there is the task of theory building, systematically classifying the facts, or colligating them by bringing them together under general laws. Such studies will usually be specialized, readable only by fellow experts in some small domain of social science, and applicable only by specially trained professionals. This, in turn, requires the training of other experts who can comprehend, evaluate, and apply this material.

2. But expertise for experts is not enough. The social scientist must not only practice his or her limited expertise but also learn how to set forth its implications in a form that the general public can assimilate to the necessary extent. To see what I mean by "to the necessary extent," we may return to the issue of technology and the physical sciences. A generally informed person will know little of combustion physics, but will want to understand something of how different combinations of engine, fuel, and emission controls can affect both fuel economy and pollution.

To provide a specific sense of the challenges for social sciences here and now, I offer a "snapshot" from the first September 1989 issue of *The Economist*, chosen because it contains a survey of the environment which shows that, across the world, the environment is becoming hot politics and suggests that sensible "green" policies will require people, governments, and companies to make immense changes. It notes that green policies do not always win votes, and suggests that economists can help governments set green priorities—a case study for the integration of economics and political science. A discussion of how to make the market clean up and of why earth and water are not free shows how economics must be integrated with a detailed understanding of geography, biology, and engineering. An article on the drug problem shows how our evaluation of social and political alternatives can come into conflict with accepted moral standards. It leads me to ponder how we can couch the political agenda in terms of social experiments instead of moral absolutes.

Clearly, we need to get the benefits of disciplinary concentration without losing the empathic understanding of what other people do, yet achieve this without lapsing into the complete relativism of "any approach goes" (e.g., we learned to reject phrenology and, in many cases, proceeded from creationism to evolutionary theory). We see here the same issue of mutual reduction that we saw in integrating the levels required to chart the human mind—neural, cognitive, individual, and social—and in integrating the schemas in an individual's head. Each level or schema or social science is possessed of many important truths, and yet is also incomplete. Their competition and cooperation yields not a total view of reality but partial views which can be continually adapted to meet the criteria (themselves evolving) of understanding, prediction, and control.

Notes

1. This paper is a revised version of a talk for the segment "Epistemology and Social Theory" of the conference on "The Notion of Knowing in the Social Sciences," University of Southern California, Los Angeles, 6-7 November 1989. My thanks to Bob Goodman, Walter Fisher, and Dallas Willard for discussions which contributed to the development of this paper.

2. Workers in artificial intelligence use such terms as "frame" and "script" for the basic structures of knowledge representation. However, I prefer not to use these terms, because there is already a rich tradition of psychologists, philosophers, and neurologists trying to analyze the mind using the terminology of schemas.

References

Arbib, M. A. 1989. *The Metaphorical Brain 2: Neural Networks and Beyond*. New York: Wiley-Interscience.

———. 1992. "Schema Theory." In *The Encyclopedia of Artificial Intelligence*, ed. S. Shapiro, 1427-43. New York: Wiley-Interscience.

Arbib, M. A., and M. B. Hesse. 1986. *The Construction of Reality*. Cambridge: Cambridge University Press.

Arbib, M. A., and J. C. Hill. 1988. "Language Acquisition: Schemas Replace Universal Grammar." In *Explaining Language Universals*, ed. J. A. Hawkins, 56-72. Oxford: Basil Blackwell.

Hesse, M. B. 1980. *Revolutions and Reconstructions in the Philosophy of Science*. Bloomington: Indiana University Press.

Matthei, E. 1979. "The Acquisition of Prenominal Modifier Sequences: Stalking the Second Green Ball." Ph.D. diss., University of Massachusetts, Amherst.

Bibliography

Arbib, M. A., and M. Hesse. 1986. *The Construction of Reality*. Cambridge: Cambridge University Press.

Arbib, M. A. 1989. *The Metaphorical Brain 2: Neural Networks and Beyond*. New York: Wiley-Interscience.

Argyris, C. 1980. *The Inner Contradictions of Rigorous Research*. New York: Academic Press.

Argyris, C., R. Putnam, and D. McLain Smith. 1985. *Action Science*. San Francisco: Jossey-Bass.

Argyris, C., and D. A. Schon. 1974. *Theory in Practice: Increasing Professional Effectiveness*. San Francisco: Jossey-Bass.

———. 1978. *Organizational Learning*. Reading, MA: Addison Wesley.

Aristotle. 1947. *Introduction to Aristotle*. 2nd ed. Trans. R. McKeon. Chicago: University of Chicago Press.

Arnold, M. B. 1984. *Memory and the Brain*. Hillsdale, NJ: Lawrence Erlbaum.

Ashmore, M. 1989. *The Reflexive Thesis: Writing Sociology of Scientific Knowledge*. Chicago: University of Chicago Press.

Austin, J. L. 1962. *How to do Things with Words*. New York: Oxford University Press.

Bacon, F. 1960. *The New Organon*. Indianapolis: Bobbs-Merrill.

———. 1965. *A Selection of His Works*. Indianapolis: Bobbs-Merrill.

Balbus, I. D. 1982. *Marxism and Domination*. Princeton: Princeton University Press.

Barrett, W. 1979. *The Illusion of Technique: A Search for Meaning in a Technological Civilization*. Garden City, NY: Anchor Books.

Bartlett, F. C. 1932. *Remembering*. Cambridge: Cambridge University Press.

Barwise, J., and J. Perry. 1983. *Situations and Attitudes*. Cambridge, MA: MIT Press.

Baynes, K., J. Bohman, and T. McCarthy eds. 1987. *After Philosophy*. Cambridge: MIT Press.

Bazerman, C. 1988. *Shaping Written Knowledge: The Genre and Activity of the Experimental Article in Science.* Madison, WI: University of Wisconsin Press.

Ben-Ze'ev, A. 1993. *The Perceptual System: A Philosophical and Psychological Perspective.* New York: Peter Lang.

Bennett, W. L. and M. S. Feldman. 1981. *Reconstructing Reality in the Courtroom: Justice and Judgment in American Culture.* New Brunswick, NJ: Rutgers University Press.

Bloor, D. 1983. *Wittgenstein: A Social Theory of Knowledge.* New York: Columbia University Press.

————. 1991. *Knowledge and Social Imagery.* Chicago: University of Chicago Press.

Bock, G. and S. James. *Equality and Difference: Gender Dimensions in Political Thought and Morality.* New York: Routledge.

Booth, W. 1974. *Modern Dogma and the Rhetoric of Assent.* Chicago: University of Chicago Press.

Bourdieu, P. 1977. *Outline of a Theory of Practice.* Cambridge: Cambridge University Press.

————. 1980. *Le Sense Pratique.* Paris: Miniut.

Boyd, R. and P. J. Richerson. 1985. *Culture and the Evolutionary Process.* Chicago: University of Chicago Press.

Bronowski, J. 1971. *The Identity of Man.* Garden City, NY: Natural History Press.

————. 1972. *Science and Human Values.* New York: Harper & Row.

Bruner, J. 1983. *In Search of Mind: Essays in Autobiography.* New York: Harper & Row.

————. 1986. *Actual Minds, Possible Worlds.* Cambridge: Harvard University Press.

————. 1990. *Acts of Meaning.* Cambridge: Harvard University Press.

Burchell, G. ed. 1991. *The Foucault Effect: Studies in Governmentality.* Chicago: University of Chicago Press.

Burk, D. M. ed. 1978. *Rhetoric, Philosophy, and Literature: An Exploration.* West Lafayette, IN: Purdue University Press.

Butler, J. 1990. *Gender Trouble: Feminism and the Subversion of Identity.* New York: Routledge.

Campbell, D. T. 1978. "Descriptive Epistemology: Psychological, Sociological, and Evolutionary." In *Methodology and Epistemology for Social Sciences*. Chicago: University of Chicago Press.

Campbell, D. T., and J. C. Stanley. 1963. *Experimental and Quasi-Experimental Designs for Research*. Skokie, IL: Rand McNally.

Carr, D. 1986. *Time, Narrative, and History*. Bloomington, IN: Indiana University Press.

Chodorow, N. 1978. *The Reproduction of Mothering*. Berkeley: University of California Press.

Chomsky, N. 1957. *Syntactic Structures*. The Hague: Mouton.

Cixous, H., and C. Clement. 1986. *The Newly Born Woman*. Minneapolis: University of Minnesota Press.

Clifford, J., and G. E. Marcus. 1986. *Writing Culture: The Poetics and Politics of Ethnography*. Berkeley: University of California Press.

Collins, H. M. 1985. *Changing Order: Replication and Induction in Scientific Practice*. London: Sage.

Collins, P. H. 1990. *The Alchemy of Race and Rights*. Cambridge: Harvard University Press.

Collins, R. 1982. *Sociological Insight: An Introduction to Non-Obvious Sociology*. New York: Oxford University Press.

Coulter, J. 1983. *Rethinking Cognitive Theory*. New York: St. Martin's.

Crapanzano, V. 1980. *Tuhami: Portrait of a Moroccan*. Chicago: University of Chicago Press.

Csikszentmihalyi, M. 1975. *Beyond Boredom and Anxiety*. San Francisco: Jossey-Bass.

———. 1990. *Flow: The Psychology of Optimal Experience*. New York: Harper & Collins.

———. 1993. *The Evolving Self: A Psychology for the Third Millennium*. New York: Harper & Collins.

Csikszentmihalyi, M. and I. Csikszentmihalyi, eds. 1988. *Optimal Experience*. New York: Cambridge University Press.

Danto, A. C. 1985. *Narration and Knowledge*. New York: Columbia University Press.

Davidson, D. 1980. *Essays in Actions and Events*. Oxford: Clarendon Press.

———. 1984. *Inquiries Into Truth and Interpretation*. Oxford: Clarendon Press.

Davies, P. 1984. *Superforce: The Search for a Grand Unified Theory of Nature*. New York: Simon & Schuster.

Dawkins, R. 1976. *The Selfish Gene*. Oxford: Oxford University Press.

———. 1982. *The Extended Phenotype*. Oxford: Oxford University Press.

Deci, E. L., and R. M. Ryan. 1985. *Intrinsic Motivation and Self-Determination in Human Behavior*. New York: Plenum Press.

Dennett, D. C. 1991. *Consciousness Explained*. Boston: Little, Brown.

Derrida, J. 1974. *Of Grammatology*. Baltimore: The John Hopkins University Press.

———. 1978. *Spurs/Eperons*. Chicago: University of Chicago Press.

———. 1981. *Dissemination*. Chicago: University of Chicago Press.

———. 1981. *Positions*. Chicago: University of Chicago Press.

———. 1982. *Margins of Philosophy*. Chicago: University of Chicago Press.

Descartes, R. 1968. *Discourse on Method and Other Writings*. Baltimore: Penguin.

Devereaux, G. 1967. *From Anxiety to Method in the Behavioral Sciences*. The Hague: Mouton.

Dewey, J. 1938. *Logic: The Theory of Inquiry*. New York: Holt, Rinehart & Winston.

———. 1988. *The Quest for Certainty: A Study of the Relation of Knowledge and Action*. In *The Later Works, 1925-1953, Vol. 4: 1929*. Carbondale, IL: Southern Illinois University Press.

Diamond, I. ed. 1983. *Families, Politics, and Public Policy*. New York: Longman.

Dinnerstein, D. 1976. *The Mermaid of the Minotaur*. New York: Harper and Row.

Dollard, J., L. Doob, N. E. Miller, O. H. Mowrer, and R. R. Sears. 1939. *Frustration and Aggression*. New Haven: Yale University Press.

Eddington, A. 1958. *The Philosophy of Physical Science*. Ann Arbor: University of Michigan Press.

Emerson, R. W. 1929. *The Complete Works of Ralph Waldo Emerson*. New York: Wise.

Fabian, J. 1983. *Time and the Other: How Anthropology Makes Its Object*. New York: Columbia University Press.

Feyerabend, P. 1978. *Against Method: Outline of an Anarchist Theory of Knowledge*. London: Verso.

✓ ———. 1988. *Farewell to Reason*. London: Verso.

Finocchiaro, M. A. 1980. *Galileo and the Art of Reasoning: Rhetorical Foundations of Logic and Scientific Method*. Dordrecht, Holland: Reidel.

Fischer, F. 1990. *Technocracy and Politics of Expertise*. Newbury Park, CA: Sage.

✓ Fischer, M. J., and M. Abedi. 1990. *Debating Muslims: Cultural Dialogues in Postmodernity and Tradition*. Madison: University of Wisconsin Press.

Fisher, W. 1987. *Human Communication as Narration: Toward a Philosophy of Reason, Value, and Action*. Colummbia, SC: University of South Carolina Press.

✓ Fiske, D. R. Shweder eds. *Metatheory in Social Science*. Chicago: University of Chicago Press.

✓ Flax, J. 1990. *Thinking Fragments: Psychoanalysis, Feminism, and Postmodernism in the Contemporary West*. Berkeley: University of California Press.

Fleck, L. 1979. *Genesis and the Development of a Scientific Fact*. Chicago: University of Chicago Press.

✓ Fodor, J. 1981. *Representation*. Cambridge: MIT Press.

✓ Foucault, M. 1980. *Power/Knowledge*. New York: Pantheon.

✓ ———. 1988. *Madness and Civilization: A History of Insanity in the Age of Reason*. New York: Vintage Books.

———. 1990. *Politics, Philosophy, Culture*. New York: Routledge.

———. 1991. *The Foucault Effect: Studies in Governmentality*. Chicago: University of Chicago Press.

✓ Fraser, N. 1989. *Unruly Practices: Power, Discourse and Gender in Contemporary Social Theory*. Minneapolis: University of Minnesota Press.

Freud, S. 1959. *Collected Papers*. J. Strachey ed. New York: Basic Books

———. 1960. *The Ego and the Id*. New York: Norton.

✓ Fuller, S. 1988. *Social Epistemology*. Bloomington: Indiana University Press.

———. 1989. *Philosophy of Science and Its Discontents*. Boulder: Westview Press.

Genesereth, M. R., and N. J. Nilsson. 1987. *Logical Foundations of Artificial Intelligence*. Palo Alto, CA: Morgan Kaufmann.

Gerstein, D. et al. 1988. *The Behavioral and Social Sciences: Achievements and Opportunities*. Washington, D.C.: National Academy Press.

✓ Gibson, J. J. 1979. *The Ecological Approach to Visual Perception.* Boston: Houghton Mifflin.

✓ Goffman, E. 1970. *Strategic Interaction.* Oxford.

✓ ———. 1971. *Relations in Public.* New York.

Goodman, N. 1951. *The Structure of Appearance.* Cambridge: Harvard University Press.

✓ ———. 1978. *Ways of Worldmaking.* Indianapolis: Hackett.

✓ Gould, S. J. 1987. *Time's Arrow Time's Cycle: Myth and Metaphor in the Discovery of Geological Time.* Cambridge: Harvard University Press.

Grassi, E. 1980. *Rhetoric as Philosophy: The Humanistic Tradition.* University Park, PA: Pennsylvania State University Press.

Gregory, D., and J. Urry. 1985. *Social Relations and Spatial Structure.* London: Macmillan.

Griffiths, M., and M. Whitford. *Feminist Perspectives in Philosophy.* Bloomington, IN: Indiana University Press.

Gross, A. G. 1990. *The Rhetoric of Science.* Cambridge: Harvard University Press.

✓ Habermas, J. 1972. *Knowledge and Human interest.* Boston: Beacon Press.

———. 1979. *Communication and the Evolution of Society.* Boston: Beacon Press.

———. 1987. *The Philosophical Discourse of Modernity.* Cambridge: MIT Press.

✓ ———. 1989. *The Theory of Communicative Action.* Boston: Beacon Press.

Hampshire, S. 1989. *Innocence and Experience.* Cambridge: Harvard University Press.

✓ Hanson, N. R. 1959. *Patterns of Discovery.* Cambridge: Cambridge University Press.

Harding, Sandra. 1986. *The Science Question in Feminism.* Ithaca, NY: Cornell University Press.

✓ Harre, R., and P. F. Secord. 1972. *The Explanation of Social Behaviour.* Oxford: Basil Blackwell.

✓ Heidegger, M. 1927. *Sein und Zeit.* Tubingen: Niemeyer.

✓ Hennessey, B. A., and T. M. Amabile. 1988. "The Conditions of Creativity." In *The Nature of Creativity.* R. J. Sternberg, ed. New York: Cambridge University Press.

✓ Herzfeld, M. 1987. *Anthropology through the Looking Glass: Critical Ethnography in the Margins of Europe.* Cambridge: Cambridge University Press.

✓ Hesse, M. 1963. *Models and Analogies in Science.* South Bend, IN: University of Notre Dame Press.

✓ ———. *Revolutions and Reconstructions in the Philosophy of Science.* Bloomington: Indiana University Press.

Hill-Collins, P. 1990. *Black Feminist Thought: Knowledge, Consciousness, and the Politics of Empowerment.* New York: Routledge.

Holliday, S. C., and M. J. Chandler. 1986. *Wisdom: Explorations in Adult Competence.* Basel, Switzerland: Karger.

Holton, G. 1973. *Thematic Origins of Modern Science.* Cambridge: Harvard University Press.

Hoover, K. R. 1988. *The Elements of Social Science Thinking.* New York: St. Martin's.

Hull, D. L. 1988. *Science as a Process: An Evolutionary Account of the Social and Conceptual Development of Science.* Chicago: University of Chicago Press.

✓ Irigaray, L. 1985. *Speculum of the Other Woman.* Ithaca, NY: Cornell University Press.

Jagger, A., and S. Bordo. eds. *Gender/Body/Knowledge.* New Brunswick, NJ: Rutgers University Press.

James, L. R., S. A. Mulaik, and J. M. Brett. 1982. *Causal Analysis: Assumptions, Models and Data.* Beverly Hills, CA: Sage.

✓ Jameson, F. R. 1981. *The Political Unconscious: Narrative as a Socially Symbolic Act.* Ithaca, NY: Cornell University Press.

Jardine, A. A. 1985. *Gynesis: Configurations of Woman and Modernity.* Ithaca, NY: Cornell University Press.

Kant, I. 1966. *Critique of Pure Reason.* Garden City, NY: Doubleday.

Kennedy, G. A. 1984. *New Testament Interpretation Through Rhetorical Criticism.* Chapel Hill: University of North Carolina Press.

Klamer, A. 1984. *Conversations With Economists.* Totowa, NJ: Rowman & Allanheld.

Klamer, A., D. N. McCloskey, and R. M. Solow. 1988. *The Consequences of Economic Rhetoric.* Cambridge: Cambridge University Press.

✓ Knorr-Cetina, K. D. 1981. *The Manufacture of Knowledge: An Essay on the Constructivist and Contextual Nature of Science.* Oxford: Pergamon.

Kuhn, T. S. 1962. *The Structure of Scientific Revolutions.* Chicago: University of Chicago Press.

———. 1977. *The Essential Tension.* Chicago: University of Chicago Press.

Lakoff, G. 1987. *Women, Fire, and Dangerous Things: What Categories Reveal About the Mind.* Chicago: University of Chicago Press.

Lakoff, G., and M. Johnson. 1980. *Metaphors We Live By.* Chicago: University of Chicago Press.

Lakotos, I., and A. Musgrave eds. 1970. *Criticism and the Growth of Knowledge.* London: Cambridge University Press.

Landes, J. B. 1988. *Women and the Public Sphere.* Ithaca, NY: Cornell University Press.

Latour, B. 1987. *Science in Action: How to Follow Scientists and Engineers Through Society.* Cambridge: Harvard University Press.

———. 1989. *The Pasterization of France.* Cambridge: Cambridge University Press.

Latour, B. and S. Woolgar. 1986. *Laboratory Life: The Construction of Scientific Facts.* Princeton: Princeton University Press.

Laudan, L. 1984. *Science and Values: The Aims of Science and Their Role in Scientific Debate.* Berkely: University of California Press.

Laudan, T. 1977. *Progress and Its Problems.* Berkeley: University of California Press.

Lepper, M. R., and D. Greene eds. 1978. *The Hidden Costs of Reward: New Perspectives on the Psychology of Human Motivation.* Hillsdale, NJ: Lawrence Erlbaum.

Levi, I. 1965. *Gambling With Truth.* New York: Knopf.

Levison, S. C. 1983. *Pragmatics.* Cambridge: Cambridge University Press.

Lewis, C. I. 1929. *Mind and the World Order.* New York: Dover.

Lindblom, C. E. and D. K. Cohen. 1979. *Useable Knowledge.* New Haven: Yale University Press.

Locke, J. 1959. *An Essay Concerning Human Understanding.* New York: Dover.

———. 1960. *The Second Treatise of Government.* New York: Cambridge University Press.

Lorde, A. 1984. *Sister Outsider.* Trumansburg, NY: Crossing Press.

Lumsden, C. J., and E. O. Wilson. 1981. *Genes, Mind, Culture: The Co-Evolutionary Process.* Cambridge: Harvard University Press.

———. 1983. *Promethean Fire.* Cambridge: Harvard University Press.

Lyotard, J.F . 1984. *The Postmodern Condition: A Report of Knowledge.* Minneapolis: University of Minnesota Press.

McClelland, J. L., and D. E. Rumelhart. 1986. *Parallel Distributed Processing: Explorations Into the Micro-Structure of Cognition.* 2 vols. Cambridge: MIT Press.

McCloskey, D. N. 1985. *The Rhetoric of Economics.* Madison, WI: University of Wisconsin Press.

———. 1990. *If You're So Smart: The Narrative of Economic Expertise.* Chicago: University of Chicago Press.

McKeon, R. 1987. *Rhetoric: Essays in Invention and Discovery.* Woodbridge, CT: Ox Bow Press.

MacCormac, E. R. 1976. *Metaphor and Myth in Science and Religion.* Durham, NC: Duke University Press.

MacIntyre, A. 1981. *After Virtue: A Study in Moral Theory.* Notre Dame, IN: Notre Dame University Press.

Madison, G. B. 1982. *Understanding: A Phenomenological-Pragmatic Analysis.* Westport, CT: Greenwood.

Malcolm, N. 1977. *Memory and Mind.* Ithaca, NY: Cornell University Press.

Marx, K. 1967. *Capital.* New York: International Publishers.

Maslow, A. H. 1968. *Towards a Psychology of Being.* New York: Van Nostrand.

Mead, G. H. 1934. *Mind, Self, and Society.* Chicago: Chicago University Press.

Medawar, P. 1984. *The Limits of Science.* Oxford: Oxford University Press.

Merleau-Ponty, M. 1945. *La Phenomenolgie de la Perception.* Paris: Gaillimard.

Mill, J. S. 1949. *A System of Logic.* London: Longmans, Green.

Mohanty, C. et al. eds. 1991. *Third World Women and the Politics of Feminism.* Bloomington: Indiana University Press.

Nietzsche, F. W. 1960. *The Will to Power in Science, Nature, and Art.* New York: Frederick Publications.

———. 1974. *The Gay Science.* New York: Vintage.

Norman, D. A. 1988. *The Psychology of Everyday Things.* New York: Basic Books.

North, D. C., and R. L. Miller. 1983. *The Economics of Public Issues.* New York: Harper & Collins.

Nussbawm, M. C. 1990. *Love's Knowledge: Essays on Philosophy and Literature.* New York: Oxford University Press.

Okin, S. M. 1989. *Justice, Gender, and the Family.* New York: Basic Books.

Olafson, F. 1979. *The Dialectics of Action.* 2nd ed. Chicago: University of Chicago Press.

Outhwaite, W. 1985. *The Return of Grand Theory in the Human Sciences.* Cambridge: cambridge University Press.

Pagels, H. 1988. *The Dreams of Reason: The Computer and the Rise of the Age of Complexity.* New York: Simon & Schuster.

Parfit, D. 1984. *Reasons and Persons.* Oxford: Oxford University Press.

Pateman, C. 1988. *The Sexual Contract.* Stanford: Stanford University Press.

Peckham, M. 1979. *Explanation and Power: The Control of Human Behavior.* New York: Seabury Pubs.

Perelman, C., and L. Olbrechts-Tyteca. 1969. *The New Rhetoric: A Treatise on Argumentation.* Notre Dame, IN: Notre Dame University Press.

Perry, W. I. 1970. *Forms of Intellectual and Ethical Development in College Years.* New York: Holt, Rinehart, and Wilson.

Piaget, J. 1954. *The Construction of Reality in the Child.* New York: Basic Books.

———. 1971. *Biology and Knowledge.* Edinburgh University Press.

Pickering, A. 1984. *Constructing Quarks: A Sociological History of Particle Physics.* Chicago: University of Chicago Press.

Plato. 1963. *The Collected Dialogues.* eds. E. Hamilton and H. Cairns. Princeton: Princeton University Press.

Polanyi, M. 1958. *Personal Knowledge.* London: Routledge & Kegan Paul.

———. 1962. *Personal Knowledge: Towards a Post-Critical Philosophy.* Chicago: University of Chicago Press.

———. 1967. *The Tacit Dimension.* Garden City, NY: Anchor Books.

Polkinghorne, D. E. 1988. *Narrative Knowing and The Human Sciences.* Albany: State University of New York Press.

Popper, K. 1965. *The Logic of Scientific Discovery.* New York: Harper & Row.

———. 1968. *Conjectures and Refutations.* New York: Harper & Row.

✓ ——— . 1972. *Objective Knowledge: An Evolutionary Approach.* Oxford: Clarendon Press.

Prelli, L. J. 1989. *A Rhetoric of Science: Inventing Scientific Discourse.* Columbia, SC: University of South Carolina Press.

Premack, D. 1986. *Gavagai!* Cambridge: MIT Press.

✓ Putnam, H. 1981. *Reason, Truth, and History.* Cambridge: Cambridge University Press.

✓ Quine, W. V. O. 1958. *From a Logical Point of View.* Cambridge: Harvard University Press.

✓ Rachman, J., and C. West. eds. 1985. *Post-Analytic Philosophy.* New York: Columbia University Press.

Rawls, J. 1971. *A Theory of Justice.* Cambridge: Harvard University Press.

Ricci, D. 1984. *The Tragedy of Political Science.* New Haven: Yale University Press.

✓ Rorty, R. 1979. *Philosophy and the Mirror of Nature.* Princeton: Princeton University Press.

✓ ——— . 1982. *Consequences of Pragmatism.* Minneapolis: University of Minnesota Press.

✓ Rosenberg, A. 1988. *Philosophy of Social Science.* Boulder, CO: Westview Press.

Rosenfield, I. 1988. *The Invention of Memory: A View of the Brain.* New York: Basic Books.

✓ Rudwick, M. J. S. 1985. *The Great Devonian Controversy: The Shaping of Knowledge Among Gentlemanly Specialists.* Chicago: University of Chicago Press.

✓ Rumelhart, D. E., and J. L. McClelland. 1986. *Parallel Distributed Processing.* vol. I. Cambridge: MIT Press.

✓ Ryle, G. 1949. *The Concept of Mind.* London: Hutchinson's University Library.

Santayana, G. 1987. *Persons and Places: Fragments of Autobiography.* Cambridge: MIT Press.

Seidelman, R., and E. J. Harpham. 1985. *Disenchanted Realists.* Albany: State University of New York Press.

✓ Simon, N. A. 1969. *The Sciences of the Artificial.* Cambridge: MIT Press.

Simonton, D. K. 1988. *Scientific Genius: A Psychology of Science.* New York: Cambridge University Press.

Smith, A. 1937. *An Inquiry Into the Nature and Causes of the Wealth of Nations.* New York: Modern Library.

Smith, B. H. 1978. *On the Margins of Discourse.* Chicago: University of Chicago Press.

————. 1988. *Contingencies of Value: Alternative Perspectives for Critical Theory.* Cambridge: Harvard University Press.

Sowa, J. F. 1984. *Conceptual Structures: Information Processing in Mind and Machine.* Reading, MA: Addison-Wesley.

Spellman, E. 1988. *Inessential Woman: Problems of Exclusion in Feminist Thought.* Boston: Beacon.

Squires, L. R. 1987. *Memory and Brain.* New York: Oxford University Press.

Steedman, C. K. 1987. *Landscape for a Good Woman: A Story of Two Lives.* New Brunswick: Rutgers University Press.

Suzuki, D. T. 1971. *What is Zen?* New York: Harper & Row.

Taussig, M. 1987. *Shamanism, Colonialism, and the Wild Man.* Chicago: University of Chicago Press.

Taylor, C. 1989. *Sources of the Self.* Cambridge: Harvard University Press.

Tedlock, D. 1989. *Days from a Dream Almanac.* Urbana: University of Illinois Press.

Tolstoy, L. 1968. *War and Peace.* [1868] Trans. by Ann Dunnigan. New York: Academic Library.

Toulmin, S. 1972. *Human Understanding.* Princeton: Princeton University Press.

————. 1990. *Cosmopolis: The Hidden Agenda of Modernity.* New York: Free Press.

Van Maanen, J. 1988. *Tales of the Field.* Chicago: University of Chicago Press.

Vickers, B. 1988. *In Defense of Rhetoric.* Oxford: Clarendon Press.

Von Hayek, F. 1979. *The Counter-Revolution of Science: Studies in the Abuse of Reason.* 2nd ed. Indianapolis, IN: Liberty Press.

Watson, J. D. 1968. *The Double Helix.* New York: New American Library.

Wiener, N. 1961. *Cybernetics: Or Control and Communication in the Animal and the Machine.* 2nd ed. New York: Wiley.

Williams, P. J. 1991. *The Alchemy of Race and Rights.* Cambridge: Harvard University Press.

Williams, R. 1977. *Marxism and Literature.* London: Oxford University Press.

Winograd, T., and F. Flores. 1977. *Understanding Computers and Cognition.* Reading, MA: Addison-Wesley.

✓ Wittgenstein, L. 1958. *Philosophical Investigations.* Trans. G. E. M. Anscombe, 3rd ed. New York: Macmillan.

✓ ———. 1980. *Remarks on the Philosophy of Psychology.* vol. I. Chicago: University of Chicago Press.

Wolf, C. 1989. *Accident: A Day's News.* New York: Farrar, Straus, & Giroux.

Ziman, J. 1968. *Public Knowledge: The Social Dimension of Science.* London: Cambridge University Press.

Contributors

Michael A. Arbib is Professor of Computer Science and Neurobiology at the University of Southern California. His current research focuses on mechanisms underlying the coordination of perception and action. This is tackled at two levels: via schema theory, which is applicable in top-down analyses of brain function and human cognition; and through the detailed analysis of neural networks, working closely with the experimental findings of neuroscientists. With Mary Hesse, he delivered the Gifford Lectures in Natural Theology at the University of Edinburgh, since published as *The Construction of Reality*, extending schema theory to provide a coherent epistemology for both individual and social knowledge.

Aaron Ben-Ze'ev is Professor in the Department of Philosophy at the University of Haifa, Israel. He has written on various topics in epistemology and philosophy of mind and, in particular, on sense-perception and the emotions. His books include *The Perceptual System* and *Aristotle on the Soul*.

Helen Couclelis is Professor in the Department of Geography at the University of California, Santa Barbara, and Associate Director of the National Center for Geographic Information. She has published widely on the philosophy and methodology of geographic research, on the study of cognition and behavior in spatial systems, and on new computer methods for simulating geographic phenomena. In the 1970s, prior to her current academic position, she was a professional planner and a policy advisor to the Greek Minister of Coordination in Athens on matters of urban and regional development.

Mihaly Csikszentmihalyi is Professor of Human Development in the Department of Psychology at the University of Chicago. He has done pioneering work in the psychology of action, and his concept of "flow" has become well known in both academic and nonacademic circles. His books include *Beyond Boredom and Anxiety*, *Optimal Experience*, *Flow: The Psychology of Optimal Experience*, and *Talented Teenagers: The Roots of Success and Failure*.

Walter R. Fisher is Professor of Communication Arts and Sciences at the University of Southern California. He has written extensively in the field of rhetoric, particularly in the areas of logic and ethics. His books include *Rhetoric: A Tradition in Transition* and *Human Communication as Narration: Toward a Philosophy of Reason, Value, and Action*.

Jane Flax is Professor of Political Science at Howard University and a psychotherapist in private practice. She has written extensively on political theory, philosophy, feminist theory, and psychoanalysis, and is author of *Thinking Fragments: Psychoanalysis, Feminism and Postmodernism in the Contemporary West*, and *Disputed Subjects: Essays in Psychoanalysis, Politics, and Philosophy*.

Robert F. Goodman is associated with the Department of Philosophy, University of Haifa, Israel. He is the co-author of *Deadlock in School Desegregation* and is the co-editor of *Good Gossip*.

George E. Marcus is Professor and Chair of Anthropology at Rice University. He is co-editor with James Clifford of *Writing Culture*, and co-author with Michael Fischer of *Anthropology as Cultural Critique*. Most recently, he has completed a volume, *Lives in Trust*, on American dynasties, and inaugurated a series of annuals, "Late Editions: Cultural Studies for the End of the Century," for the University of Chicago Press.

Donald N. McCloskey is John F. Murray Professor of Economics, Professor of History, and Director of the Project on Rhetoric of Inquiry at the University of Iowa. Well known as an economic historian, he has written also on the rhetoric of inquiry, as in *The Rhetoric of Economics*, *If You're So Smart: The Narrative of Economic Expertise*, and *Knowledge and Persuasion in Economics*.

Donald A. Schon is Ford Professor Emeritus and Senior Lecturer in the Department of Urban Studies and Planning at the Massachusetts Institute of Technology. He is widely known for his work in the fields of organizational learning, professional knowledge and education, and theory of designing. Among his recent books are *The Reflective Practitioner*, *Educating the Reflective Practitioner*, and *The Reflective Turn*.

Barbara Herrnstein Smith is Braxton Craven Professor of Comparative Literature and English at Duke University and Director of its Center for Interdisciplinary Studies in Science and Cultural Theory. Her publications, which focus on issues in contemporary literary theory, include *Poetic Closure*, *On the Margins of Discourse*, and *Contingencies of Value*.

Charles Taylor is Professor of Philosophy and Political Science at McGill University. Among his books are *Hegel and Modern Society*, *The Malaise of Modernity*, and *Sources of the Self*.

Stephen Toulmin is Henry R. Luce Professor of Multiethnic and Transnational Studies at the University of Southern California. Originally trained in physics, he has written about the philosophy of science, the history of ideas, epistemology, and professional ethics. His most recent books are *The Abuse of Casuistry* (with A. R. Jonsen) and *Cosmopolis: The Hidden Agenda of Modernity*.

Index